MOSAIC
FOR
DUMMIES

References for the Rest of Us

COMPUTER BOOK SERIES FROM IDG

Are you baffled and bewildered by programming? Does it seem like an impenetrable puzzle? Do you find that traditional manuals are overloaded with technical terms you don't understand? Do you want to know how to get your PC to do what you want? Then the ...*Programming For Dummies* book series from IDG is for you.

...*Programming For Dummies* books are written for frustrated computer users who know they really aren't dumb but find that programming, with its unique vocabulary and logic, makes them feel helpless. ...*Programming For Dummies* books use a humorous approach and a down-to-earth style to diffuse fears and build confidence. Lighthearted but not lightweight, these books are a perfect survival guide for first-time programmers or anyone learning a new environment.

> *"Simple, clear, and concise. Just what I needed."*
> —Steve P., Greenville, SC

> *"Finally, someone made learning to program easy and entertaining. Thanks!"*
> —Diane W., Chicago, IL

> *"When I saw this book I decided to give programming one last try. And I'm glad I did!"*
> —Paul G., St. Louis, MO

Millions of satisfied readers have made ...*For Dummies* books the #1 introductory-level computer book series and have written asking for more. So if you're looking for a fun and easy way to learn about computers, look to ...*For Dummies* books to give you a helping hand.

IDG BOOKS

MOSAIC FOR DUMMIES
WINDOWS EDITION

David Angell

and

Brent Heslop

IDG Books Worldwide, Inc.
An International Data Group Company

Foster City, CA • Chicago, IL • Indianapolis, IN • Braintree, MA • Dallas, TX

Mosaic For Dummies

Published by
IDG Books Worldwide, Inc.
An International Data Group Company
919 East Hillsdale Boulevard, Suite 400
Foster City, CA 94404

Library of Congress Catalog Card No.: 94-072742

ISBN: 242-2

Printed in the United States of America

First Printing, January, 1995

10 9 8 7 6 5 4 3 2

Distributed in the United States by IDG Books Worldwide, Inc.

 is a registered trademark of IDG Books Worldwide, Inc.

Welcome to the world of IDG Books Worldwide.

IDG Books Worldwide, Inc. is a subsidiary of International Data Group, the world's largest publisher of computer-related information and the leading global provider of information services on information technology. IDG was founded more than 25 years ago and now employs more than 7,200 people worldwide. IDG publishes more than 233 computer publications in 65 countries (see listing below). More than sixty million people read one or more IDG publications each month.

Launched in 1990, IDG Books Worldwide is today the #1 publisher of best-selling computer books in the United States. We are proud to have received 3 awards from the Computer Press Association in recognition of editorial excellence, and our best-selling ...For Dummies™ series has more than 15 million copies in print with translations in 24 languages. IDG Books, through a recent joint venture with IDG's Hi-Tech Beijing, became the first U.S. publisher to publish a computer book in the People's Republic of China. In record time, IDG Books has become the first choice for millions of readers around the world who want to learn how to better manage their businesses.

Our mission is simple: Every IDG book is designed to bring extra value and skill-building instructions to the reader. Our books are written by experts who understand and care about our readers. The knowledge base of our editorial staff comes from years of experience in publishing, education, and journalism — experience which we use to produce books for the '90s. In short, we care about books, so we attract the best people. We devote special attention to details such as audience, interior design, use of icons, and illustrations. And because we use an efficient process of authoring, editing, and desktop publishing our books electronically, we can spend more time ensuring superior content and spend less time on the technicalities of making books.

You can count on our commitment to deliver high-quality books at competitive prices on topics consumers want to read about. At IDG, we value quality, and we have been delivering quality for more than 25 years. You'll find no better book on a subject than an IDG book.

John J. Kilcullen

John Kilcullen
President and CEO
IDG Books Worldwide, Inc.

WINNER
Eighth Annual
Computer Press
Awards 1992

WINNER
Ninth Annual
Computer Press
Awards 1993

IDG
BOOKS

For More Information...

For general information on IDG Books in the U.S., including information on discounts and premiums, contact IDG Books at 800-434-3422.

For information on where to purchase IDG's books outside the U.S., contact Christina Turner at 415-655-3022.

For information on translations, contact Marc Jeffrey Mikulich, Foreign Rights Manager, at IDG Books Worldwide; fax number: 415-655-3295.

For sales inquiries and special prices for bulk quantities, contact Tony Real at 800-434-3422 or 415-655-3048.

For information on using IDG's books in the classroom and ordering examination copies, contact Jim Kelly at 800-434-2086.

The ...For Dummies book series is distributed in Canada by Macmillan of Canada, a Division of Canada Publishing Corporation; by Computer and Technical Books in Miami, Florida, for South America and the Caribbean; by Longman Singapore in Singapore, Malaysia, Thailand, and Korea; by Toppan Co. Ltd. in Japan; by Asia Computerworld in Hong Kong; by Woodslane Pty. Ltd. in Australia and New Zealand; and by Transword Publishers Ltd. in the U.K. and Europe.

About the Authors

David Angell started his computing adventures in 1985 with one of the first IBM PC clones, and has dedicated his efforts to demystifying computers and technology. **Brent Heslop** bought his first IBM PC back in 1983 and continues to follow the never-ending path to digital enlightenment.

David and Brent have coauthored more than a dozen books on various computer topics. Both are Internet consultants and partners in Bookware, a technical communications company. You can contact David at dangell@bookware.com and Brent at bheslop@bookware.com.

Credits

Vice President and Publisher
Christopher J. Williams

Publishing Director
Trudy Neuhaus

Brand Manager
Amorette Pedersen

Project Editor
Susan Pink

Manuscript Editor
John Pont

Technical Reviewer
Jeff Bankston

Managing Editor
Beth Roberts

Proofreader
Vicki L. Hochstedler

Indexer
Liz Cunningham

Composition and Layout
Publishers' Design and Production Services, Inc.

Book Design
University Graphics

Cover Design
Kavish + Kavish

Acknowledgments

Just as the World-Wide Web is a network that draws its strength from individual players, so too was the writing of *Mosaic For Dummies*. A lot of people helped us through this project. We would like to thank both Chris Williams for giving us the opportunity to work on this exciting project and our literary agent Matt Wagner at Waterside Productions for putting the project together. Our special thanks to a talented IDG team including Trudy Neuhaus, Amy Pedersen, and John Pont. Thanks also to the technical reviewer, Jeff Bankston. A special thanks to Susan Pink for skillfully navigating us through this project. At InterNex, our ISDN-based service provider, we'd like to thank Robert Berger, Randy Bias, and Geoff White for all their help throughout this project. Other people who deserve mention include Desiree Madison-Briggs at Netcom, Bill Sohl at Bellcore, Dan Baumbach at Canyon Software, Scott Etheredge at Combinet, Jerri Emm at Ascend Communications, Rich White at Portal Communications, Bob Williams at NetManage, Rebecca Michals at Adobe Systems, and last but definitely not least our wives, Joanne Angell and Kim Merry-Heslop.

(The publisher would like to give special thanks to Patrick McGovern, without whom this book would not have been possible.)

Contents at a Glance

Cartoons at a Glance

by Rich Tennant

page 1

page 341

page 51

page 261

page 169

page 213

page 294

page 184

page 113

page 7

Table of Contents

· ·

Introduction

Mosaic is changing the face of the Internet from a barren, text-only world of UNIX commands to a rich, multimedia environment of hypertext links, graphics, sounds, and videos. The World-Wide Web (called the Web for short) and Mosaic, the Web's graphical interface, are sweeping over the Internet like a powerful tidal wave. It's time to get off the beach and dive in to catch this Web wave. Using Mosaic for Windows as your surfboard and *Mosaic For Dummies* as your guide, you'll be surfing the thousands upon thousands of hypermedia Web sites right from your computer. New sites are springing up daily, as individuals, businesses, government agencies, universities, and many other types of organizations stake a claim in the multimedia cyberspace of the Web. Surf's up!

The 5th Wave — By Rich Tennant

PORTRAIT OF A CYBERHOLIC

HEY, MISTER! WHEN I SAY PUT YOUR HANDS UP, I MEAN BOTH OF THEM!

About This Book

To get you working and playing on the World-Wide Web with Mosaic for Windows, we use plain English and straightforward, hands-on instructions. Using our certified Web surfing course, you'll learn how to:

- ✔ Get the right Internet connection to run Mosaic
- ✔ Obtain your copy of Mosaic for Windows, which is free for the downloading
- ✔ Install and set up Mosaic
- ✔ Navigate the World-Wide Web using Mosaic
- ✔ Use Mosaic to work with Gopher, FTP, and other Internet tools
- ✔ Find hundreds of World-Wide Web sites for business, after-hours entertainment, and more
- ✔ Build your own lists of your favorite World-Wide Web sites
- ✔ Customize Mosaic to get more out of your Web surfing adventures
- ✔ Add full multimedia power to Mosaic, including sound players, video viewers, and other useful tools
- ✔ Create your own Web documents and make them available to millions of Internet users
- ✔ Understand the jargon of the World-Wide Web, Mosaic, and the Internet

How to Use This Book

You should use this book as combination how-to guide and reference. When we want you to type something, it appears in the book like this:

```
http://www.ncsa.uiuc.edu/SD/Software/Mosaic/Docs/What's-new.html
```

Type it in, just as it appears. Use the same capitalization we do, because in some situations there's a difference between upper- and lowercase.

In Windows, you have the option of using either the mouse or the keyboard to execute commands. When we say "choose a command," we leave it to you to decide how you want to execute the command. If you need to choose an item in a list in Windows, we tell you to select the item, which means click on the item to highlight it. To help you become as efficient as possible with Mosaic, we'll point out keyboard shortcuts and buttons you can click as alternatives to navigating through Mosaic's menus.

Who Are You?

In writing this book, we assumed a few things about you:

- ✓ You want more from the Internet than the old-fashioned, unfriendly UNIX interface can deliver.

- ✓ You're not afraid of working with Windows. That doesn't mean you're a technoweenie wearing a propeller beanie. It just means you know how to copy a file using the File Manager, and perform such common Windows tasks as resizing a window.

- ✓ You want to get the results of working with Mosaic and the World-Wide Web as fast as possible, but without skimping on any information you might need.

- ✓ You want to know in specific, practical terms, what's available on the World-Wide Web, and how you can get it.

- ✓ You want to know how you can use the World-Wide Web as an affordable means for promoting yourself, a business, or any organization on the Internet.

How This Book Is Organized

Mosaic For Dummies has six parts. We organize the material in a progression of what you need to know at the time you need to know it. Each part builds on the previous part, but each part also stands on its own.

Part I: Before You Go Web Surfing

Part I tells you everything you need to know about getting up and running with Mosaic. In concise terms, we give you the big picture of how the Web and Mosaic work. We explain the type of connection you need to run Mosaic, and we tell you how to get one. We wrap up this part by giving you step-by-step instructions for getting your own copy of Mosaic and installing it.

Part II: Web Surfing Fundamentals

In Part II, you learn the basics of using Mosaic to surf the World-Wide Web. You also master creating your own lists (called *hotlists*) of Web sites while you surf. Rounding out your surfing skills, we explain how to download documents and files, how to interact with forms, and how to use Mosaic as a pretty face for other Internet tools.

Part III: Power Surfing

Part III is where we show you how to customize your Mosaic surfboard for better Web surfing. We also take you into the multimedia realm of the World-Wide Web so you can play movies, hear sounds, and view all kinds of pictures directly from Mosaic. You also learn other powerful capabilities of Mosaic, such as working with annotations.

Part IV: Building Your Own Home Page for Fun and Profit

In Part IV, you make the transformation from a Web user to a Web provider. You learn how to create your own Web document and publish it on the Internet, where other Mosaic users can enjoy your Web creation. We tell you how to design and build documents using a simple editor program. Not only are you having fun, you're staking your claim in cyberspace.

Part V: The Part of Tens

The Part of Tens, as its name implies, provides you with tens upon tens of Mosaic and Web surfing resources. We point you to Internet service providers, software goodies, and server services that offer low-cost Web publishing options for putting your own Web document on the Internet. Part V also provides you with resources for obtaining and setting up an ISDN connection for faster surfing, and tips for promoting your Web document on the Internet.

Part VI: The Web Surfer's Guide

Mosaic is your surfboard for navigating the Web. Once you know how to ride it, you'll want to surf to all kinds of Web sites. Part VI provides an extensive, annotated listing of Web sites with links to thousands more. We break down Web sites into three categories: jumpstations (sites that act like directories to other sites), practical business sites, and after-hours sites. Almost any topic you can imagine is covered in your Web Surfer's Guide.

Icons Used in This Book

Several icons are sprinkled throughout this book. These icons highlight important or useful tidbits of knowledge. Here's what they look like and why they're used:

We use this icon to point out something that you should try to remember. We also use it to remind you about something that you've already learned. ▪

This icon identifies interesting, but nonessential information. We use these icons to provide you with the sort of background information that techno-people love to recite. You can skip them if you'd like. ▪

If you're looking for tips and tricks that can save you time, keystrokes, and possibly some aggravation, here's where you'll find them. ▪

Watch out! In addition to loads of entertaining and useful information, Mosaic and the World-Wide Web also present numerous potential pitfalls. This icon points out these potential problems, and tells you how to avoid them or how to solve them. ▪

This icon marks a special point of interest or supplementary information about a feature or task. ▪

And a little gray square, like the one at the end of this sentence, is used to indicate the end of the iconed text. ▪

Where to Go from Here

That's all you need to know to get started. Throughout the book, we try to anticipate problems you might encounter and show you how to solve them. However, if you hit a snag, just look up the problem in the Table of Contents or Index of this book. Let's get going on the ultimate Web surfin' safari.

Part I

Before You Go Web Surfing

The 5th Wave   By Rich Tennant

"ALL RIGHT, STEADY EVERYONE. MARGO, GO OVER TO TOM'S PC AND PRESS 'ESCAPE'...VERY CAREFULLY."

In This Part...

Before you start surfing the World-Wide Web, you need to get your Mosaic surfboard ready to go. This part shows you what it takes to ride the Web. We help you understand what it means to catch the Web wave, and we take you on a virtual surfing expedition. Then, we guide you through the maze of getting the right connection for working with Mosaic. Mosaic requires a different type of Net connection than the old-fashioned UNIX-based accounts. We also show you where to get your free copy of Mosaic, and how to install it on your Windows PC. After this part, you're ready to start surfing the World-Wide Web.

Chapter 1

Catching the Web Wave

. . . .

In This Chapter

▶ What Mosaic is and why it's so cool

▶ What the World-Wide Web is all about

▶ What you can see and do on the World-Wide Web using Mosaic

▶ How you can use Mosaic to explore the World-Wide Web

▶ How to choose your path for getting started with Mosaic

. . . .

*U*nless you've been away from the planet for awhile, you've heard about the Internet. It's the mother of all networks — the colossal, global network of networks — universally known as the *Net*. The World-Wide Web is a system of interlinked information that lets you use Mosaic for Windows to work with multimedia information on the Internet.

The World-Wide Web is sweeping the Net like a powerful tidal wave. Don't be afraid and don't try to fight it. Let's dive in and catch the wave for the best surfing in cyberspace.

We're Not in ASCII Anymore, Toto

For most Windows users, working on the Net might seem like a step backward. Without tools such as Mosaic, you work in an unfriendly, barren, ASCII text terrain using a strange UNIX language. As shown in Figure 1-1, life is stark in this outdated, command-line world.

The World-Wide Web, which is universally nicknamed the *Web*, and its graphical interface Mosaic have transformed the Net into a rich, cyberdelic world of hypertext links, graphics, fonts, sound, and video. Thanks to Mosaic, the Net finally has a pretty Windows face. To see what the Net looks like through the eyes of a Mosaic for Windows user, take a peek at Figure 1-2.

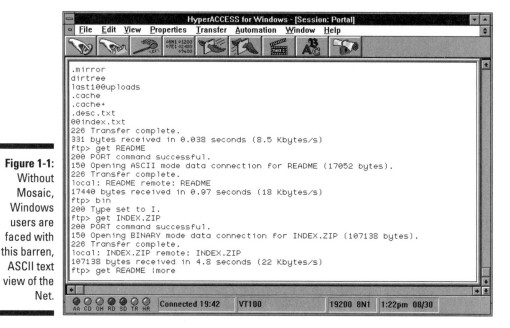

Figure 1-1: Without Mosaic, Windows users are faced with this barren, ASCII text view of the Net.

Figure 1-2: The pretty, hypermedia face of the Net as seen through the eyes of the Mosaic beholder.

Gone are all those UNIX commands; they've been replaced by buttons and menus in that familiar Windows environment that we all know and love — well, most of the time. Clicking a highlighted word, a picture, or an icon transports you to a resource that might be located anywhere on the Net. From your perspective, the sources of information appear seamless. This automatic linking is the power of the Web. When combined with multimedia, it makes the Web one exhilarating ride after another.

Mosaic: Your Window on the Web

Mosaic for Windows is your surfboard for riding the Web wave. It's the program you run to navigate and work on the Web. The generic term for Mosaic or any program that lets you work on the World-Wide Web is *Web browser.* Mosaic lets you:

- ✔ Work on the Net using common Windows menu commands, buttons, and dialog boxes as well as your mouse.

- ✔ Display electronic documents with text in a variety of formats, including numbered and bulleted lists, paragraphs, and numerous fonts in normal, bold, and italic styles.

- ✔ Connect to programs that let you view pictures, play audio sounds, and watch videos in a wide variety of file formats.

- ✔ Use interactive, electronic forms that include such easy-to-use elements as fields, check boxes, and radio buttons. For example, you might fill out an order form to request delivery of a dozen roses to your significant other.

- ✔ Use as many as 256 colors for formatting documents and displaying vibrant pictures.

- ✔ Keep track of your Web travels and create customized menus that let you automatically connect to your favorite destinations.

- ✔ Download copies of Web documents as files to your computer, where you can use Mosaic to work with them locally without a live connection to the Net.

- ✔ Handle all your Web connections automatically.

But wait, there's more

Mosaic is your Swiss army knife for working on the Net. You can use it as a full-featured program to work with the other common tools of the Net, including FTP, Gopher, Telnet, Network News, and others. Table 1-1 describes these tools. You can't send e-mail directly from Mosaic.

Table 1-1: Tools of the Net that you can work with using Mosaic

Tool	Description
FTP	The File Transfer Protocol, which is used for transferring files from one computer to another across the Net.
Gopher	A menu-driven system that lets you search for and retrieve files across the Net. The space of thousands of servers acting as one giant pool of seamless information is called Gopherspace.
Telnet	A remote log-in system that is used to connect a client to a host computer on the Net.
News	A tool that lets you access newsgroups that are part of the USENET distributed messaging system, which is heavily used on the Net.
WAIS	Wide-Area Information Server, which lets you search databases using keywords.
Finger	A tool that lets you get information about other users on the Net.

Mosaic makes even these tools look a lot better. Figure 1-3 shows what a Gopher menu looks like in Mosaic. Gopher is a popular Net tool for searching and retrieving information across thousands of servers connected to the Net. You can navigate Gopher in Mosaic by clicking the Gopher menu items.

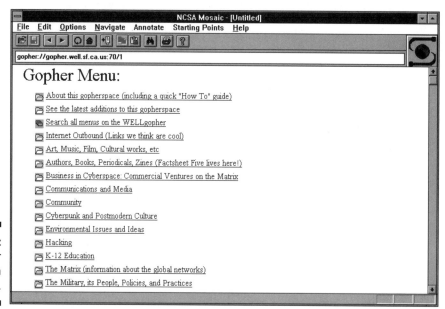

Figure 1-3:
A Gopher
sighting in
Mosaic.

Mosaic commercials

Mosaic is the killer application of the Net, and many commercial software publishers are jumping on the Mosaic clone bandwagon. A growing number of TCP/IP software programs — the programs that let Windows communicate with the Net — now include their own built-in Mosaic clones. Other software publishers are creating stand-alone versions of the Mosaic program. For example, Mosaic Communications has developed a Web browser called NetScape. We cover the alternative Web browser options in Chapter 15.

Mosaic is the standard among Web browsers. By mastering Mosaic, you'll be a better consumer of other programs if you decide that you want to upgrade to a commercial version. All your skills are easily transferable to other Web browsers. Our best advice is to learn now, and pay later to use a commercial version.

How the Web Is Weaved Together

The Web is a universe of information that's weaved together from several interrelated parts. The elements of the Web include text and multimedia documents, the rules and tools that link these documents to form hypertext and hypermedia, and the addresses that hold the whole thing together and allow you to find your way around the World-Wide Web. Most of the Web lingo springs forth from these core pieces, which are described in the following sections.

Once upon a time...

You're at a party, and someone asks the question, Where did the Web and Mosaic come from? Here's your chance to impress everyone with your deep understanding of the Web and Mosaic. Little do they know that you read this *Cliff's Notes* version of how it all began.

The World-Wide Web originated in the realm of physics. It began conceptually in March 1989, when Tim Berners-Lee of the European Particle Physics Laboratory — a collective of European high-energy physics researchers — proposed a project to develop a means for transporting research and ideas effectively throughout the organization (which is known as CERN). By the way, here's a little trivia: CERN stands for Conseil European pour Récherche Nucleaire, which was the previous name for the European Particle Physics Laboratory.

By the end of 1990, the first piece of Web software was introduced. It had capabilities for viewing hypertext documents and transmitting them to other people on the Internet. Over time, developers added to the capabilities of the World-Wide Web. These developers created the *protocol* that forms the foundation of the Web. A protocol is a set of rules and specifications that different computer systems follow in order to communicate with each other. This protocol lets Mosaic communicate with computers that store Web documents.

Although the Web had been in existence for over four years, 1993 is the year its use exploded across the Internet. Most of the credit for this sudden popularity belongs to the introduction of Mosaic, the graphical World-Wide Web client program. Mosaic was developed at the National Center for Supercomputing Applications (NCSA) at the University of Illinois at Urbana-Champaign. The NCSA Mosaic effort was funded by the National Science Foundation (NSF), a key U.S. government player in the Internet. Because of Mosaic's public funding, it's available free of charge to anyone who wants to use it. Mosaic comes in three flavors: Microsoft Windows, X Windows (UNIX), and Macintosh. Your tax dollars at work!

The Web is a hyper place

Hypermedia is the foundation of the Web. As you probably guessed, hypermedia comprises hypertext and multimedia. The term *hypertext*, which was coined by Ted Nelson, describes text that when selected makes a connection to another source of related information. For example, clicking on a phrase in a document takes you to related information located at another source. Hypertext allows you to follow information in a non-linear manner.

Multimedia can include ASCII text, formatted text, graphic images, audio files, or any other sort of data stored as computer files. Hypermedia is a way of connecting this data. A hypermedia document has non-linear links or connections to other documents. You can jump around in hypermedia documents and explore related documents at your own pace, navigating in whatever direction you choose. For example, when you click an icon in a hypermedia document, Mosaic might display a picture file, play a video file, or play a sound file that is stored at another computer on the Net.

Hyperlink is a comprehensive term that describes the use of both hypertext and hypermedia on the Web. These hyperlinks, which are also called *links*, are embedded in Web documents. When you choose a hyperlink by clicking it, Mosaic instantly takes you to another source of information. This new source of information can be any type of media, and it can be located on any computer on the Net. Hyperlinks are the heart and soul of the Web. They're so elegantly simple, yet so powerful.

The Web is at your service

Just like the Net, the Web is a client-server networking system. When you use Mosaic to request information from another computer on the Net, your computer and Mosaic are acting as a *client*. The computer that responds to your request is a *server*. A server can be accessed by any number of users who have client programs that are supported by the server.

Mosaic is the client program that sends requests for documents and files to any Web server (or other type of server). A Web server is a program running on a computer that, upon receipt of a request, sends the requested document or file back to the client.

Web server programs are relatively simple, because Mosaic does most of the work for displaying Web documents. Web servers deliver codes and compressed files, not fully assembled documents. This approach eases the workload on the server.

A typical session between Mosaic and a Web server goes something like this:

1. Running Mosaic for Windows on your system with a direct connection to the Net, you send a request to a Web server. Using the server's unique address, the request is routed across the Net to the Web server.

2. The Web server receives the request and responds by sending the hypermedia Web document codes and related files, such as pictures, to your computer.

3. Mosaic receives the information and draws the Web document on your screen.

Every time you go to a new Web server or display a different Web document at the same Web server site, the same series of events happens. The Web is a vast digital grid that handles the huge volume of these transactions, which are taking place all the time, throughout the world.

Web servers are at sites that have full-time (dedicated), high-speed, digital line connections to the Net. Dedicated connections are needed to handle the volume of many clients accessing the site at one time. Web servers can be on an organization's own computer system that is connected to the Net, or at a server service company, which sells space on a Web server for publishing Web documents.

The lords of the files

Most Web sites have a designated keeper of the realm called a *Webmaster*. Like a network system administrator, a Webmaster keeps everything running at a Web site. A Webmaster has the added responsibility of choreographing the way the Web server appears to Mosaic users. Because there are no professional Webmaster licensing requirements or standards, the quality of Web sites varies according to the Webmaster's skills and tastes. By default, many Webmasters are from the technoweenie tribe, which is known for its lack of design skills. However, more and more people from the desktop publisher and designer tribes are becoming involved in the design of Web sites.

The glue that holds the Web together

The *HyperText Transfer Protocol* (HTTP) is the language that Web clients and servers use to communicate with each other. Think of *protocols* as a kind of Robert's Rules of Order for communication between clients and servers. To send and receive hypermedia documents, Mosaic and any Web server (called an HTTP server) must be able to speak HTTP. The phrase *World-Wide Web* refers to the collective network of servers speaking HTTP as well as the global body of information available via this protocol.

HTTP supports most of the other tools you use on the Internet, such as the File Transfer Protocol (FTP). However, you get the multimedia richness of Web documents only when you are connected to an HTTP server — in other words, a true Web server. The other tools appear in their native, ASCII text format.

The Zen of URLs

To find almost any resource on the Net, the Web uses *Uniform Resource Locators*, or *URLs*. Nearly everything on the Net has a URL, which is a unique address. For example, you use URLs to point to Web sites, files, newsgroups, Gopher sites, and FTP sites. A URL is a one-line address for a resource on the Net. Just think of URLs as an electronic addressing system for connecting to resources on the Net.

Mosaic lets you enter a URL to go directly to a specific site or resource. URLs also lurk beneath any hyperlink within a Web document. When you click on the hyperlink in a Web document, Mosaic automatically connects to the URL that's encoded in the Web document.

A typical URL address for a Web site might be:

```
http://sailfish.peregrine.com/surf/surf.html
```

The first part of the URL (the characters preceding the colon) specifies the Net tool you want to access. The preceding example uses http, which is the standard access method for connecting to a Web server. Notice that http is also the name of the Web protocol. The sailfish.peregrine.com entry is the site address, which is usually the domain name address. The /surf/surf.html entry is the file pathname — that is, the location of the file on the server.

If you're connecting to an FTP site, the URL starts with ftp://. For example, an FTP URL might be:

```
ftp://ftp.mcsnet.users/barnhart/letterman
```

The ftp:// access method tells Mosaic it's connecting to an FTP server. The ftp.mcsnet.users entry is the domain name address for the site, and /barnhart/letterman is the file pathname that takes you to the letterman directory on the server.

What's behind those pretty Web documents?

The standard language used for creating Web documents is the *HyperText Markup Language*, or *HTML*. HTML codes are document formatting instructions that tell Mosaic how to create the document on your screen. The Web server sends these codes to Mosaic. These codes are in an ASCII text file, which is called an *HTML document*, or source document. Once Mosaic gets the HTML file, it creates the Web document. HTML document files end with the extension .html. In DOS and Windows, the extension is truncated to .htm.

URLs use domain name addresses for easier reading

URLs usually use domain names, which are based on the Domain Name System (DNS). DNS is a text-based addressing scheme that is easier to understand than Internet Protocol (IP) addresses. An IP address is a collection of four numbers separated by dots — for example, 198.67.38.22. Using the DNS, the name for this IP account might be ns.internex.net. For the most part, domain names are usually indicative of the name and type of organization that owns or supports the system. For example, microsoft.com is the domain name for Microsoft Corporation, a very successful commercial (.com) entity.

Figure 1-4 shows the naked HTML instructions behind a Web document, and Figure 1-5 shows the Web document in full plumage. Mosaic lets you view the code behind any document — if it's available — by choosing a command from a menu.

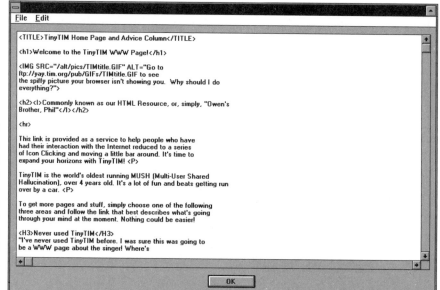

Figure 1-4:
What's behind a Web document's pretty face? Nothing but naked HTML codes.

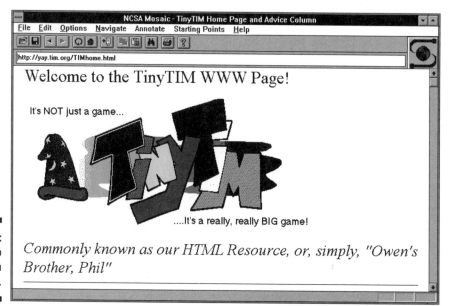

Figure 1-5:
The Web document in all its glory.

HTML+, Son of HTML

The current HTML standard offers limited layout capabilities. A new version of HTML, called HTML+, will add new formatting and other capabilities to the Web. HTML+ will provide more versatile layout and formatting options, such as tables and styles. HTML+ will also include support for e-mail, so hyperlinks can be used to send e-mail automatically. For example, selecting an e-mail address in a piece of hypertext would open a mail program, ready to send e-mail to that address.

What You Can See and Do on the Web

The Web is the digital version of the wild west; it's vast and untamed. It doesn't take a rocket scientist to figure out why the Web is taking the Net by storm. Anyone with a little time and effort or a small fistful of dollars can strike a claim in the cyberdelic realm of the Web.

Numbers don't lie. In June 1993, there were approximately 100 Web sites. As of May 1994, there were more than 4,500 Web sites. This number has undoubtedly doubled in the meantime, with new sites popping up daily.

Millions of individuals, schools, businesses, and other organizations are turning to the multimedia Web to deliver their message via on-line publishing. Others are setting up electronic storefronts to conduct virtual commerce. Everyone is getting into the act:

- Businesses are finding that the Web is a low-cost, multimedia means for publishing information or conducting virtual commerce. Hundreds of businesses of all sizes have set up a Web presence to market all kinds of products and services. Other companies are establishing on-line malls that house the virtual storefronts of many businesses.

- Educational and governmental institutions are major sources of Web sites.

- Individuals from all walks of life, from admirals to zoologists, are publishing everything imaginable on-line.

There's no end in sight to the numbers and types of Web sites. All these Web sites combine to form the great melting pot of the Net. Everyone is doing their own thing, with different sites focusing on different interests. Some sites act as gateways to other sites, providing a kind of free directory service. For example, one Web document might list and link hundreds of commercial sites that are available on the Web.

We'll tell you how to stake your own claim on the Web in Part IV. Designing your own Web documents is lots of fun. You can create Web documents using a wide variety of free or inexpensive HTML editors. Once you create a document, you can inexpensively place it on the Web. ■

Enough Talk, Let's Surf the Web

You've got a grasp of the Web and all its marvels; now it's time to experience the Web firsthand. Don't worry about the technical details. We're taking you on a ride on our Mosaic surfboard to see what it's like to surf the Web, which is riding the Web from site to site. You don't have to learn anything here, just come along for the ride. In the following chapters, we'll cover all the tools and techniques you need to surf the Web yourself. Let's ride.

You start surfing the Web by making a connection to the Net, and then launching Mosaic on your computer. By default, Mosaic automatically connects to a Web server at NCSA (the folks that developed Mosaic).

You enter the URL for the site you want to visit in the URL box at the top of the Mosaic window. For example you might enter the following (see Figure 1-6):

```
http://www.directory.net/dir/directory.html
```

Figure 1-6: To connect to a Web site, you enter the site's URL in the URL box at the top of the Mosaic window.

When you press Enter, the Commercial Services on the Net document appears on your screen, as shown in Figure 1-7. It's not a pretty page, but it's packed with hyperlinks to the business side of the Web.

You scroll down the Commercial Services on the Net page to a hyperlink titled Future Fantasy Bookstore. When you click this hyperlink, Mosaic displays the home page shown in Figure 1-8. This on-line bookstore specializes in science fiction, fantasy, and mystery books.

After checking out the latest in sci-fi books, you navigate back to the Commercial Services on the Net page by simply clicking the left-arrow button on the toolbar at the top of the Mosaic window (above the URL box and below the menus).

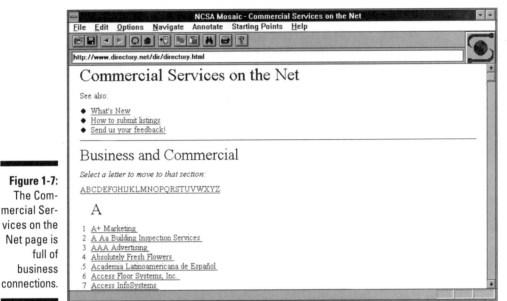

Figure 1-7:
The Commercial Services on the Net page is full of business connections.

Figure 1-8:
The Future Fantasy Bookstore Web site offers an on-line catalog.

Next, you decide to go software shopping at the Internet Shopping Network, a member-based discount shopping mall that's shown in Figure 1-9.

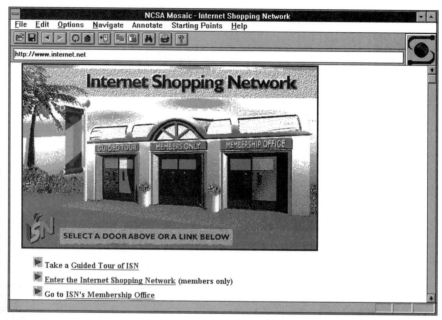

Figure 1-9:
The Internet
Shopping
Network
lets you
shop on-line
at discount
prices.

You could spend hours checking out more business sites on the Web, but it's time for some after-hours Web surfing. To go directly to Adam Curry's Cyber-Sleaze Report, which is an entertainment industry rag, you enter the following URL in Mosaic's URL box and press Enter (yes that's an s before html):

```
http://metaverse.com/vibe/sleaze/index.shtml
```

Mosaic displays the Cyber-Sleaze page, which contains hyperlink dates. Click the date hyperlink for today's Sleaze report. Figure 1-10 shows a typical Cyber-Sleaze Report.

Rounding out your evening at the Web, it's time for some rock 'n' roll. You head over to The Grateful Dead home page by entering the following URL and pressing Enter:

```
http://www.cs.cmu.edu:8001/afs/cs.cmu.edu/user/mleone/web/dead.html
```

As shown Figure 1-11, Mosaic displays The Grateful Dead page. Clicking the Graphics hyperlink in the Grateful Dead home page takes you to the visual feast of images shown in Figure 1-12.

The Cyber Sleaze Report

Cyber Sleaze for Friday, October 21, 1994

The following materials are copyrighted by CurryCo Ltd. and may not be re-distributed or Duplicated for any other means than personal entertainment. Failure is subject to prosecution.

* REM are considering releasing a live album of totally new material - directly on the back of their latest best selling record MONSTER. PETE BUCK from the group says, "It could be a live album of 12 new songs. We might include soundchecks, playing in hotel rooms. We don't know yet. MICHAEL STIPE says it was vital for his group REM to get back on the road after their break of several years. "If we hadn't got back on the road we would have turned into some kind of punk version of STEELY DAN. That wouldn't have worked." (IRV/MM)

* BON JOVI guitarist RICHIE SAMBORA has agreed to a no-sex promise with live in lover HEATHER LOCKYEAR. Locklear has agreed to avoid sex scenes on TV show MELROSE PLACE, while Sambora agrees to avoid fooling around, at least before the wedding. Locklear was so hurt by infidelities of her now ex-husband TOMMY LEE that she insisted on the "love pact" with Sambora. (DA/WNW/JAG)

Figure 1-10: A typical Cyber-Sleaze Report keeps you up-to-date on the seamy side of the entertainment industry.

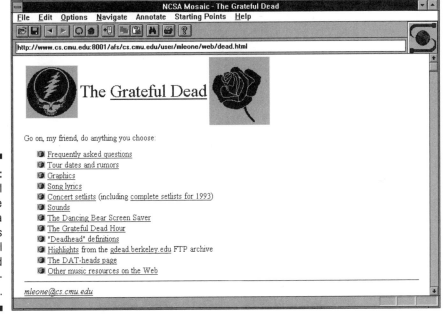

The Grateful Dead

Go on, my friend, do anything you choose:

- Frequently asked questions
- Tour dates and rumors
- Graphics
- Song lyrics
- Concert setlists (including complete setlists for 1993)
- Sounds
- The Dancing Bear Screen Saver
- The Grateful Dead Hour
- "Deadhead" definitions
- Highlights from the gdead.berkeley.edu FTP archive
- The DAT-heads page
- Other music resources on the Web

mleone@cs.cmu.edu

Figure 1-11: The Grateful Dead home page is a site that's chock-full of Dead paraphernalia.

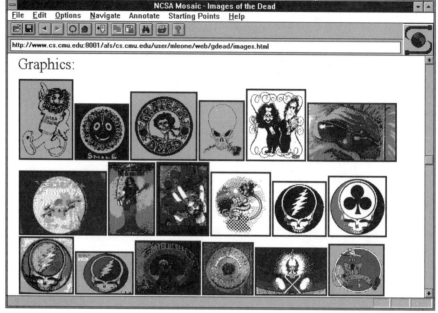

Figure 1-12:
A feast of
tie-dye
visuals
awaits you
at the
Grateful
Dead Web
site.

Finally, you decide to come back to the shore. You choose File I Exit in Mosaic and return home from yet another endless surfin' safari adventure. Tomorrow's another day.

What Do You Need to Run Mosaic?

By now, you probably want to do your own Web surfing. However, before you can enter the cyberdelic world of the Web, you need to pass through a few technical rites of passage. Here are the key things you'll need to make the metamorphosis to the Web using Mosaic. Don't panic. We cover these topics in more detail later. To run Mosaic, you'll need:

- ✔ A PC-compatible with at least a 386 processor, 4MB or more of memory, and Windows 3.1 or Windows for Workgroups.

- ✔ An Internet Protocol (IP) account with a service provider. This class of account makes your computer part of the Net. That old UNIX command-line account won't do.

- ✔ A dedicated or dial-up telecommunications link between your computer or local network and an Internet service provider. If you're using a dial-up link over a voice telephone line, which is the case for most single computers and small businesses, you'll need a fast modem (14.4Kbps or faster).

✔ Windows TCP/IP software, which allows your computer to communicate in the language of the Net when it sends and receives information. This software comes with the networking protocol and usually includes Windows-based client tools for working on the Internet, such as e-mail, FTP, and Gopher.

✔ PKZIP or any other program that can compress and decompress files using the PKZIP compression format.

✔ The Win32s program, which allows Windows 3.1 and Windows for Workgroups to work with 32-bit applications, of which Mosaic is one.

✔ A copy of Mosaic for Windows.

Moving On

To clear up any confusion, we'll tell you where to go in this book to get started with Mosaic. Where you start depends on what you know or don't know. Here are the paths you can take:

✔ If you don't have a clue about any of the items in the preceding section, start by reading Chapter 2. It gives you a handle on all these pieces of the Mosaic puzzle.

✔ If you know all about IP connections and TCP/IP software, but you need to get Mosaic and install it, start by reading Chapter 3.

✔ If you've got a connection, TCP/IP software, and the latest version of Mosaic already up and running on your system, you can start with Chapter 4.

We've hit you with a lot of information in this chapter. Here are the key points you should remember: Mosaic for Windows is a client program that you run on your computer. When you connect to the Net, you use Mosaic to connect to a Web server. The Web server sends instructions (HTML codes) to Mosaic, telling Mosaic how to assemble the Web document on your system. The World-Wide Web is the system on which Mosaic (or other Web browsers) and servers interact with each other based on the HTTP protocol.

Chapter 2

Connecting with the Net

● ●

In This Chapter

▶ Getting into IP connections

▶ Choosing your own domain name

▶ Shopping for an IP connection

▶ Managing the telecommunications factor

▶ Making Windows speak TCP/IP

● ●

*B*efore you can run Mosaic, you must have an Internet Protocol (IP) connection. If you don't have one, you have to take the plunge into the cold waters of setting up an IP connection. Think of this chapter as a wet suit that insulates you from the technical chill of hooking into the Net.

What's an IP Connection?

One of the most common ways to access the Net is command-line access through a local Internet service provider. This is the least expensive type of access, but it's also the most primitive. You dial into the service provider's computer using a communications program and a modem. Once you're connected, you work and play on the Net using the unfriendly command-line client programs on the service provider's host system, which is typically a UNIX computer system.

With this approach, your computer isn't directly part of the Net because it doesn't speak the language of the Net. As a result, you can't use Mosaic and other client programs — for example, e-mail programs, FTP, Gopher, and Telnet — that run in your native Windows environment.

To use a Windows-based client program such as Mosaic, your computer needs to speak TCP/IP (Transmission Control Protocol/Internet Protocol).

This is the standard protocol that glues together all the different computers on the Internet. To communicate directly with any other computer on the Internet, your computer must speak TCP/IP.

To give your computer this capability, you need an IP connection, Windows TCP/IP software running on your system, and a telecommunications link to a service provider.

The Net is more fun with a Windows connection

Accessing the Net using Windows is more elegant and fun than command-line access. It also means more than simply being able to use Mosaic. An IP connection lets you use the familiar Windows interface for all your Net activities. Cruising the Net becomes as easy as clicking your mouse and choosing commands from menus. With an IP connection, you can run Windows client programs for e-mail, FTP, Telnet, Gopher, Network News, and other tools.

Another big benefit of an IP connection is that information arrives at your computer nonstop from the server. For example, let's say you want to download some files from an FTP server to your computer. Because you are using FTP with an IP account, the files can be transferred directly from the server to your computer without stopping at the service provider's computer. Without an IP address, the files are downloaded from the server to the service provider's computer, and then downloaded again from the service provider to your machine.

Addressing yourself to the Net

The Net uses an addressing scheme called the Domain Name System (DNS). A domain name is a unique Internet address for a computer that is directly connected to the Net. When you establish an IP connection with a service provider, you choose your own domain name or your service provider assigns a name.

Domain names have a hierarchical structure. From left to right, a domain name goes from the most specific (that is, user or computer name) to the most general top-level domain. For example, dangell@bookware.com translates to a user named dangell at the bookware host computer. The top-level domain specification is .com, which means it's a commercial organization. Table 2-1 lists the different categories of top-level domains used in DNS.

Table 2-1: The top-level domains used in the Domain Name System

Domain	Organization type
com	Commercial
edu	Education
gov	Government
mil	Military
net	Networking
org	Anything that doesn't fit in the other categories; often non-profit groups
au (Australia)	Geographical
ca (Canada)	Geographical
uk (United Kingdom)	Geographical

Creating your own domain address

A domain name is your vanity address. Keep the following rules in mind if you're choosing your own name:

- ✔ A domain name consists of two or more alphanumeric fields. Fields are separated by a period (called a dot).

- ✔ You can use any of the following characters in the fields that make up a domain name: the letters A through Z (upper- or lowercase), the digits 0 through 9, and the hyphen (-).

- ✔ Don't use spaces in a domain name. However, you can use an underscore (_) to indicate a space.

- ✔ Don't use any of the following characters: . @ % !

- ✔ Domain names are case-insensitive, so it doesn't matter whether letters are upper- or lowercase.

Finding out if a domain name is available

If you're choosing your own domain name, you need to make sure the name you want is available. Your service provider will actually register your domain name, but you can check to see if the domain name you want is available. InterNIC is the center for registration of domain names.

Domain names are registered on a first-come, first-serve basis. Registering a domain name implies no legal ownership of the name. For example, you may be able to register a domain name that is the name of another company, but that company might send its lawyers after you for using its trade name.

Here are three ways you can find out whether a domain name is available:

- ✔ You can call InterNIC registration services at 703-742-4777 and ask if the name or names you're considering are already registered.
- ✔ If you have an e-mail account that has access to the Net — for example, an account with America Online, CompuServe, or MCI Mail — you can check the domain name by sending an e-mail message to hostmaster@rs.internic.net.
- ✔ If you already have a connection to the Net, Telnet to rs.internic.net. At the system prompt, type whois. This connects you to InterNIC's on-line database. Type a name and press Enter. If there's a match, information appears about the company that has registered the domain name. If there's no match, the domain name is available.

Are you dedicated or on demand?

With an IP connection, you can connect to the Net using either a dedicated, digital telecommunications line or a dial-up, on-demand connection.

A dedicated connection means your computer, as part of a network at your location, is always connected to the Net. This type of connection uses a high-speed digital telecommunications link. These high-speed links can move a lot of information between local computers and the Net. However, high-speed, dedicated connections are expensive. Most universities, government agencies, corporations, and many other large organizations use dedicated connections to link their networks to the Net.

For the rest of us, a dial-up, on-demand connection is the only affordable option. This type of connection to the Net uses standard telephone lines and a modem. Using a modem and a voice-grade telephone line is at the bottom of the data transmission food chain — it's just plain slow.

The good news is that regional telephone companies are offering a new service called ISDN, which stands for *Integrated Services Digital Network*. ISDN is coming on-line in a big way, and it promises to free us from the bondage of slow, voice-grade telephone line connections. More on this later.

PPPing or SLIPing on the Net

For dial-up IP connections, you have to choose between PPP (point-to-point), SLIP (Serial Line Internet Protocol), and CSLIP (Compressed SLIP) access. These protocols allow your computer to speak TCP/IP using a dial-up connection.

The protocol you choose depends on the TCP/IP software you're using and what your service provider offers. There are three types of dial-up IP accounts:

- PPP is the connection of choice because it's faster and more reliable. It's not as widely available as SLIP, but that is changing rapidly.

- SLIP is built into most UNIX systems. Like UNIX, it's everywhere on the Net. However, SLIP is not as sophisticated as PPP.

- CSLIP is a modified version of SLIP that compresses data for transfers between your computer and the service provider's network. If your service provider doesn't offer PPP, ask for CSLIP. Compared to SLIP, CSLIP can save you time.

Most Windows TCP/IP programs include support for PPP, SLIP, and CSLIP. However, not all service providers support the three types of IP accounts.

IP connection shopping

IP connections are very affordable. In many places, you can get an account for less than $30 a month with 20 or more hours of free connection time. However, prices can vary substantially, so you need to shop around. Beyond the service provider's costs, you also need to consider other charges that might come into play. Be aware of the following factors when shopping for an IP account:

- Some service providers, such as NetCom, provide TCP/IP programs when you establish an IP account. NetCom's TCP/IP program, Net-Cruiser, includes features that streamline the process of getting started with a single-user IP account.

- Some service providers offer toll-free phone connections. Be sure to consider the telecommunications costs of connecting to your service provider.

- Many service providers charge a set-up fee to establish an IP account.

- The cost of an IP account usually involves a flat rate that covers a specified amount of connection time, and an hourly rate for connection time in excess of that initial amount. For example, a service provider might charge a base rate of $30 a month to provide you with up to 20 hours of connection time. If you use the IP connection for more than 20 hours in a month, your bill would include the $30 base rate and hourly charges for the additional connection time. You should estimate your expected use of an IP account so you can project your approximate costs. Be liberal in your estimate of expected Net use. The amount of time you spend surfing the Net invariably increases over time.

Chapter 13 provides an extensive listing of Net service providers that offer IP connection accounts. ■

The Telecommunications Factor

Between your computer and the Net is the telecommunications link. The type of link you use and the location of the service provider's computer play a big role in the cost and speed of your Web surfing. Two telecommunications options are available for most users:

- ✔ A standard voice telephone line and a modem
- ✔ ISDN

And the bandwidth played on

The term *bandwidth* refers to the data traffic capacity of any connection. A graphics or sound file requires considerably more bandwidth than a simple ASCII text message. All the whizbang technology of Mosaic and the Web — the graphics, sounds, pictures, and videos — requires immense amounts of bandwidth. The more bandwidth your connection supports, the faster you can ride the Web.

In general, the greater the bandwidth, the more expensive the line. The two types of telecommunications lines are *analog* (voice) and *digital*. Analog lines are at the low end of the bandwidth spectrum. At the high end are leased digital lines. Leased lines are usually too expensive for small businesses and individuals.

In addition to their impressive bandwidth, digital lines are more reliable. AT&T estimates a reliability rate of 75% for analog lines and 99% for digital lines.

Web surfing on POTS

In telecommunications jargon, a voice-grade telephone line is Plain Old Telephone Service, or *POTS*. An analog telephone line is the slowest way to connect to the Net. To surf the Web on POTS, you also need a modem. You'll want a fast modem because Mosaic downloads all those pretty pictures and formatted text in Web documents to your computer. The faster your modem connection, the faster you get the Web documents.

In the graphics-intensive world of the Web, you'll want to use at least a 14.4 Kbps or 28.8 Kbps modem. However, you need to remember that your modem can transfer information only as fast as the modem at the other end of the analog line. Check with your service provider to make sure you can connect to a modem that matches your modem's speed.

The ultimate ride on ISDN

ISDN is the next generation of telecommunications for the rest of us. It's being offered by all the regional telephone companies (Baby Bells). Most U.S. telephone companies expect ISDN to be 85% to 95% deployed by 1995. Depending on your location and telephone company, ISDN services range from $25 to $100 a month. If you are calling within a local calling area, as defined by your local telephone company, a call can cost from one to four cents a minute. For residential ISDN service, some telephone companies don't charge after 5:00 P.M. and on weekends.

An ISDN connection lets you surf the Web at the warp speeds of a digital line, but at very affordable prices. Each ISDN line includes two digital 64 Kbps channels, called *bearer* channels (B channels for short), which combine for a total capacity of 128 Kbps without any compression. But, like everything else in life, ISDN isn't perfect. Here's a list of caveats, exceptions, and peculiarities of ISDN:

- The location of the phone company's central office determines whether you will be able to get 64 Kbps or 56 Kbps per channel. If you're within a certain distance from the central office that provides the ISDN service, you will enjoy 64 Kbps or 128 Kbps speeds.

- Some phone companies and service providers offer ISDN with only a single 64 Kbps channel.

- The speed of your ISDN connection also depends on the hardware and software you're using at your end of the connection.

- ISDN equipment at your premises connects to an Ethernet card in your computer. If you use a serial connection, the speed of the ISDN line is reduced to 38.4 Kbps.

✔ You can divide the ISDN line to have a channel for your data transmissions and a channel for voice. However, this leaves you with a single 64 Kbps connection (or 56 Kbps, depending on your location).

✔ You need to make sure that a service provider supports ISDN and it's within your local calling area; otherwise, you'll have expensive toll charges.

For more detailed information on ISDNing your connection to the Net, see Chapter 14. This chapter explains all the components you need for establishing an ISDN connection. ■

POP goes the connection

To keep your telecommunications costs down, you should always try to have a local telephone number that you can call for making a connection. Most large service providers have *Point of Presence* (POP) facilities, which allow you to connect to the service provider from major metropolitan areas by using a local access number. A POP facility is leased from a telephone company that provides access to the service provider. With a local POP, you can use a local number to connect to your service provider, even though the service provider's site is hundreds or thousands of miles away.

Residential telephone service typically includes unlimited message units within a local calling area. For business service, telephone companies usually charge for all the calls you make. Check with your telephone company for specific rate information. Some service providers offer an 800 telephone number for access but add a surcharge to their hourly charges. Although it's more expensive than using a local access number, an 800-number service can save money if you're using your IP account on the road. Calls made on telephone credit cards can get expensive.

Teaching Windows to Speak TCP/IP

TCP/IP software lets Windows communicate with the Net using an IP account. It allows your computer to send and receive information in the form used on the Net. Most Windows TCP/IP programs include the TCP/IP software that runs behind the scenes. They also include a communications program for connecting to a service provider via a modem, and a set of Windows client applications for working with e-mail, FTP, Telnet, Gopher, and other tools.

Several commercial TCP/IP programs are available for Windows. TCP/IP support is also being added to popular communications programs such as HyperAccess for Windows. Chapter 12 provides more information on commercial Windows TCP/IP packages.

NetManage's Chameleon is a popular Windows TCP/IP product that we use. Figure 2-1 shows the Chameleon window with its icons for the various Net tools. Clicking the e-mail icon displays the friendly mail program window shown in Figure 2-2. Clicking the Gopher icon displays the gopher client application shown in Figure 2-3.

Figure 2-1:
The
Chameleon
group
window.

If you're using a stand-alone computer, you can buy the non-network version of TCP/IP software. Compared with the network version, it's cheaper and easier to install and run. If you have a modem hooked directly to your computer, you can use the stand-alone version of TCP/IP software, even if you're connected to a network.

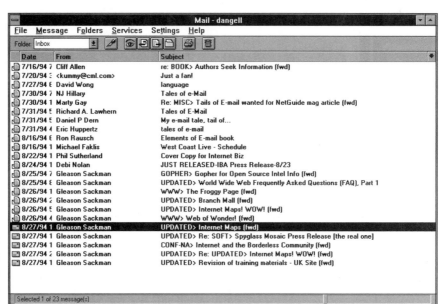

Figure 2-2:
E-mail the
GUI way.

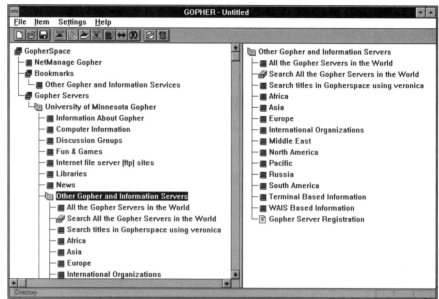

Figure 2-3:
Gopher gets
graphical.

If your computer is part of a network and your system operates through a server or a router, you need to run a network version of the TCP/IP software. You need to install a separate copy of the program on each computer on a network that wants to use TCP/IP.

Stacking up TCP/IP

The technoweenie term for TCP/IP software is a *TCP/IP stack* that handles the data traffic between your computer and the Net. WinSock is the software that enables TCP/IP software packages to work with Windows. Most Windows TCP/IP software comes with the TCP/IP stack and WinSock built in.

The bottom line on what you need to use Mosaic is an IP connection with a Net service provider using a SLIP or PPP dial-up Internet account. The telecommunications connection to your Net service provider can use a 14.4Kbps (or faster) modem or an ISDN line. On your computer, you need a TCP/IP package that includes the Winsock and TCP/IP stack software. With these key components in place, you're ready to get Mosaic and install it on your system.

Chapter 3

Installing Mosaic

● ●

● ●

*B*efore you can start Web surfing, you need to get a copy of Mosaic and set it up. It takes a little effort to get through the process of obtaining the software and installing it on your system. After you install Mosaic, you should order the coveted technoweenie celebration pizza and Jolt cola — you've earned it.

Here's the Game Plan

Before you can start working with Mosaic, you need to get everything in place. Here are the steps you need to complete:

    ✔ Connect to the Net with access to the FTP program, which lets you transfer files across the Net.

    ✔ Download up to three programs — PKUNZIP, Win32s, and Mosaic — from FTP servers.

    ✔ Use the PKUNZIP program to decompress the files you download.

    ✔ Install the Win32s program, which allows Windows 3.1 or Windows for Workgroups to run the 32-bit version of Mosaic.

    ✔ Install Mosaic.

Let's get to it.

Before You Install Mosaic

Before you go to all the effort of getting Mosaic up and running, it's time for a quick system check. Does your system have what it takes?

- An absolute minimum of an 80386SX-based computer with a color monitor. A faster 386 machine, a 486, or a Pentium processor is better.
- At least 4MB of RAM. However, NCSA recommends 8MB.
- A Windows TCP/IP package.
- An Internet Protocol (IP) connection to the Internet — that is, an IP account.
- To play audio, you need a sound card or an installed speaker driver for your computer's speaker, which usually sounds like people talking in cans connected by a string.
- More of everything. In this graphical environment, more is better: more memory, more disk space, more processing power, more graphics card power, and so on.

Downloading What You Need with FTP

The FTP program is the application you use to get the files you need for installing Mosaic. With your IP connection and TCP/IP software in place, you're ready to get the files you need using the FTP program.

Each TCP/IP program comes with its own version of the FTP program, and no two are exactly alike. However, the different versions generally work in the same way. The following steps show you how to get the files you need from the FTP site at NCSA using Chameleon's FTP tool. If the NCSA's FTP site is busy, Table 3-1 lists other FTP sites from which you can get these files.

Table 3-1: Alternative FTP sites for getting the Mosaic program

FTP site	Directory path
ftp.sunset.se	/pub/pc/Mosaic
ftp.luth.se	/pub/clients/PCmosaic/pub/infosystems/www/ncsa/Windows
ftp.vmedia.com	/pub/companions/mosaicqt/mosaic
sunsite.unc.edu	/pub/packages/infosystems/WWW/clients/Mosaic/Mosaic-NCSA/Windows

NetManage's Chameleon is the leading Windows TCP/IP program. The following steps show you how to get the files you need using Chameleon's FTP tool:

1. Create a directory or set aside a directory to store your downloaded files. For example, you might create a directory named c:\transfer.

2. Double-click the FTP icon in the Internet Chameleon group window. As shown in Figure 3-1, the FTP window is displayed.

3. Choose Settings | Connection Profile, and click the New button in the dialog box that's displayed. As shown in Figure 3-2, the Connection Profile dialog box is ready for you to enter the log-in information for the FTP sites to which you plan to connect.

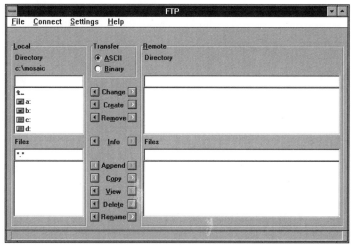

Figure 3-1:
The
Chameleon
FTP
window.

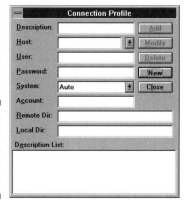

Figure 3-2:
The Con-
nection Pro-
file dialog
box.

4. Enter the following log-in information to define the connection profile for getting the Mosaic and Win32s programs:

Field	*Entry*
Description	NCSA Mosaic
Host	ftp.ncsa.uiuc.edu
User	anonymous
Password	Your e-mail address — for example, bob@book-ware.com
Remote directory	/Web/Mosaic/Windows
Local directory	The complete pathname for the directory you've created on your computer for storing downloaded files — for example, c:\transfer

5. Save this connection profile by clicking the Add button. To define the connection profile for getting the PKUNZIP program, click the New button, and enter the following log-in information:

Field	*Entry*
Description	PKZIP Software
Host	oak.oakland.edu
User	anonymous
Password	Your e-mail address — for example, bob@book-ware.com
Remote directory	/pub/msdos/zip
Local directory	The complete pathname for the directory you've created on your computer for storing downloaded files — for example, c:\transfer

6. Click the Add button, then click Close, which returns you to the FTP window.

7. Minimize the FTP window to an icon.

8. Double-click the Custom icon in the Chameleon group window, and choose the Connect command on the menu bar to connect to your service provider.

9. Double-click the FTP tool icon, and choose Connect from the FTP menu. As shown in Figure 3-3, the Connect dialog box is displayed.

10. In the Description list, select the NCSA Mosaic entry, and choose OK. The FTP tool makes the connection to the NCSA host computer at ftp.ncsa.uiuc.edu, and places you in the /Web/Mosaic/Windows directory, ready to copy the Mosaic and Win32s files from this remote site to

Figure 3-3:
The Con-
nect dialog
box.

your local computer. You may need several attempts to make a connection, because the ftp.ncsa.uiuc.edu site is a very busy place.

11. Choose the Binary radio button in the Transfer settings section of the
FTP window, which tells the FTP program that you're downloading a
program file.

12. Scroll down in the Remote Files area of the FTP window until you find
the file wmos20a7.zip. This is the file that contains Mosaic. Click on this
filename to select it, and then scroll down to find the win32s.zip file,
which contains the compressed Win32s program. Hold down the Ctrl
key while clicking on this filename.

13. Click the Copy button that's pointing to your local directory (c:\transfer
or any other directory you want to use). The selected files are downloaded to your computer. Now that you've downloaded Mosaic and the
Win32s program, you can disconnect from NCSA's FTP site.

14. Choose Disconnect (when you're connected to an FTP site, the Connect
option changes to Disconnect), and then click the Disconnect button in
the Disconnect dialog box. To get a copy of PKUNZIP, you need to connect to the FTP site at oak.oakland.edu.

15. Choose Connect. In the Connect window's Description list, choose the
PKZIP Software entry, and choose OK. The FTP window now lists the
files in the /pub/msdos/zip directory of the host computer named
oak.oakland.edu.

16. Scroll down the list of files in the Remote Files area and click on the file
pkz204g.exe.

17. To download pkz204g.exe to your computer, click the Copy button
that's pointing to your local directory and files.

18. Choose Disconnect, and then choose the Exit button in the Disconnect
dialog box to exit the FTP connection and close the FTP window. A dialog box is displayed asking whether you want to save your changes to

the file c:\netmag\ftp.cfg. Choose Yes to save the entries you made in the Connection Profile dialog box for the FTP sites from which you just got your software. You can now disconnect from your service provider.

Keep in mind that Mosaic's filename changes with each new release and update. It's always in the format wmos*version*.zip, where *version* represents the current version number. As you probably guessed, "wmos" is short for Windows Mosaic. For example, wmos20a7.zip is the filename for NCSA Mosaic for Windows version 2.0, Alpha version 7.0. ■

It's Time to Decompress with PKUNZIP

Most FTP sites compress files to save storage space and reduce the time it takes to transfer files. The Mosaic and Win32s files are no exception. You use the pkunzip.exe utility to decompress the wmos20a7.zip and win32s.zip files that you downloaded. Here's how you set up the PKZIP program:

1. Create a directory for your PKZIP program. Here's a creative name: PKZIP.

2. Move the pkz204g.exe file into the PKZIP directory.

3. At the DOS prompt, enter pkz204g.exe. The PKZIP self-explodes into five files. The file that's important to you for installing Mosaic is pkunzip.exe.

4. Open your autoexec.bat file and add the PKZIP directory path to your Path statement, so you can run PKZIP and PKUNZIP from any directory.

Get Your 32 Bits Worth

If you're using Windows 3.1 or Windows for Workgroups, you must install Win32s before you can run Mosaic. Win32s allows you to run 32-bit Windows applications under Windows 3.1 and Windows for Workgroups. You get this 32-bit power by upgrading your Windows software with Win32s.

Because Mosaic is a 32-bit application, you must have Win32s running on your system. After you install the Win32s program, it resides in your C:\windows\system\win32s directory, with the exception of the WIN32S.INI file, which resides in the \system subdirectory.

If you already use other 32-bit Windows applications under Windows 3.1, the Win32s software is already installed on your computer. However, it may be an older version. In this case, you still need to install Win32s. In order for Mosaic to work, you must be using version 1.1.5a or higher of the Win32s software. You can check for the proper version by examining the contents of

More on 32-bit systems

Microsoft developed Win32s, and it's currently available for free to licensed users of Windows 3.1 and Windows for Workgroups. You don't need to use the Win32s software with Windows NT because it is a true 32-bit operating system — everything is already built in. The bottom line is that 32-bit operating systems and applications are faster than their 16-bit counterparts. Machines based on the Intel 80386 microprocessor or higher support 32-bit processing.

the WIN32S.INI file, which is stored in the \windows\system subdirectory. To check the version of your Win32s software, open the Windows File Manager, find the WIN32S.INI file in the C:\windows\system directory, and double-click this filename. Windows displays the contents of this text file in Notepad. Under the [Win32s] heading there should be the entry Version=1.15.111.0; if not, you need to get the updated version of Win32s.

Installing Win32s

The Win32s program comes in a single compressed file, which contains two compressed files that you can decompress to fit on two disks. However, it's easier to create a temporary directory and install Win32s from your hard disk. Here are the steps for installing Win32s:

1. Create a temporary directory for decompressing the Win32s files — for example, c:\win32tmp.

2. Change to the directory containing the win32s.zip file.

3. At the DOS prompt, enter:

```
pkunzip win32s.zip \win32tmp
```

This command unzips the win32s.zip file into two unzipped files and a text file and puts them in the \win32tmp directory. Specifically, this command extracts three files from win32s.zip — w32s1_1.bug, w32s115A.zip, and README.TXT — and puts these files in your \win32tmp directory.

4. Change to the \win32tmp directory.

5. Enter the command:

```
pkunzip -d w32s115a.zip
```

PKUNZIP inflates the files and displays the message Inflating *filename* for each directory and file that is decompressed. PKUNZIP creates two directories, Disk1 and Disk2. Now that you have unzipped all the necessary files, you can run the Win32s setup program. This program installs Win32s and automatically updates your Windows configuration files.

6. Start Windows, and choose File|Run from the Program Manager window. Enter the path of the setup program in the Command Line text box — for example, c:\win32tmp\disk1\setup. Choose OK and the Win32s setup program automatically upgrades your Windows files. After installing Win32s, the setup program asks if you want install a 32-bit card game called Freecell.

7. Choose Yes, and try the Freecell card game. It's more than just a card game; if it works, you know that Win32s is also working.

Installing Mosaic

OK, you're finally at the Mosaic installation stage. You can smell the pepperoni. Mosaic isn't a big program; it's around 650K. Here's how you install it:

1. Use the Windows File Manager or DOS to create a separate directory for Windows Mosaic — for example, c:\mosaic.

2. Change to the directory containing the wmos20a7.zip file.

3. At the DOS prompt, unzip the wmos20a7.zip file into the directory you've created for Mosaic. For example, if you plan to put Mosaic in c:\mosaic, you would enter the following command:

```
pkunzip wmos20a7.zip c:\mosaic
```

4. Start Windows and open the group window in which you want to add the Mosaic icon. For example, you can add a Mosaic icon to the group containing your TCP/IP software.

5. Choose File|New in the Program Manager window. Windows displays the New Program Object dialog box.

6. Make sure the Program Item radio button is on and click OK. As shown in Figure 3-4, Program Manager displays the Program Item Properties dialog box.

7. Fill out the fields using the following entries (press Tab to move from one field to the next):

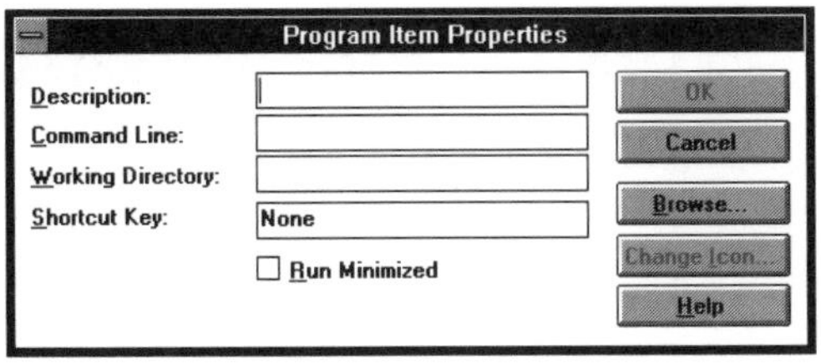

Figure 3-4:
The Program Item Properties dialog box.

```
┌──────────────────── Program Item Properties ─────────────────────┐
│ Description:       [                    ]      [   OK   ]          │
│ Command Line:      [                    ]                          │
│ Working Directory: [                    ]      [ Cancel ]          │
│ Shortcut Key:      [None               ]      [ Browse... ]       │
│                    ☐ Run Minimized            [ Change Icon... ]  │
│                                               [  Help  ]          │
└───────────────────────────────────────────────────────────────────┘
```

Field	Entry
Description	Mosaic
Command Line	c:\mosaic\mosaic.exe
Working Directory	c:\mosaic

8. Click the OK button. The Mosaic icon appears in the current group window. If the icon isn't visible, use the scroll bar to move to the bottom of the window.

9. Copy the mosaic.ini file from your Mosaic directory to your Windows directory using the Windows File Manager. This is an important step. If you don't put mosaic.ini in your Windows directory, Mosaic won't recognize and save your configuration changes.

TECHNICAL STUFF

Putting mosaic.ini in another directory

It is possible to store your mosaic.ini file in another directory by defining a mosaic.ini environment variable in your autoexec.bat file. For example, if you wanted to point to the mosaic.ini file in your mosaic directory, you could edit your autoexec.bat file to include the following line:

```
set mosaic.ini=c:\mosaic\mosaic.ini
```

If you use the environment variable, be sure to make a backup copy of the mosaic.ini file. For example you might copy it to a backup file named mosaic.bak.

What are Those Files in my Mosaic Directory?

When you unzip the wmos20a7.zip file, six files appear in your Mosaic directory. Table 3-2 describes these files. All the files with .wri extensions are information files. To read any of these files, use the Write program in the Windows Accessories group.

Table 3-2: The files in your Mosaic directory

File	Description
update.wri	Current list of the version's enhancements and bug fixes in Write format. A techie file.
install.wri	Mosaic installation and configuration guide.
mosaic.exe	The Mosaic program.
mosaic.ini	The initialization and configuration file for Mosaic.
devnote.wri	Version introduction information. This is another techie file.
faq.wri	A list of frequently asked questions (FAQs) about Mosaic and the World-Wide Web.

A Mosaic Shakedown Ride

Well, you've done it. Mosaic is ready and waiting. Let's take it for a shakedown cruise to make sure all systems are go. At this point, you need to have an IP connection working with the TCP/IP software.

1. Connect to your service provider.

2. Double-click the Mosaic icon.

3. If the Mosaic program starts, and the default home page appears as shown in Figure 3-5, go directly to celebration pizza. If Mosaic doesn't start, displays an error message, or doesn't appear correctly, get a can of Jolt cola and go directly to "Troubleshooting Common Installation Problems."

4. To close the Mosaic window, choose File|Exit or double-click the Control menu box in the upper-left corner of the Mosaic window.

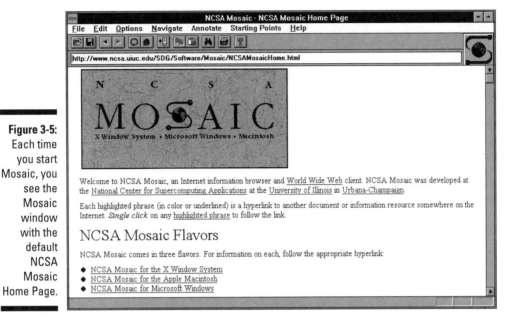

Figure 3-5:
Each time
you start
Mosaic, you
see the
Mosaic
window
with the
default
NCSA
Mosaic
Home Page.

Troubleshooting Common Installation Problems

Several problems might prevent Mosaic from starting properly. Mosaic installation problems can be related to your TCP/IP software, Win32s, or Mosaic itself. In the worst case, you'll have to get an upgrade or reinstall one of these programs. Here are the most common problems and how to fix them.

The "Failed DNS Lookup" message

If you don't see the default home page displayed in Figure 3-5 and Mosaic displays the error message "Failed DNS Lookup," you need to consider a few possible causes. First, it's possible that Mosaic is unable to display the default home page that's specified in your mosaic.ini file. Try another site by entering a URL address directly in the URL text box at the top of the Mosaic window. For example, you can enter http://galaxy.einet.net and press Enter. It's possible that you've given your TCP/IP software the wrong IP address for the service provider's Domain Name System (DNS) server. The DNS server keeps track of DNS addresses on the Net. It's also possible that you made a typing mistake or the URL address doesn't exist. Finally, it's possible that your service provider's DNS server is down.

No menus in the Mosaic window

If no menus appear in your Mosaic window, it's likely that the mosaic.ini file isn't in your Windows directory. To correct this problem, either copy the mosaic.ini file to your Windows directory or verify that you've defined the environment variable properly in your autoexec.bat file.

An exclamation point

If a blank dialog box appears with an exclamation point and no text, your Win32s software probably isn't installed correctly. When you close this dialog box, Windows displays a general protection fault dialog box. Try reinstalling the Win32s software.

The "Unable to load TCP/IP" message

If you see the error message "Unable to load TCP/IP," you may be using an obsolete version of WinSock. This message is also displayed if your TCP/IP program can't find files that it needs to load. It's also possible that you do not have enough system resources; such as memory, to launch the TCP/IP program; try rebooting and don't open any other applications. If you still see this error message and all else fails, try reinstalling your TCP/IP software.

The "Cannot find winsock.dll" message

If the message "Cannot find winsock.dll" is displayed, it's possible that your TCP/IP software's winsock.dll file isn't in the \windows\system directory. Another possibility is that the path to the winsock.dll file isn't included in the Path statement of your autoexec.bat file.

Getting Mosaic Upgrades

If you already have Mosaic, but want to obtain a newer version of Mosaic or Win32s, you can download the files directly using Mosaic. Of course, you can use FTP to go to the NCSA FTP site, but using Mosaic is a lot easier.

Mosaic for Windows is an *alpha* stage product (currently in alpha version 7.0). Alpha is a software development term used to describe a piece of software that's in the early stages of development. To you, alpha means further releases of Mosaic for Windows are imminent. As a result, you'll want to check the NCSA site periodically to see if a new version is available. Each new version of Mosaic for Windows adds improvements over the previous version, and sometimes adds some new problems. ■

Here's how you get your Mosaic upgrades:

1. With Mosaic running, choose Starting Points | Windows Mosaic home page or enter the following address in the Mosaic URL text box:

   `http://www.ncsa.uiuc.edu/SDG/Software/WinMosaic/HomePage.html`

   Mosaic displays the Mosaic for Microsoft Windows Home Page. Find the bulleted list labeled User Support Information, and click The Latest Release of Mosaic.

2. Scroll down to the Windows 3.2 and WfW header, hold down the Shift key, and click the Win3.1, WfW, NT for the Intel iX86 processor link. You can also choose Options | Load to Disk, and then click the link. As shown in Figure 3-6, the Save As dialog box is displayed. The name of the file is listed in the File Name box.

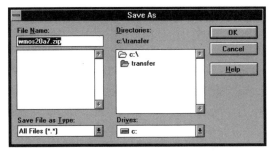

Figure 3-6: The Save As dialog box lets you specify where you want to put the downloaded file.

3. Choose the drive and directory in which you want to put the downloaded file, and choose OK. The Mosaic program is downloaded to your computer.

Once you get the new version of Mosaic for Windows, you can install it on your system. Before you install it, make a backup copy of your previous Mosaic for Windows version, including the mosaic.ini file in your C:\windows directory. This is just insurance in case the new version causes problems and you need to return to the old version. Also, remember to add the new mosaic.ini file to your C:\windows directory to replace the old one.

Part II
Web Surfing Fundamentals

The 5th Wave   By Rich Tennant

Arthur inadvertently replaces his mouse pad with an Ouija board. For the rest of the day, he receives messages from the spectral world.

YOU WILL FORGET YOUR PASSWORD. YOUR HARD DISK WILL CRASH AAAHAHAHAHA

In This Part...

This is the cool part, where you learn how to go Web surfing. After a hands-on orientation to the Mosaic window terrain, you'll master the basics of working with Mosaic, including connecting to a Web site, working with Mosaic's commands, using hyperlinks and URLs, and other essential navigation skills. You're also introduced to hotlists, the great Kahunas of Web surfing. A hotlist is a powerful, yet easy-to-use feature that lets you quickly capture hundreds of Web site addresses (URLs) while you surf. In no time, you'll have your own list of sites that you can visit by simply choosing a menu item. We round out your essential surfing skills with a variety of Mosaic techniques, including downloading Web documents and other files, printing and searching Web documents, interacting with on-line forms, and using Mosaic as an interface for other Internet tools.

Chapter 4

Let's Go Web Surfing

*Y*ou've made it through the boot camp of getting your IP connection, setting up your TCP/IP software, and installing Mosaic. It's time to start surfing the Web and having some fun. This chapter covers the essential techniques you need to start surfing the Web using Mosaic. In no time, you'll feel the exhilaration of riding one Web hyperlink after another. Surf's up!

Launching Mosaic

Before you launch Mosaic, you need to connect to the Net. Once you're connected to the Net, you launch Mosaic the same way you start any Windows application. No big surprises here.

Here are the most common ways to launch Mosaic:

▸ Double-click the Mosaic icon, which looks like this:

MOSAIC

✔ Double-click the mosaic.exe file in the File Manager window.

✔ Choose File | Run in the Program Manager window, enter the path to Mosaic in the Run dialog box, and then click OK or press Enter.

After you launch Mosaic, your mouse pointer changes to an hourglass, your computer's processor and hard disk grind, and the Mosaic window appears. But wait; there's more. After a few moments, Mosaic automatically connects to the NCSA Web site and displays the NCSA Mosaic Home Page. Figure 4-1 shows what initially appears on your screen if you make the connection without a hitch.

Figure 4-1:
With the NCSA Mosaic Home Page displayed, Mosaic is launched and ready for you to start surfing.

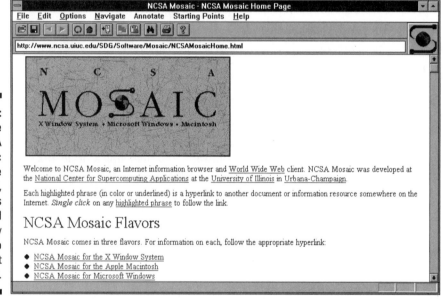

Hey, I got an error message in Greek!

If Mosaic fails to connect to the NCSA Mosaic Home Page, the unfriendly message in Figure 4-2 splashes across your screen.

Don't panic — just click OK. You can still make another connection attempt. This error message just tells you that the attempted connection to the Web server failed. The Failed DNS error message crops up frequently when you're surfing the Web. You might see this error message for several reasons:

Figure 4-2: Relax, this message simply means that a connection attempt failed.

✔ Mosaic got a wrong IP address associated with the domain name of the site to which you're trying to connect from the Domain Name Service server at your service provider.

✔ You entered the wrong URL address or the domain name doesn't exist.

✔ The Web site is unplugged from the Net for repairs, updates, or some other reason.

✔ Mosaic is just acting funky. How's that for a technical reason? Retrying the connection usually takes care of the problem.

Here's what you should do if you are constantly running into the Failed DNS Lookup error message:

1. When the error message is displayed, click OK or press Enter.

2. Choose File | Exit to close the Mosaic window.

3. Check your connection using your TCP/IP program, and, if necessary, reconnect to your service provider. Most TCP/IP programs include a ping program, which allows you to send a message to a computer to see if it's running. In this case, you should ping your service provider's computer to make sure it's running.

4. Restart Mosaic.

There's no place like the default home page

The NCSA home page that appears on your screen is the default home page specified at the factory. Each time you launch Mosaic, the software takes you to the default home page. You'll want to change this default home page, because it's not that exciting and it's located at one of the most heavily used Web sites on the planet.

For example, you might want to change your default home page to the EINet Galaxy home page shown in Figure 4-3. This home page offers an extensive listing of Web sites covering a variety of topics. You can go directly to any of those sites by clicking the hyperlinks on the EINet Galaxy home page.

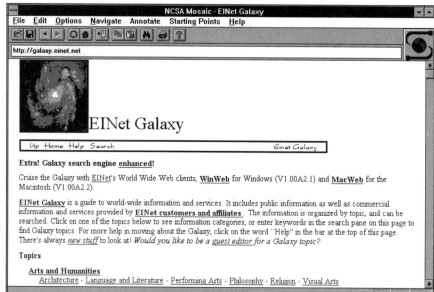

Figure 4-3:
An alternative default home page might be EINet Galaxy, which is a gateway to hundreds of Web sites.

You change the default home page by editing an entry in the mosaic.ini file (the Mosaic initialization file). You can even tell Mosaic that it shouldn't connect to any home page when you start it. See Chapter 7 if you can't wait to change your default home page or turn it off. Trust us; it's not that hard to do.

Adjusting the Mosaic Window

When you first launch the Mosaic window, it comes up stunted. You don't want to work with a cramped Mosaic window, because Web documents will lose their shape. Like any window in Microsoft Windows, you can manipulate the Mosaic window to find a better size.

To refresh your window-arranging skills, here are the easiest ways to manipulate the Mosaic window:

 ✔ To resize the window, use the mouse pointer to click and drag an edge or corner of the window to the location you want.

✔ To move the window, click and drag the window title bar to the new location.

✔ To expand the Mosaic window to its maximum size, double-click its title. (You can also click the maximize button in the upper-right corner of the Mosaic window.) The window explodes to fill the vacuum of your entire screen. The Mosaic window loses its borders when it fills the entire screen. To bring the window back to its previous size, double-click its title bar again.

✔ To reduce the Mosaic window to an icon, click the minimize button in the upper-right corner of the Mosaic window.

Tiling the Mosaic window by itself is a handy working arrangement for saving memory. To do this, you minimize all open windows except the Mosaic window to icons. Then, double-click anywhere on the desktop to display the Task List dialog box, and click the Tile button. Figure 4-4 shows the Mosaic window using this window arrangement scheme.

Once you have the Mosaic window set up just the way you like it, you can save that look for the next time you launch Mosaic by choosing File I Save Preferences. ■

Figure 4-4: Tiling the Mosaic window saves memory and makes it easier to access other tools.

Welcome to Mosaic

Mosaic has all the key components found in most Windows applications, including the window title bar, the menu bar, the toolbar, the document display area, vertical and horizontal scroll bars, and the status bar. Figure 4-5 identifies these key parts of the Mosaic window.

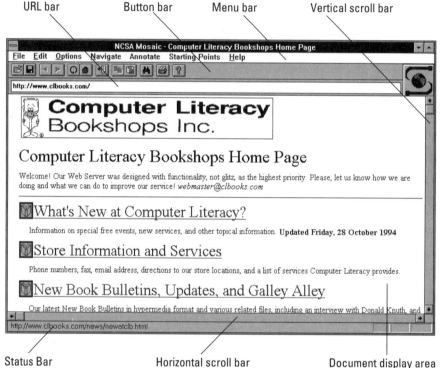

Figure 4-5:
The key elements of the Mosaic window are standard fare for most Windows applications.

Commanding Mosaic by the menus

The menu bar is familiar to any Windows user. It has all the commands for working with Mosaic. Table 4-1 gives you a brief summary of the major functions found in each menu.

For keyboarders, you can open a menu by pressing the Alt key while typing the first letter of the menu item. With a menu open, you can execute a command by typing the first letter or the underlined letter in that menu option.

Table 4-1: Mosaic's menus and their major functions

Menu	Major functions
File	Opening, saving, and printing documents.
Edit	Copying text to and from the clipboard, and searching Web documents for specific text.
Options	Customizing Mosaic — for example, hiding the toolbar — and saving Web documents to files.
Navigate	Navigating among the documents you've viewed in the current session.
Annotate	Adding Post-It notes to Web documents while you surf.
Starting Points	Surfing the Web by choosing menu items that automatically connect you to various Web sites. This menu is customizable; you can add your own items.
Help	Getting help for working with Mosaic. These menu items connect to NCSA help documents.

You'll notice that Mosaic doesn't exactly follow the Windows convention of underlining the letter that executes a menu option. Just remember that you execute a command from the keyboard by typing either the underlined letter in that menu option or the first letter in a menu option that doesn't have an underlined letter.

A few menu commands in Mosaic have keyboard shortcuts. For example, you can execute the Print command from the File menu by pressing Ctrl-P.

A right-pointing arrow next to a menu item means that a submenu lurks beneath that menu item. An ellipsis (...) next to a menu item means that a dialog box appears when you choose that command.

For mouse-based surfers, Mosaic uses the standard click-and-drag methods for opening menus and choosing commands.

Clicking commands on the toolbar

Unless you're a diehard keyboarder, the toolbar is a real convenience. Buttons stand by, ready and waiting for a click of your mouse. The toolbar includes buttons for performing the most commonly used Mosaic commands. Of course, all these commands are also found in the menus. Table 4-2 describes the function of each button. Moving the pointer over any toolbar icon displays a label that identifies the button.

Table 4-2: Know your toolbar buttons

Button	Description	Menu command
	Opens the Open URL dialog box, which lets you enter or choose an address for a Web site.	File|Open URL
	Saves the current document to a file, which you can display off-line using Mosaic.	File|Save As
	Displays the previous document.	Navigate|Back
	Displays the next document.	Navigate|Forward
	Reloads the current document.	Navigate|Reload
	Returns Mosaic to the default home page.	Navigate|Home
	Adds the current URL to a hotlist.	Navigate|Add Current To Hotlist
	Copies the current selection to the clipboard.	Edit|Copy
	Pastes the contents of the clipboard into the active window.	Edit|Paste
	Opens the Find dialog box, which lets you search for specific text in the current document.	Edit|Find
	Prints a copy of the current document, pictures and all.	File|Print
	Displays the About NCSA Mosaic for Windows dialog box.	Help|About Windows Mosaic

Document titles, the URL bar, and the spinning Mosaic logo

The title of the Web document currently displayed in Mosaic appears in the Window title. The title of a document is the user-friendly, English name of the site, not the document's URL address.

The URL address appears in the URL bar, which is located under the toolbar. You can go to any Web site (or other resource) by entering its URL address in the URL bar's text box and pressing Enter.

The NCSA Mosaic logo appears immediately to the right of the URL bar. When Mosaic is connecting to a server or transferring a file, this logo comes alive, with the earth spinning and yellow lights moving around it As long as the earth is spinning, Mosaic is working on one of these tasks. For more detailed messages about what's going on with any process, you can check the status bar at the bottom of the Mosaic window.

Seeing is believing in the document display area

The document display area does what its name implies. After being down-loaded and rendered, Web documents are displayed in this area. The term *rendered* simply means drawn on your computer screen. By default, Mosaic displays Web documents with a grey background. As detailed in Chapter 7, you can change it to a white background by editing the mosaic.ini file.

Scrolling along

Most Web documents are larger than a single screen. You can move around in Mosaic's document display area using either your mouse and the scroll bars or keyboard commands.

Mosaic automatically displays scroll bars if a Web document is either longer (vertical scroll bar) or wider (horizontal scroll bar) than the Mosaic window. These scroll bars work exactly like the scroll bars in any Windows applica-tion. To work at the bars:

  ✔ Move the document in small steps, typically about one line or character at a time, by clicking the small arrow at either end of the scroll bar.

  ✔ Move through the document in larger increments by clicking on either side of the button in the scroll bar.

If you're a keyboarder, Table 4-3 lists the keyboard commands that let you move around in Web documents.

Keeping posted with the status bar

The status bar keeps you informed about Mosaic's activities by displaying the following information:

  ✔ The status of a document. Messages in the status bar tell you what's happening while Mosaic is attempting to access, transfer, or display documents.

Table 4-3: Keyboard commands for scrolling through a document

Key	Scrolls
Up-Arrow	Up one line
Down-Arrow	Down one line
PgUp	Up one page
PgDn	Down one page
Home	To the top of the document
End	To the bottom of the document

✔ The URL associated with a hyperlink. When you move the pointer to any hyperlink, the status bar displays the URL for that link.

✔ The current settings for caps lock, number lock, and scroll lock. Indicators for these settings are found in the three boxes on the right side of the status bar.

By default, the status bar displays the URL for any hyperlink you point to in Mosaic. This status information is useful because it allows you to see what type of file is behind the hyperlink before you click. For example, you might discover that a hyperlink is connected to a large video file that you don't want.

You can turn off the display of URLs in the status bar by choosing the Options | Show Anchor URLs command. However, our advice is to keep the Options | Show Anchor URLs command active at all times. Surfing without seeing URLs in the status bar is like riding with your eyes closed.

Show Anchor URLs and most of the other commands in the Options menu are toggle commands. In other words, you turn them on and off by selecting the menu items. Check marks appear to the left of menu items that are active. Any changes you make to these toggle commands remain in effect for the current session or until you choose the command again. By choosing File | Save Preferences, you can save any changes to the default settings so they'll be in effect the next time you launch Mosaic. ■

Getting a better view

To maximize your document viewing area, you can tell Mosaic to hide the toolbar, the status bar, and the URL bar. Figure 4-6 shows a Web Document as it appears in the Mosaic window with the toolbar, status bar, and URL bar turned on, which is the default setting. Figure 4-7 shows the same Web

Figure 4-6:
The GNN home page as it appears in the Mosaic window with the toolbar, status bar, and URL bar displayed.

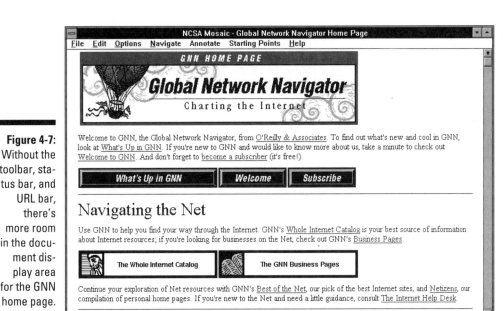

Figure 4-7:
Without the toolbar, status bar, and URL bar, there's more room in the document display area for the GNN home page.

document in the Mosaic window with the toolbar, status bar, and URL bar turned off.

Here are the menu options that let you toggle the display of the toolbar, the status bar, and the URL bar:

- ✔ Options|Show Toolbar
- ✔ Options|Status Bar
- ✔ Options|Show Current URL

Although shutting off the toolbar, the status bar, and the URL bar enlarges your viewing area, you pay a price for your expanded view:

- ✔ Without the toolbar, you have to use the menus to select commands, which usually takes a few extra steps.
- ✔ Without the URL bar, extra steps are needed to direct Mosaic to Web sites.
- ✔ Without the status bar, you don't have information about the status of downloading, hyperlink sources, and other Mosaic tasks. What's more, turning off the status bar doesn't add much space to the document display area. ■

Basic Web Surfing Techniques

Put on your baggies. It's time to learn some essential Web surfing techniques. Mosaic lets you ride the Web using two different methods:

- ✔ You can connect to a Web site by clicking a hyperlink in a Web document.
- ✔ You can go directly to a Web site by entering a URL address or choosing one from a menu.

Daddy, where do Web site addresses come from?

You might be wondering, How do I find Web site addresses? Good question. As you surf the Web, you'll pick up lots of addresses from hyperlinks in Web documents. Many Web sites are collections of hyperlinks to other Web sites. These starting-point sites act as gateways to lots of other sites on the Web. To help you fill up your address book, we'll mention many URL addresses throughout this book. We also provide an extensive, annotated list of our favorite Web sites at no extra charge in Part VI.

Web surfing via hyperlinks

As you read through a Web document, you'll see words and phrases highlighted by color or an underscore (or both). These highlighted words and phrases are hyperlinks. Each hyperlink points to another document, image, video, sound, or file. Pictures and icons also can act as hyperlinks.

A hyperlink uses the URL address for a Web site or other resource, such as a file. When you move the mouse pointer to a hyperlink, Mosaic displays the corresponding URL address in the status bar. When you click on a hyperlink, you are instantly transported to the Web site at the other end of that hyperlink.

You use your mouse to navigate through the hyperlinks in Web documents. There are no keyboard equivalents for navigating through hyperlinks. When you move the mouse pointer to any hyperlink object on the screen, the pointer changes from an arrow into a pointing finger.

The author of a Web document defines your options for surfing via hyperlinks. Most Web sites offer a collection of hyperlinks that focus on a particular topic or area of interest. Other sites act as gateways to a whole range of topics. If you exhaust the links at any Web site, you can simply catch a ride to another different Web site by pointing Mosaic in the right direction.

The Options | Change Cursor Over Anchors command lets you change the way the pointer appears when it's on a hyperlink. If this menu item is active, which is the default setting, the pointer changes from an arrow to a pointing hand when it's on a hyperlink. If you deactivate this command, your pointer doesn't change shape when it's on a hyperlink. We recommend that you leave this command active. Why not use the visual cue to recognize hyperlinks?

Web surfing with menus

The options in the Starting Points menu correspond to a variety of Web sites. All the items in this menu are hotlist entries. A *hotlist* is a list of Web or other resource addresses that you can define. The initial list of items in the Starting Points menu was installed for you, but you can change this menu or add your own menu of hotlists. Chapter 5 shows you how to do this.

You can connect to a Web site simply by choosing an item in the Starting Points menu. NCSA set up these menu items, but you can, and will, change them to reflect your interests. Most of the items in this menu connect you to Web sites. The only exceptions are the Gopher Servers, Finger Gateway, Whois Gateway, and Archie Request commands. These menu items are quick connections to other Internet tools. We show you how to use these tools in Chapter 6. The World-Wide Web Info, Home Pages, and Other Documents menu items display submenus of Web sites from which you can choose.

To get the feel of surfing with the Starting Points menu, choose Starting Points I NCSA Mosaic's 'What's New' Page. Mosaic connects to a site maintained by NCSA, which announces new Web sites on an almost daily basis. Figure 4-8 shows the What's New With NCSA Mosaic home page. Each entry includes a brief description and the hyperlink to a new site. If you scroll to the bottom of this home page, you'll find hyperlinks that let you access the What's New listings for the past 12 months.

You can also choose any menu item by using the Open URL dialog box, which is shown in Figure 4-9. You access this dialog box by choosing File I Open URL, by clicking the Open URL button, or by pressing Ctrl-O. To select the menu you want, click the small arrow to the right of the Current Hotlist field and drag the cursor to select the desired menu — for example, Starting Points. You can choose the menu items from the selected menu using either of the fields at the top of the Open URL dialog box. The URL field lists the sites by their URL addresses. The other drop-down list lets you choose sites by their friendlier, English titles. After choosing the desired menu item, choose OK or press Enter.

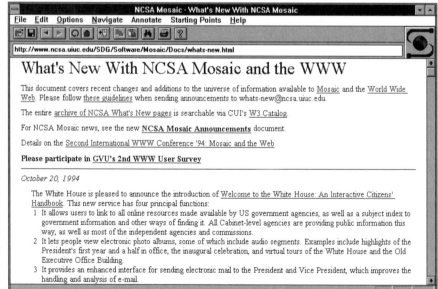

Figure 4-8:
The NCSA What's New home page is a great place to keep up with the latest additions to the Web.

Figure 4-9: You can use the Open URL dialog box to choose the same menu items that appear in the Starting Points menu.

Web surfing by manually entering URL addresses

A common term in Web surfing is *pointing*, which means entering the URL address for a Web site that you want to visit using Mosaic. To go directly to a Web site for the first time without using a hyperlink, you have to enter a URL address in Mosaic's URL bar or the Open URL dialog box.

Once you enter the URL and connect to the Web site, and the Web document appears in Mosaic, you can add the URL to Mosaic's hotlist. With the address in a hotlist, you can choose it from a menu. Chapter 5 shows you how to add URLs to Mosaic's hotlist menus.

Before you press Enter to execute the URL you've entered in the URL box, select the address with the mouse, or press Shift-End, and then press Ctrl-C. This copies the URL address to the clipboard. If the connection fails, which removes the address from the URL box, you can press Ctrl-V to copy the URL address into the URL box and make another connection attempt. This saves you the trouble of manually reentering the URL. ▪

The easiest way to surf manually is to use the URL bar in the Mosaic window. Here's how you do it:

1. Click in the URL text box on the URL bar. The URL address is high-lighted.

2. Select the current URL address in the text box and press Delete.

3. Type one of the Web site addresses listed in Table 4-4 — for example, http://mistral.enst.fr:80/~pioch/louvre.

4. Press Enter. As shown in Figure 4-10, Mosaic displays the Le WebLouvre home page.

5. To go to another Web site, repeat the preceding steps.

The other way to surf the Web manually is by using the Open URL dialog box. You open this dialog box by pressing Ctrl-O, clicking the Open URL button, or choosing File | Open URL. To enter the URL address for a Web site, click in the

---

Table 4-4: A Web site sampler

URL address	Contents
http://cybersight.com/cgi-bin/cs/s?main.gmml	The CyberSights home page is a starting point for the alternative, Generation X side of the Web.
http://sunsite.unc.edu/elvis/elvishom.html	The Elvis Presley home page is a musical and visual tribute to the king. You can tour Graceland, view Elvis photos, and listen to sound bites.
http://www.directory.net/dir/directory.html	The Commercial Services on the Net site is a great starting point for checking out hundreds of businesses that have established a Web presence on the Net.
http://www.commerce.digital.com/palo-alto/FutureFantasy/home.html	Future Fantasy Bookstore is an on-line bookstore that sells science fiction, fantasy, and mystery books.
http://bingen.csbsju.edu/letterman.html	The Late Show with David Letterman site is a collection of Dave memorabilia. It includes a vast archive of Top Ten lists.
http://sailfish.peregrine.com/surf/surf.html	SurfNet is a true surfer's Web site, complete with shots of beaches and ultimate rides.
http://mistral.enst.fr:80/~pioch/louvre	The Le WebLouvre site won the Best of the Web '94 award for Best Use of Multiple Media. It's a virtual museum of famous paintings.
http://www.microsoft.com	This is the home page for the lord of the Windows realm, Microsoft Corp.
http://www.eff.com	The Electronic Frontier Foundation is a non-profit organization dedicated to protecting on-line civil rights.

URL text box to select the text in the box, type a URL address, and choose OK.

Moving back in history

Mosaic maintains a history of your current session so you can retrace your steps and review documents that you've already seen. You can navigate through these documents using buttons and menu commands or the History window.

Figure 4-10:
The Le
WebLouvre
home page,
which deliv-
ers art
direct from
France.

You can easily navigate among the documents you've seen in your current
session by using the following buttons and menu commands:

✓ Clicking the left-arrow button on the toolbar or choosing Navigate⎜Back
displays the previous document. If no previous document exists, the
button is dimmed.

✓ Clicking the right-arrow button on the toolbar or choosing Navigate⎜For-
ward displays the next document. If there isn't a next document, the button is dimmed.

✓ Clicking the Home button on the toolbar or choosing Navigate⎜Home
takes you back to where it all began, your default home page.

✓ Clicking the Reload button on the toolbar or choosing Navigate⎜Reload
reloads the current document. Pages sometimes get scrambled during
transmission or rendering, and Reload lets you quickly reload the document to your system.

If you navigate back to a Web document and then choose a new hyperlink in
that document, history is rewritten. After navigating back to a previously displayed document, any hyperlinks you select will overwrite the existing history from that site. In other words, any sites in your history list after the
original visit to that site are removed from the list.

When you use the navigation buttons or menu commands to navigate through
documents you've viewed, you're flying blind through Mosaic's history list.

Those who can't store enough history are destined to repeat it

Mosaic uses a feature called *document caching* to store the last two Web documents in your computer's memory. Mosaic can quickly redisplay these documents because they are cached (stored) in your computer's memory. Without caching, Mosaic would have to transfer the documents from the Web site to your computer again before displaying them. For the other sites in your history list,

Mosaic keeps only the URL addresses in memory. As a result, Mosaic must reconnect to the Web site when you go back to one of those documents. If your computer has sufficient memory, you can increase the number of documents Mosaic keeps in memory beyond the default of two by editing the mosaic.ini file. We show you how to do this in Chapter 7.

You can see all the URL addresses you've visited in your current surfing session by displaying Mosaic's history list for your current session. You can return to any site you've visited by choosing it from this list.

Here's how you use Mosaic's history list:

1. Choose Navigate | History from Mosaic's menu. As shown in Figure 4-11, Mosaic displays the History window. The current history list is displayed and the current document's URL is highlighted.

2. To view a document from the history list, double-click the document's URL, or select it and click the Load button.

3. To close the History window without loading a new document, click Dismiss.

You can keep the History window open at all times while you surf. Just reduce the History window to a smaller size and move it into a corner of your screen. From this shrunken window, you can continue to jump around as you please while you surf the Web. ■

Wipeout! Aborting a document transfer

You may find yourself in a situation where you don't have enough time to finish downloading a very large document containing lots of pictures or a video or sound clip file. If your TCP/IP software supports interrupts (which most do, but some don't), you can abort the transfer.

Figure 4-11: The History window lets you navigate through the documents you've viewed in the current session by choosing a URL address item.

To abort a document transfer, click the Mosaic icon while the earth on this icon is spinning. If the Web document is transferring pictures, you have to click the Mosaic icon once for each image. In other words, if the Mosaic icon continues to spin, keep clicking until it stops.

Mosaic isn't picture perfect

Mosaic lets you view GIF (Graphics Interchange Format) files as inline images. GIF is a bitmap file format created by CompuServe, and it's one of the most widely used file formats on the Net. *Inline images* are pictures that are actually connected to the Web document. You can display these pictures in Mosaic without an external viewer program. GIF has a built-in compression scheme that reduces the size of files while they are being transferred.

To view and work with other picture formats and other forms of multimedia, such as sounds and video, you need to install special viewers. We show you how to install these viewers in Chapter 8. But for now, you can do a lot of surfing without using external viewers.

If for any reason, a picture isn't transferred, you'll see the standard Failed DNS error message, and Mosaic will display a picture placeholder icon like this:

If a picture doesn't get transferred, it usually means the URL for the picture file is incorrect in the Web document, or the telecommunications line is experiencing problems. In such cases, you might be able to correct the problem by clicking the Reload button or choosing Navigate|Reload to reload the document.

Watch out for crowded surfing conditions

Traffic on the Net is getting worse and worse. With its heavy downloading of data, the Web doesn't help. If possible, try to use the Net after rush hours. The standard 9–5 routine seems to carry over to cyberspace. If traffic on the Net is heavy, the information coming to your computer can slow to a crawl. In addition, Web sites can become overcrowded and you can't connect to them. After normal business hours, traffic drops, and surfing the Web usually becomes smoother and faster.

Getting Help in Mosaic

The current version of Mosaic isn't equipped with the standard Windows on-line help system. In other words, you can't get help by pointing to something on the screen and pressing F1. To access Mosaic's help system, you have to connect to a Web document at NCSA by choosing Help | Online Documentation.

If you're thinking you can get telephone support like you do with most commercial software programs, forget it. NCSA doesn't offer a technical support hotline. ▪

Here's what you'll find in Mosaic's Help menu:

✔ The Online Documentation item connects to an NCSA Web document called the Mosaic for Windows User's Guide, which is shown in Figure 4-12. The table of contents is hyperlinked for your convenience. You can download this documentation to your system using the Options | Load to Disk command, as explained in Chapter 6.

✔ The FAQ Page item connects to an NCSA Web document of Frequently Asked Questions. You may want to download this document; it includes some useful information.

✔ The Bug List item connects to an NCSA Web document that lists all the known bugs for the current version of Mosaic. This document is a good one to keep handy. If you have a problem doing something, chances are it's listed here, which means you're not alone.

✔ The Feature Page item connects to an NCSA Web document that lists the features of the current version of Mosaic.

✔ The About Windows Mosaic item displays a dialog box that identifies which version of Mosaic you're using. This is the same dialog box that appears when you click the Help button.

✔ The Mail to Developers item lets you fire off an e-mail message to the developers if you've discovered a bug or need some help. However, it

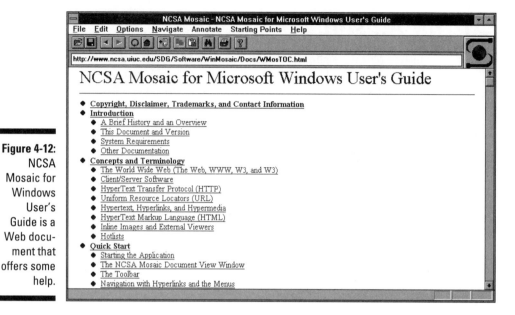

Figure 4-12:
NCSA
Mosaic for
Windows
User's
Guide is a
Web docu-
ment that
offers some
help.

can take weeks to get a response to your question. Choosing Help | Mail to Developers displays the Mail to Developers window, which is shown in Figure 4-13. You can fill out an e-mail message, choose the Send button, and wait a few weeks for a response.

Figure 4-13: The Mail to Developers window lets you send an e-mail message to the developers of Mosaic; however, don't expect a quick response.

Exiting Mosaic

Quitting Mosaic is simple. You can choose File | Exit or double-click the Control-menu box in the upper-left corner of the Mosaic window. Keyboarders can press Alt-F4. No matter which you method you use, the Mosaic window closes. After you exit Mosaic, you're still connected to the Net. If you want to disconnect, use your TCP/IP software.

Chapter 5

Hotlists: The Great Kahunas of Web Surfing

. . . .

In This Chapter

▶ Getting into hotlists

▶ Navigating Mosaic's factory-installed hotlists

▶ Creating your own hotlist menus

▶ Adding items to hotlists

▶ Editing hotlists to keep up with the times

. . . .

*H*otlists are the Web surfer's best friend. They let you store hundreds of your hottest or coolest Web site addresses as menu items. Hotlists make your Web surfing safari easier and faster — all you do is choose a menu item.

What Are Hotlists?

Hotlists are simply Web sites or other Net resources that are listed as menu items. By putting a Web site in a hotlist menu, you can choose it like any menu command, and off you go. Menus that include these hotlist entries are called *user-configurable menus*, which simply means they're menus that you can create and customize. After you add a URL as a menu item, you don't have to type in the URL each time you want to go to the Web site.

You can build up an impressive array of hotlist entries by entering them manually or storing them as you surf the Web. To store your hotlists, Mosaic lets you create up to 20 top-level menu items that can each contain submenus. A top-level menu appears on the menu bar in the Mosaic window. Under each top-level menu item, you can create a submenu containing as many as 40 entries. With 800 possible menu items, you can organize your Web sites according to almost any criteria.

With the exception of a special hotlist called the Quicklist, all hotlists are accessible via menus. The Quicklist is the only hotlist that never shows up as a menu. We show you how to work with this odd hotlist feature at the end of this chapter.

Mosaic's Factory-Installed Hotlists

You've already used a hotlist to go to Web sites. The Starting Points menu is a top-level menu of hotlist items and submenus created by the folks at NCSA. Some items in this menu connect to a single site, while others display a sub-menu of more items. Table 5-1 describes the items and submenus in the Start-ing Points menu. Over time, you'll want to change these hotlist items because many of them won't be of interest to you.

Choosing Hotlist Items

When you choose a hotlist item, Mosaic automatically connects to that site. The act of choosing a hotlist item is not one of your more taxing tasks. There are two ways to choose a hotlist item:

✔ Directly from the menu. This is the easiest way to choose a hotlist item. A right-pointing arrow next to a hotlist menu item indicates that the menu item contains a submenu. You can display the submenu by click-ing the menu item or dragging the cursor over it. To choose a menu item, either drag the cursor to the menu item and release the mouse but-ton, or click the menu item.

✔ Using the Open URL dialog box, which is shown in Figure 5-1. To access this dialog box, choose File|Open URL, click the Open URL button, or press Ctrl-O. To select a hotlist, click the down-arrow icon to the right of the Current Hotlist field, and highlight the hotlist you want. You can choose an item from the selected hotlist using either of the top fields in the dialog box. The drop-down list on the right side of the dialog box lists the sites by their titles. The URL field lists sites by their URL addresses. After choosing the hotlist item you want, choose OK or press Enter. Because the Quicklist doesn't appear as a menu, the Open URL dialog box is the only method for choosing an item from the Quicklist.

Table 5-1: The hundred points of sites from the Starting Points menu

Menu item	Description
Starting Points Document	Displays an NCSA Web document containing hyperlinks to various sites on the Web. It's OK, but there are better ones on the Web.
NCSA Mosaic Demo Document	Displays a Web document to test external viewers that you have installed.
NCSA Mosaic's 'What's New' Page	Displays a Web document that identifies new Web sites. This is a definite keeper because it provides an extensive, regularly updated monthly listing of new Web sites.
NCSA Mosaic home page	Displays the mothership home page, the NCSA's Mosaic home page that appears by default each time you launch Mosaic. This home page includes updates on developments at NCSA, as well as hyperlinks to all kinds of Mosaic user information.
Windows Mosaic home page	Displays the Mosaic for Windows home page. This home page keeps you up to date on new releases of Mosaic and supporting software.
World Wide Web Info	Displays a submenu of items about the World-Wide Web that are stored on the CERN Web server. CERN developed the HTTP protocol that is the basis of the Web.
Home Pages	Displays a submenu of mostly academic Web sites. Most of these sites won't be on your list of keepers.
Gopher Servers	Displays a submenu of Gopher sites to which you can connect using Mosaic. Gopher is an Internet search and retrieval tool for accessing information that's located on hundreds of servers scattered across the Net.
Finger Gateway	Displays a Web document for working with the Finger command in Mosaic. The Finger command lets you find information about users on the Internet.
Whois Gateway	Displays a Whois Web document for working with the Whois command, which lets you access databases of sites and users on the Internet.
Other Documents	Displays a submenu that lists a variety of Web sites. You might want to check out some of these sites, but most of them are academic sites.
Archie Request Form	Displays a Web document for working with Archie, which is an Internet file searching program.

Figure 5-1: The Open URL dialog box lets you choose both a hotlist and hotlist items.

Your Own Personal Menus of Hotlists

You can create and manage your hotlists by using the Personal Menus dialog box, which is shown in Figure 5-2. To open this dialog box, choose Navigate | Menu Editor from the Mosaic menu.

Here are the main parts of the Personal Menus dialog box:

> ✔ The Menus list displays the current set of hotlist menus. Initially, this list contains only the Starting Points menu, its submenus, and the Quick-list hotlist. The submenus for the Starting Points menu are indented under the Starting Points entry.

> ✔ The Items list displays the contents of the menu or submenu that's selected in the Menus list. For example, if you select Starting Points in the Menus list, the Items list displays all the items found in the Starting Points menu. Greater-than signs (>) precede the names of submenus in the Items list.

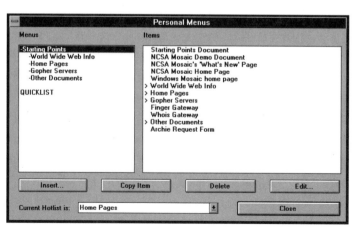

Figure 5-2: The Personal Menus dialog box lets you create and renovate your hotlists.

✔ The Insert, Copy Item, Delete, and Edit buttons let you perform editing actions on the selected item in either list.

✔ The Current Hotlist drop-down list box lets you choose the current hotlist. This is the hotlist Mosaic uses when you add hotlist items while you surf.

✔ The Close button closes the Personal Menus dialog box and saves your changes.

Creating Hotlist Menus

Hotlist menus are the containers for organizing and storing your hotlist entries. Mosaic lets you construct a hierarchy of hotlist menus. Like the Starting Points menu, your hotlist menus can include a top-level menu and submenus. You can even create submenus within submenus.

Creating top-level hotlist menus

Mosaic lets you create multiple top-level menus. However, if you add more menus than can fit in the width of your Mosaic window, they'll wrap around on the menu bar. In most cases, a few top-level menus are more than enough.

For now, it's easier to build your own top-level hotlist menu from scratch instead of editing the Starting Points menu. At a later time, you can change the Starting Points menu, including its top-level name. ▪

Here's how you add your own top-level menu to the Mosaic menu bar:

1. Choose Navigate|Menu Editor to open the Personal Menus dialog box.

2. Click in the blank space above the QUICKLIST option in the Menus list.

3. Click Insert. As shown in Figure 5-3, Mosaic displays the Add Item dialog box. Only the Title field and the Menu control button are active.

Figure 5-3: You use the Add Item dialog box to enter a name for your new menu item.

4. Enter a name for your new top-level menu item in the Title field. For example, you can name your top-level menu Web Fun or Business. Try to keep it short so you'll have room for adding more top-level menu items in the future.

5. Choose OK to close the Add Item window. You are returned to the Personal Menus dialog box, which now lists the new item in the Menus list.

6. Choose Close to save your changes and exit the Personal Menus dialog box. Figure 5-4 shows the Mosaic window with two top-level menus added to the right side of the menu bar, just before the Help menu.

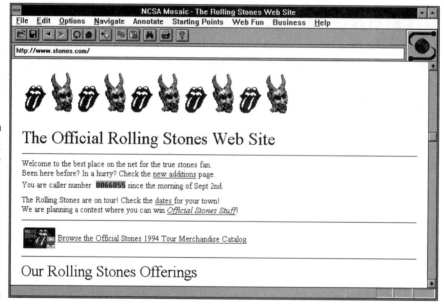

Figure 5-4:
The new top-level menus are ready for adding submenus or individual hotlist items.

Creating hotlist submenus

Creating submenus is just as easy as creating a top-level menu item. In the Mosaic window, a submenu shows up as an option in a top-level menu. An arrow to the right of a menu option indicates that it opens a submenu containing more options. Here's how you create a submenu:

1. Open the Personal Menus dialog box by choosing Navigate | Menu Editor from the Mosaic menu.

2. In the Menus list, click a top-level menu for which you want to create a submenu.

3. Click the Insert button, which opens the Add Item dialog box.

4. Click the Menu radio button. The URL text box disappears.

5. Enter the name of your submenu in the Title text field. Remember, the name you're entering is a menu item, so you shouldn't make it too long.

6. Choose OK to close the Add Item dialog box and return to the Personal Menus dialog box. The submenu item you created appears at the bottom of the Items list, with a greater-than sign (>) to the left of the item name. The submenu also appears in the Menus list at the end of any submenus for the top-level menu you specified. Figure 5-5 shows the addition of several submenus under a new top-level menu.

7. Choose Close to save your changes and exit the Personal Menus dialog box.

Figure 5-5:
Using the Personal Menus dialog box, several submenus have been added under a new top-level menu item.

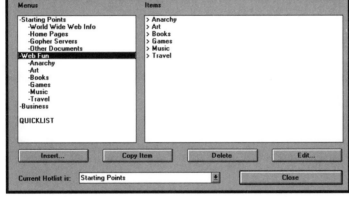

Adding Sites as Hotlist Items

So far, the menus you've created are nothing but shells. Now it's time to add content to those menus. You can add any Web document or other Net resource, such as a Gopher site, as a menu item. If you frequently go to particular sites, you can enter those sites as items in a top-level menu rather than going through a submenu.

Mosaic lets you add hotlist menu items using two methods. You can enter the site's URL address and your own title for the site using the Personal Menus dialog box. You can also add the site to a hotlist while you're viewing the site in the Mosaic window.

Table 5-2 lists some interesting Web sites you can use to get some practice adding hotlist items. Part VI provides an extensive, annotated surfer's guide to all kinds of Web sites, including the sites listed in Table 5-2.

Table 5-2: Some Web sites you might want to add to your hotlists

Web site	URL
Internet Business Center	http://www.tig.com/IBC/
Global Network Navigator	http://nearnet.gnn.com/GNNhome.html
Branch Information Services	http://branch.com:1080/
Career Mosaic	http://www.careermosaic.com:80/cm/
ElNet Galaxy	http://galaxy.einet.net
The Asylum	http://www.galcit.caltech.edu/~ta/asylhome.html
The Virtual Tourist	http://wings.buffalo.edu/world
CommerceNet	http://www.commerce.net/

Adding hotlist items using Personal Menus

By using the Personal Menus dialog box, you can add hotlist items without first connecting to the site. You need to have the site's URL address and a name for the site, which will be used as the menu item. Here's how you add an item to a menu:

1. Open the Personal Menus dialog box by choosing Navigate|Menu Editor from the Mosaic menu.

2. In the Menus list, click on the top-level menu or the submenu in which the new hotlist item is to appear.

3. In the Items list, click to indicate where you want the menu item to appear. The new item will be inserted above the item you select.

4. Choose the Insert button. Mosaic displays the Add Item dialog box, and the Document item radio button is already selected.

5. Select the text in the Title field if necessary and enter the name of your menu item. Remember to make it concise.

6. Select the text in the URL field if necessary and enter the URL address for your site.

7. Click OK. Your entry is added to the Items list in the Personal Menus dialog box. Figure 5-6 shows a collection of items added to a submenu.

8. Choose Close to save your changes and exit the Personal Menus dialog box.

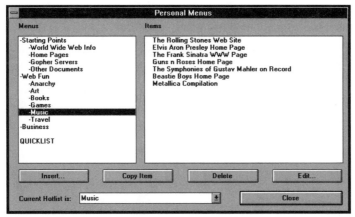

Figure 5-6:
A collection of hotlist items added to a sub-menu in the Personal Menus dialog box.

Adding hotlist items while you surf

Mosaic makes it easy to add URL addresses and document titles to your hotlists while you surf the Web. Adding entries this way lets you check out the site first to make sure it's worth saving as a hotlist item. When you add a Web site to a hotlist, the document title appears as the menu item.

Mosaic keeps one hotlist active until you change it. This active hotlist is called the current hotlist. If you want to add entries while you surf the Web, you need to make sure you have the right hotlist active as the current hotlist.

Fortunately, you can change the current hotlist while you surf. There are two ways to choose the current hotlist in Mosaic:

> ✔ Choose File|Open URL, click the Open URL button, or press Ctrl-O. Click the arrow in the Current Hotlist field, and select the hotlist you want.

> ✔ Choose Navigate|Menu Editor, click the arrow in the field labeled Current Hotlist is, and select the hotlist you want.

Let's go surfing and capture some hotlist entries:

1. Choose File|Open URL. Mosaic displays the Open URL dialog box.

2. Click the down-arrow button to the right of the Current Hotlist field, and drag the cursor to select the hotlist to which you want to add entries.

3. Choose OK. The selected hotlist is now the current hotlist.

4. Enter a URL address for a site you want to visit in Mosaic's URL text field, and press Enter. For example, you can enter the following:

```
http://wings.buffalo.edu/world
```
This takes you to The Virtual Tourist home page.

5. Click the Add to Hotlist button or choose Navigate|Add Current to Hotlist. Bingo, the site becomes an item in the current hotlist.

6. Navigate to other sites by using hyperlinks or entering URLs. Each time you find a site that you want to add to the current hotlist, choose Navigate|Add Current to Hotlist.

Managing Your Hotlists

The one thing that never changes is change. The Web is no exception; it's always changing, and so will your hotlists. Sites come and go, your tastes change, some sites lose their appeal, or maybe you'll want to rearrange some hotlists. Whatever the reason, you can edit your hotlists using the Personal Menus dialog box. Mosaic also lets you group related items in your menus by adding separators, which are lines that separate items in menus.

You can share your hotlists with other Mosaic users by using the Windows Notepad to extract hotlists from your mosaic.ini file and save them as a file. Chapter 9 gives you the nuts-and-bolts details of using the mosaic.ini file and the Windows Notepad to share hotlists. ▪

Editing a menu title or a hotlist item

The Edit button in the Personal Menus dialog box allows you to edit a top-level menu name, a submenu name, or a menu item. You can't edit the hotlist named Quicklist.

Here's how you edit a hotlist menu name or menu item:

1. From the Menus list in the Personal Menus dialog box, select the menu you want to change. If you want to change an item on this menu, select the item from the Items list. To edit a menu item in the Items list, you must select both the item and the corresponding menu in the Menus list.

2. Click the Edit button. Mosaic displays the Edit Item dialog box. As shown in Figure 5-7, the Edit Item dialog box doesn't include the URL field if you selected a menu or submenu. Figure 5-8 shows the Edit Item dialog box with the URL text box, which is displayed if you selected a menu item.

3. Enter your changes in the Title and URL text boxes.

4. Choose OK. The changes are displayed in the Personal Menus dialog box.

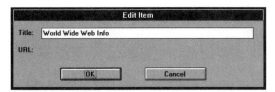

Figure 5-7: The Edit Item dialog box looks like this if you're editing a menu or submenu title.

Figure 5-8: If you're editing a menu item, the Edit Item dialog box includes the URL text box.

5. Choose Close to save your changes and exit the Personal Menus dialog box.

A quick way to display the Edit Item dialog box for editing a menu or menu item is to double-click the entry in either the Menus list or the Items list. ■

Copying hotlist items

Mosaic makes it easy to copy items from one hotlist to another in the Personal Menus dialog box. However, Mosaic won't let you copy menus. Here's how you copy an item from one hotlist to another:

1. Select a hotlist from the Menus list, and select an item from that hotlist in the Items list.

2. Click the Copy Item button.

3. In the Menus list, select the hotlist to which you want to copy the item.

4. Click in the Items list to specify where the item should be copied. It will be inserted immediately before the item you select in the Items list.

5. Click the Insert button. Mosaic displays the Add Items dialog box, with the copied item's Title and URL information, and the Document item radio button already chosen.

6. Click OK. The item is added to the Items list for the selected hotlist.

Deleting hotlist items

You can remove a selected hotlist menu or menu item by clicking the Delete button in the Personal Menus dialog box. To delete a hotlist item, select the item in the Items list, and click the Delete button. Mosaic displays a dialog box asking you to confirm that you want to delete the item. Click the Yes button to delete the selected item from the hotlist menu.

Before you can delete a menu, you must delete any items or submenus that are contained in that menu. After deleting the items, you delete a menu by selecting it from the Menus list and clicking the Delete button. When you click the Delete button, Mosaic displays the message shown in Figure 5-9.

Figure 5-9: The menu deletion message warns you about deleting a menu that still contains items.

This message means that you need to delete the items in the menu before deleting the menu. Although you can choose OK and delete a menu that still contains items, the items in the menu aren't removed from your mosaic.ini file. Because the items remain in your mosaic.ini file without a menu name, you may need to edit the mosaic.ini file if you choose the OK button. The best advice is don't delete a menu that still contains items. We tell you how to edit hotlists from the mosaic.ini file in Chapter 9.

Moving hotlist items

Mosaic doesn't automatically sort hotlist menu items, but you can move items around using the Copy Item button in the Personal Menus dialog box. After copying the menu item to its new location, you can remove the original item using the Delete button. You can't move submenus using this method. However, as explained in Chapter 9, you can change the order of submenu entries by editing the mosaic.ini file.

Here's how you use the Personal Menus dialog box to move an item in a hotlist:

1. In the Menus list, select the menu in which you want to rearrange items.

2. In the Items list, select the menu item you want to move.

3. Click the Copy Item button.

4. In the Menus list, select the menu to which you want to move the selected item.

5. Click in the Items list to specify where the item should be copied. It will be inserted immediately before the item you select in the Items list.

6. Click the Insert button. The item is copied to the selected menu.

7. Select the old item at its original location.

8. Click the Delete button. Mosaic displays a dialog box asking you to confirm that you want to delete the selected item. Choose OK. Mosaic deletes the item from its original location.

9. Choose Close to save your changes and exit the Personal Menus dialog box.

Making your menus easier to read

Menu separators are simply lines that are displayed in a menu to group related menu items. You can add separators to top-level hotlist menus and submenus. They're handy visual aids for working with menus because they let you organize related menu items into groups. For example, Figure 5-10 shows how you can use separators in the Starting Points menu to add a visual element to the organization of different types of sites.

Here's how you add a separator to a menu:

1. Open the Personal Menus dialog box by choosing Navigate | Menu Editor from the Mosaic menu.

Figure 5-10: You can add separators to the Starting Points menu to break up the items into visual groupings.

Starting Points Document
NCSA Mosaic Demo Document
NCSA Mosaic's 'What's New' Page
NCSA Mosaic Home Page
Windows Mosaic home page
World Wide Web Info ▶
Home Pages ▶
Gopher Servers ▶
Finger Gateway
Whois Gateway
Other Documents ▶
Archie Request Form

2. Select the menu in the Menus list.

3. In the Items list, select the menu item immediately after the last item you want included in the first separated group.

4. Click the Insert button. Mosaic displays the Add Item dialog box.

5. Click the Separator radio button and choose OK. The line appears in the Items list. If the line is not in the right place, select the line, click the Delete button, and try again.

6. Click the Close button to save your changes and exit the Personal Menus dialog box. When you open the menu, the separator appears in the menu.

Working with the Quicklist

The Quicklist is the only hotlist that never shows up as a menu. Because the Quicklist can contain an unlimited number of entries, you can use the Quicklist as a holding bin for surfing the Net. At best, however, the Quicklist is only a marginal feature. Even so, you can't delete the Quicklist.

The only way to access items from the Quicklist is by selecting it as the current hotlist and then choosing the items from the Open URL dialog box. You can add or delete sites in the Quicklist just as you do for any other hotlist.

The Quicklist hotlist comes with several entries already in place. Like any other hotlist, you can edit, remove, or add Quicklist items. Figure 5-11 shows the items in the Quicklist as they appear in the Personal Menus dialog box.

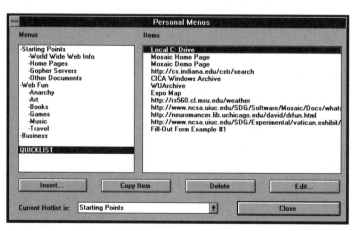

Figure 5-11: The items in the Quicklist hotlist as they appear in the Personal Menus dialog box.

Moving On

Now that you've mastered the essentials of surfing the Web on your Mosaic
surfboard, you might want to do some surfing and build up your own hotlists.
If you go to the Web Surfer's Guide in Part VI, you can get all the URLs you
want for surfing the Web and building your own hotlists. After you finish your
surfing adventures, return to the next chapter, which tells you how to customize your Mosaic surfboard by editing the mosaic.ini file.

Chapter 6

Rounding Out Your Basic Surfing Techniques

• •

In This Chapter

▶ Transferring Web documents to your computer

▶ Launching Web documents directly from your computer

▶ Printing and searching Web documents

▶ Turning off pictures

▶ Interacting with electronic forms

▶ Using Mosaic as a pretty face for other Net tools

• •

*Y*ou understand the surfing basics and you know how to be a hotlist hot-dogger. This chapter rounds out your basic Web surfing skills. It delivers new techniques to give you more control over your rides, and it opens up new surfing experiences.

Making Web Documents and Other Files Yours

While you're Web surfing, you can capture any Web documents and hyperlinks you see and transfer copies to your computer. Mosaic lets you retrieve Web documents that appear in the Mosaic window or documents and other files from hyperlinks within a Web document. Mosaic delivers all of them right to your computer.

As you might recall, Mosaic creates Web documents on your computer by processing an ASCII text file containing HTML codes, as well as any inline pictures that appear in the Web document. A Web server sends the HTML codes and inline pictures to your computer. Once these codes and pictures arrive at your computer, Mosaic renders them into the Web documents you see on your screen.

By downloading a Web document and saving it as a file on your computer, you can view the document on your computer without being connected to the Web. In addition, you can load the document on your computer and use it as a starting point for working on the Web. The benefit of storing the Web document file on your computer is that you don't have to wait for the Web server to download the HTML codes and inline pictures each time you want to display the Web document. With the Web document loaded on your computer and a live connection to the Net, you can start surfing by choosing any of the hyperlinks in the document.

Mosaic lets you retrieve all the Web documents and files you navigate to during a Web surfing session, or you can retrieve Web documents and files on a one-by-one basis.

Not all filenames are created equal

The Net is the great melting pot of computers. As a result, many files you download don't conform to the DOS/Windows filename standard. Remember that DOS/Windows filenames consist of up to eight alphanumeric characters, optionally followed by a dot (a period) and an extension of up to three alphanumeric characters.

If you save a file that has a long name without assigning a new name that conforms to the DOS/Windows file-naming rules, DOS/Windows automatically creates a new filename as follows:

✔ If there are more than eight characters before the first period in the original filename, DOS/Windows uses the first eight characters as the new filename.

✔ If there are more than three characters after the last period in the original filename, DOS/Windows uses the first three characters after the last period as the filename extension.

✔ If the original filename contains more than one period, DOS/Windows deletes everything between the periods. Only one period is used in the new DOS/Windows filename.

For example, the HTML file SurfChronicles.html becomes SurfChro.htm. DOS/Windows filenames are not case sensitive. Filenames that are automatically truncated to satisfy the DOS/Windows filename rules can become fairly cryptic, so you may want to rename the files that you download.

Retrieving Web documents and files from a surfing session

By choosing the Load to Disk command from the Options menu, you instruct Mosaic to retrieve every Web document, hyperlink, and file to which you navigate. As long as the Load to Disk option is active, Mosaic saves the Web documents as files on your computer.

To tell Mosaic that you want to stop saving the Web documents and files to your disk, you must turn off the Load to Disk option. After turning off the Load to Disk command, you can return to displaying Web documents and viewing hyperlinks.

Load to Disk is a toggle command. In other words, each time you choose this command, you turn it either on or off. By default, it's shut off.

To keep the Load to Disk command active for subsequent Mosaic sessions, turn it on and then choose File I Save Preferences. In most cases, you'll want to leave this option turned off, which is the default setting. ■

Here's how you use Mosaic's Options I Load to Disk command to retrieve Web documents or other files and store them as files on your computer for a surfing session:

1. Choose Options I Load to Disk from the Mosaic menu bar.

2. Go to a Web document or click a hyperlink. As shown in Figure 6-1, Mosaic displays the Save As dialog box to allow you to save the previous document.

3. Choose the drive and directory in which you want to save the file. The default filename is displayed in the File Name text box. You can accept the default name or enter another filename. If it's a Web document file, make sure you add the .HTM filename extension. Without this extension, Mosaic won't be able to load this file.

4. Choose OK. Mosaic saves the file on your computer.

5. Repeat steps 2–4 for each Web document or file you want to transfer to your local system.

6. To turn off the Load to Disk command and return to viewing Web documents, choose Options I Load to Disk or click the Disk button in the toolbar.

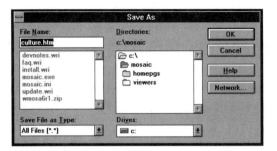

Figure 6-1: The Save As dialog box lets you specify where to save your file and what to name it.

Retrieving Web documents and files one at a time

It's easy to retrieve the current Web document or the Web document or file that's behind a hyperlink. To determine what's behind a hyperlink, just point to it without clicking it. The status bar lists the URL for the hyperlink, including the type of file. To retrieve the current Web document or the Web document or file that's behind a hyperlink:

1. Do one of the following:

   a. Display the Web document you want to retrieve.

   b. Point to the hyperlink in a Web document. You can check the status bar to see what type of file it is.

2. Do one of the following:

   a. If you're retrieving the current Web document, click the Load to Disk button.

   b. If you're retrieving what's behind a hyperlink, hold down the Shift key and click the hyperlink. Mosaic displays the Save As dialog box.

3. Choose the drive and directory in which you want to save the file. Either accept the default filename or enter another filename in the File Name text box. Remember, if the file is a Web document, you must keep the .HTM filename extension so Mosaic can read it.

4. Choose OK. Mosaic saves your file.

Retrieving Web documents at the source

Behind each Web document lies its HTML source code. This source document is a text file containing instructions that tell Mosaic how to generate the Web document on your computer. The File I Document Source command lets you view and retrieve this HTML file for any currently displayed Web document.

If you are building your own Web documents with an HTML editor, using an existing HTML file as a starting point is a real time-saver. Part IV shows you how to use these files as templates for creating your own Web documents. ■

Here's how you retrieve a Web document's source file:

1. Display a Web document you want to retrieve. Figure 6-2 shows a typical Web document in the Mosaic window.

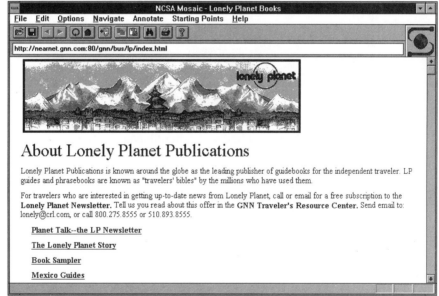

Figure 6-2:
A Web document as it usually appears in the Mosaic window. You get the picture.

2. Choose File I Document Source. As shown in Figure 6-3, Mosaic displays the Source Document window with the Web document's HTML codes exposed.

3. Choose File I Save in the Source Document window. Mosaic displays the Save As dialog.

File Edit

```
<HTML><HEAD>
 <TITLE>Lonely Planet Books</TITLE>
 <LINK REV=made HREF="mailto:forum@gnn.com">
</HEAD><BODY>

<IMG SRC="graphics/logo2.gif" ALT="">

<H1>About Lonely Planet Publications</H1>

Lonely Planet Publications is known around the globe as the leading
publisher of guidebooks for the independent traveler. LP guides and
phrasebooks are known as "travelers' bibles" by the millions who have
used them. <P>

For travelers who are interested in getting up-to-date news from Lonely
Planet, call or email for a free subscription to the <B>Lonely Planet
Newsletter.</B> Tell us you read about this offer in the <B>GNN Traveler's
Resource Center.</B> Send email to: lonely@crl.com, or call 800.275.8555 or
510.893.8555. <P>

<DL>
<DD> <A HREF="news.html"><B>Planet Talk--the LP Newsletter</B></A> <P>

<DD> <A HREF="story.html"><B>The Lonely Planet Story</B></A> <P>

<DD> <A HREF="books.html"><B>Book Sampler</B></A> <P>

<DD> <A HREF="mex.html"><B>Mexico Guides</B></A> <P>

<DD> <A HREF="order.html"><B>Ordering Information</B></A> <P>
</DL>

<HR>
<A HREF="/gnn/meta/travel/index.html">
```

[OK]

Figure 6-3:
The naked HTML codes behind the Web document.

4. Choose the drive and directory for saving the file, and either accept the default filename or enter another filename in the File Name text box. If you enter a new filename, don't forget the .HTM filename extension.

5. Choose OK. Mosaic saves the file.

When you choose the File | Document Source command, Mosaic doesn't always display the Web document's HTML text file. As shown in Figure 6-4, if the

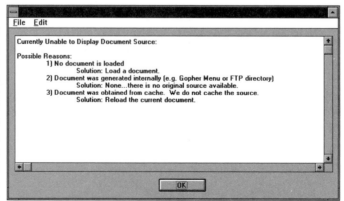

File Edit

```
Currently Unable to Display Document Source:

Possible Reasons:
            1) No document is loaded
                        Solution: Load a document.
            2) Document was generated internally (e.g. Gopher Menu or FTP directory)
                        Solution: None...there is no original source available.
            3) Document was obtained from cache.  We do not cache the source.
                        Solution: Reload the current document.
```

[OK]

Figure 6-4:
You'll see the Source Document message if Mosaic is unable to display the source document.

source document isn't available, Mosaic displays information in the Source Document window. If Mosaic displays this message, you can try to reload the current Web document. In some cases, the source document isn't available.

Opening Web Documents Locally

Loading Web documents locally is useful because it saves time and connection charges. Launching a Web document locally saves time because Mosaic doesn't have to download it from the Web server for you to begin surfing. Here's how it's done:

1. Launch Mosaic and choose File I Open Local File. As shown in Figure 6-5, Mosaic displays the Open dialog box.

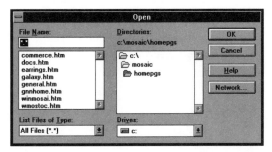

Figure 6-5: The Open dialog box lets you load a Web document locally.

2. Select the Web document file you want to load. In DOS/Windows, Web documents have filenames that end with .HTM, which is short for HTML.

3. Choose OK. Mosaic displays the Web document.

4. Connect to the Net and start using the hyperlinks in the Web document that's displayed in Mosaic.

You can automatically load a local Web document and make a connection at the same time when you launch Mosaic. You set this up by editing the mosaic.ini file. We'll show you how to do this in Chapter 7. ■

Get It in Writing

You can print any Web document that's displayed in Mosaic. It's like taking a Polaroid picture — fast and easy. With a laser printer, the printed output is a good likeness of the actual Web document, including the pictures. Mosaic prints the entire Web document.

Like any Windows application, Mosaic's printing functions are handled by the Windows Print Manager. See your Windows documentation for help with setting up your printer in Windows.

Mosaic uses the following standard Windows printing functions:

> ✔ Choosing File|Print, clicking the Print button, or pressing Ctrl-P displays the standard Windows Print dialog box, which is shown in Figure 6-6. Make any changes you want, and choose OK to print the document. Mosaic displays a dialog box telling you that it's printing.

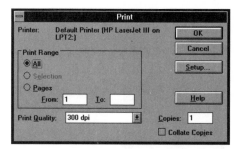

Figure 6-6: The Print dialog box. It's the same one you use in your other Windows applications.

> ✔ Choosing the File|Print Setup command displays the Print Setup dialog box, which is shown in Figure 6-7. This dialog box lets you choose a printer and select other options for your specific printer.

Figure 6-7:
The Print
Setup dialog
box lets you
change your
printer
settings.

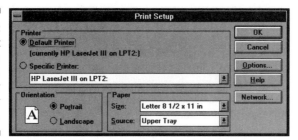

✔ Choosing the File | Print Preview command displays the current document in the Print Preview window, which is shown in Figure 6-8. The Print Preview window lets you scan through a Web document to see how many pages it includes and what's on them. Table 6-1 lists the buttons you use in the Print Preview window.

Figure 6-8:
The Mosaic
Print Pre-
view win-
dow gives
you a bird's-
eye view of
the pages in
a Web
document.

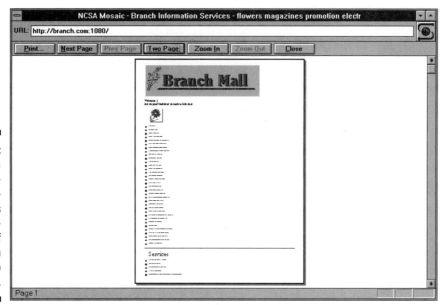

Mosaic's Print Preview feature is finicky. A document may appear scrambled in the Print Preview window. If this happens, try reloading the document and choosing File | Print Preview again. ∎

Table 6-1: Buttons in the Mosaic Print Preview window

Button	Description
Print	Returns to the Mosaic window and displays the Print dialog box.
Next Page	Displays the next page of the document. The button is dimmed if there's no next page.
Prev Page	Displays the previous page of the document. The button is dimmed if there's no previous page.
One Page	Changes from a two-page display to a one-page display.
Two Page	Changes from a one-page display to a two-page display.
Zoom In	Displays the page in a readable size.
Zoom Out	Returns to the reduced page size.
Close	Closes the Mosaic Print Preview window.

Searching High and Low through Web Documents

Mosaic includes a search capability that lets you find a character string, a word, or a phrase in the current Web document. The term *character string* is just another techie way of saying any combination of letters, numbers, or punctuation. Mosaic searches for text only in the current Web document.

To find a character string:

1. Choose Edit I Find or click the Find button. As shown in Figure 6-9, Mosaic displays the Find dialog box.

2. Enter the text you want to search for in the Find What field.

3. Choose the Match Case check box if you want the search to be case-sensitive. For example, if you choose the Match Case check box and tell Mosaic to find the text *HANG TEN* in the current document, the search will be unsuccessful if the document contains *hang ten*.

4. Choose Find Next. Mosaic searches the entire document. If Mosaic finds the string, it positions the document so that the first occurrence of the string appears within the document display area. To find the next occur-

rence of the string, click again on Find Next. If Mosaic doesn't find the
string, you'll see the ominous message displayed in Figure 6-10. If you
see this message, just click OK.

Figure 6-9: The Find dialog box lets you search
for text in your Web document.

Figure 6-10: This message informs you that
Mosaic failed in its search for matching text.

No Pictures, Please

Sometimes you run into choppy surf when you're transferring the pictures
with your Web documents. If Mosaic has problems getting inline images, a
timeout or the Failed DNS error message typically appears, and Mosaic displays the following error picture placeholder icon for each picture that isn't
downloaded:

If you're having trouble retrieving a Web document or you're using a slow
modem, you can tell Mosaic that it shouldn't download any pictures. This
speeds up the transfer of Web documents. Mosaic still displays the text and
hyperlinks in the Web document, but an icon of the NCSA logo is displayed in
place of the inline images. Figure 6-11 shows a Web document with graphics,
and Figure 6-12 shows the same Web document with the inline images turned
off. Placeholder icons appear in place of the inline images.

Figure 6-11:
A Web doc-
ument with
inline
pictures
displayed.

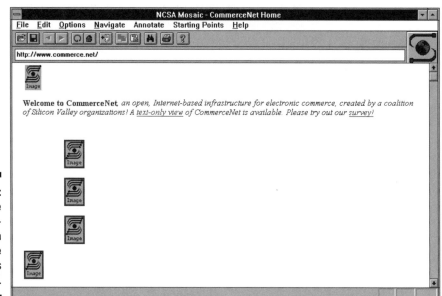

Figure 6-12:
The same
Web docu-
ment with
inline
pictures
turned off.

To turn off the inline images, choose Options | Display Inline Images. Mosaic turns off the check mark next to the Display Inline Images option, which means this toggle command is inactive. The default setting is active.

If you've turned off the inline images, you can display one of these pictures by clicking its placeholder icon with the right — that's right, the *right* — mouse button. A border around a placeholder icon indicates that the inline image is a hyperlink. You can move to the link by clicking the icon using the left button on your mouse.

As we explained in Chapter 4, inline images are pictures that are part of the Web document. Mosaic lets you view inline images in the GIF file format. GIF stands for Graphics Interchange Format. GIF comes from CompuServe, and it's the standard for displaying graphics on the Web in Mosaic. GIF has built-in compression to reduce the size of files for faster transfer rates. ■

Interacting with Forms

At this point, you might be thinking that the Web is all one-way. Think again. With the introduction of forms in Mosaic, the Web has gone interactive. Forms appear in Mosaic much like a form might appear on paper. Instead of using a pen or pencil to fill out the form, you simply point to a text box, click, and enter your text.

Forms can include a variety of features such as drop-down lists and buttons. Figure 6-13 shows a form that lets you order flowers. After you complete this form, it is sent as an e-mail message to Grant's Flowers.

Other Web forms let you enter keywords for searching a database. Figure 6-14 shows a search form in a Web document.

Forms also act as interfaces for working with different tools on the Net using Mosaic. For example, Figure 6-15 shows a form that lets you use Archie, a tool for finding files on the Net.

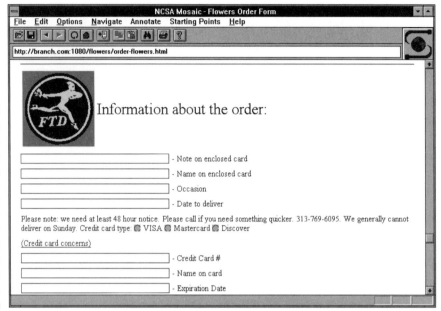

Figure 6-13:
Thanks to
Grant's
Florist &
Green-
house, you
can order
flowers for
Mom using
a form via
the Web
and Mosaic.

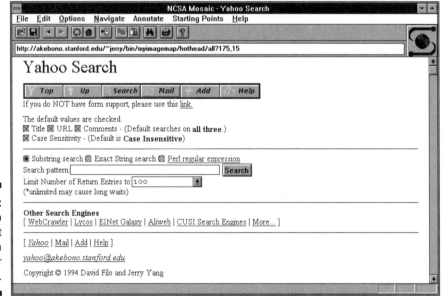

Figure 6-14:
This Web
document
form is a
front end for
a database.

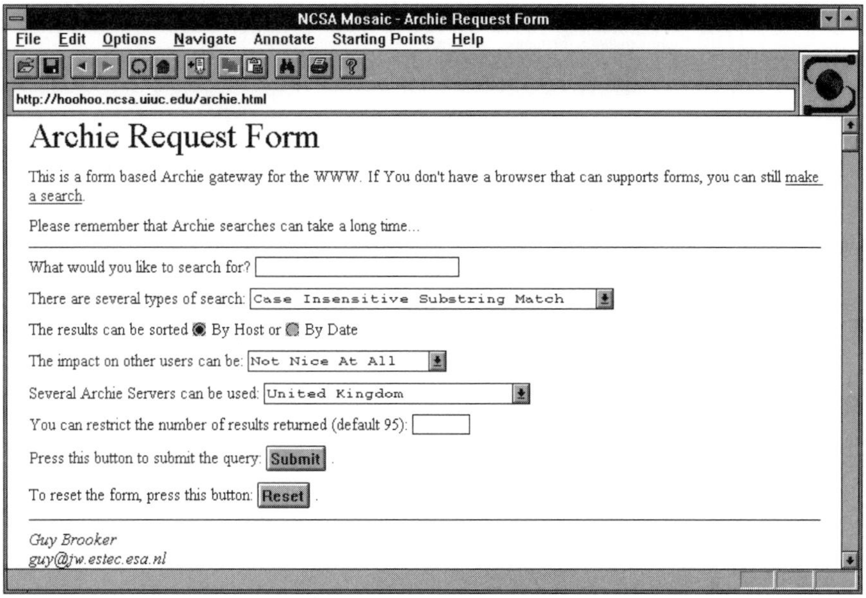

Figure 6-15:
This Web document is a form-based interface for the Archie tool.

Using Mosaic with Other Internet Tools

Mosaic is like a Swiss army knife tool for working on the Net. You can use it to connect to other types of servers, such as Gopher or FTP. Of course, Mosaic shines when it's connected to a Web server, but other tools also look better when you work with them using Mosaic. For example, Figure 6-16 shows a Gopher menu as it appears in Mosaic.

Mosaic lets you connect to the following Internet applications:

- Archie — a tool that lets you search for files.

- Finger and Whois — tools that let you search for user and site information.

- FTP (File Transfer Protocol) — the standard Internet tool for copying files between computers.

- Gopher — a tool that is similar to the Web, but lacks its powerful hypertext features. Information accessible from Gopherspace (Gopher servers) consists of ASCII menus.

- NNTP (Network News Transport Protocol) — the protocol behind network news, which is a vast bulletin board for sharing information across the Internet.

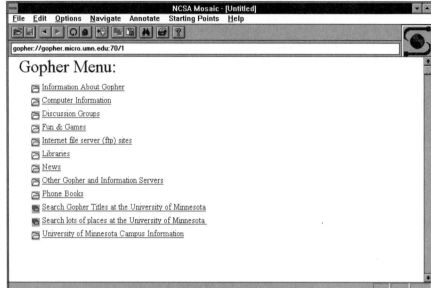

Figure 6-16:
A Gopher
menu as it
appears in
Mosaic.

✔ Telnet — the tool that lets users log in from remote sites and work on other computers on the Internet.

✔ WAIS (Wide-Area Information Server) — a text-based database retrieval tool that lets you find documents by entering keywords.

The Starting Points menu includes a submenu of Gopher hotlist items, a Finger Gateway item, a Whois Gateway item, and an Archie Request Form item. ■

Mosaic, FTP, and Gopher: A Great Combination

Directories, files, and menus in tools such as FTP and Gopher appear in Mosaic as hyperlinks. Using Mosaic, you can retrieve the files behind these hyperlinks in the same way you retrieve Web documents.

By default, Mosaic represents the files in an FTP or Gopher listing with icons that identify the file type or a directory. Table 6-2 identifies the most common icons that can appear at an FTP or a Gopher site.

You can turn off the display of these icons in Mosaic by choosing Options | Extend FTP Directory Parsing. Figure 6-17 shows a list of files with the

Table 6-2: Icons used for common file types

Icon	Filename extension	File description
	n/a	Directory on an FTP server. You can't download a directory.
	.zip	Compressed file in the PKZIP format, which is the most popular compression format on the Net.
	.txt	ASCII text file.
	.mpg	MPEG movie file.
	.mov	QuickTime movie file.
	.au	Audio file.
	.jpg	JPEG image file.
	.gif	GIF image file.
	n/a	File format that the server is unable to identify.
	n/a	Telnet access, which is available only at Gopher sites.
	n/a	Searchable WAIS index, which is available only at Gopher sites.

Options I Extend FTP Directory Parsing command active. Figure 6-18 shows the same file list with the Options I Extend FTP Directory Parsing command turned off.

If you click a hyperlink that points to any file other than text or another Web document, Mosaic transfers the file to your system for purposes of viewing or playing it with an external viewer program. In such cases, Mosaic must be set up to launch the external program that lets you work with the file. Otherwise, Mosaic will display an error message indicating that the file can't be viewed. Chapter 8 explains how you can add the external viewers and players you need for working with these files. ■

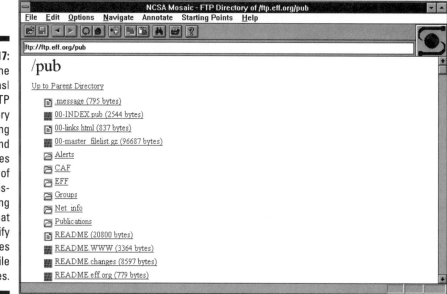

Figure 6-17:
The
Optionsl
Extend FTP
Directory
Parsing
command
enhances
this list of
files by dis-
playing
icons that
identify
directories
and file
types.

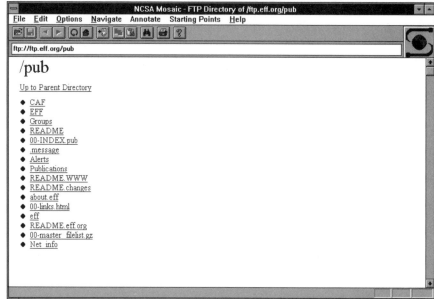

Figure 6-18:
With the
Extend FTP
Directory
Parsing
command
turned off,
the list of
files looks
pretty
barren.

To access an FTP server via Mosaic, you need the FTP server's URL. The URL format for pointing Mosaic to an FTP site is:

```
ftp://site/file path
```

For example, if you enter ftp://ftp.ncsa.uiuc.edu in Mosaic's URL box and press Enter, Mosaic takes you to NCSA's FTP server. Once you're connected to the FTP site, all the directories and files are displayed as hyperlinks. You can navigate through directories by clicking directory hyperlinks. When you find the file you want, choose Options|Load to Disk or click the Load to Disk button. Mosaic displays the Save As dialog box. Specify where you want the file on your system, and choose OK.

Mosaic lets you browse gopherspace and transfer files to your computer. Connecting to a Gopher server using Mosaic works exactly the same as connecting to an FTP site, except you specify gopher instead of ftp. You point Mosaic to a Gopher site using the following URL format:

```
gopher://site[/filepath]
```

For example, if you enter gopher://micro.umn.edu, Mosaic connects you to the University of Minnesota's Gopher server. You navigate the gopher server the same way you navigate an FTP server; by clicking directory links. You also download files the same way you do at an FTP site.

Lurking in USENET newsgroups

Mosaic lets you view articles that are posted in USENET newsgroups. USENET newsgroups are very popular on the Net, and they number in the thousands. These discussion groups cover every imaginable topic. A network news server is called an NNTP (Network News Transport Protocol) server. Before you can use Mosaic to read network news articles, you need to tell Mosaic the URL for your service provider's NNTP server. As explained in Chapter 7, you do this by changing an entry in the mosaic.ini file. To access a newsgroup, you need to know its address. Table 6-3 provides a sampling of newsgroups you can try after you set up Mosaic to work with network news.

The URL form for connecting to a newsgroup is different from the other tools because it lacks the two slashes (//). To connect to a newsgroup, you use the following URL format:

```
news:newsgroupname
```

For example, if you enter news:comp.infosystems.www.users in the URL box and press Enter, Mosaic displays a hyperlinked list of the titles of the 20 most

Table 6-3: Web-related newsgroups

Newsgroup	Description
comp.infosystems.announce	Announces new Web sites.
comp.infosystems.www.providers	Provides information on setting up and administering a Web server.
comp.infosystems.www.misc	Covers topics not addressed by other Web newsgroups.
comp.infosystems.www.users	Provides information on browser software, questions from new users, general news, and other topics.

recent postings (articles) to a newsgroup, as shown in Figure 6-19. At the top of the window is a hyperlink named (Earlier articles...), which lets you view earlier articles. To read the messages, just click the title and Mosaic displays the full article.

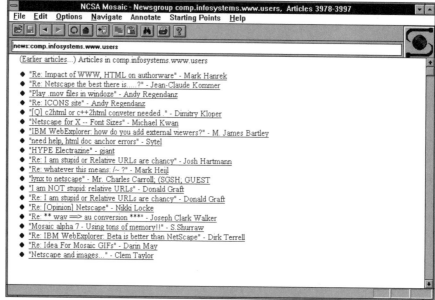

Figure 6-19: The 20 most recent postings of the comp.info-systems. www.users newsgroup appear as hyperlinks in Mosaic.

Working with WAIS

WAIS (Wide-Area Information Server) is a text search and retrieval system. WAIS allows you to search databases of text documents by entering keyword queries. The URL format for connecting to a WAIS server is as follows:

```
waisindex wais://site/database
```

An easy way to connect to the WAIS system is to point Mosaic to the following URL:

```
http://info.cern.ch/hypertext/Products/WAIS/Sources/Overview.html
```

As shown in Figure 6-20, this site provides a master list of WAIS databases.

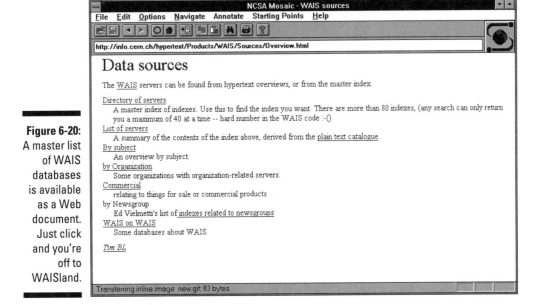

Figure 6-20: A master list of WAIS databases is available as a Web document. Just click and you're off to WAISland.

Putting the Finger on another user

Finger is a utility program that lets you look up information about users on UNIX systems. In most cases, a user's Finger file tells you the user's log-in name, their real name, the last time they accessed their account, and whether they have any unread mail. There's also an area in the Finger file to show a plan, which can be any text that a user wants others to see when they finger that user.

You can access Finger files with Mosaic by going through a gateway that accesses Finger, such as the following site:

```
http://cs.indiana.edu/finger/gateway
```

This site is a menu item (Finger Gateway) in Mosaic's Starting Points menu. At this site, you can read more information about Finger files and the Web gateway through which they are accessed. You can also search for a Finger file from anywhere on the Web by pointing Mosaic to following URL:

```
http://www.cs.indiana.edu/finger/hostname/username
```

Telneting via Mosaic

You can't remotely log in to another computer via Telnet directly from Mosaic. You need to install and set up a Telnet program to work in conjunction with Mosaic. We explain how to install an external Telnet program in Chapter 9. Once you have a Telnet program in place, you can point Mosaic to a Telnet server using the following URL form:

```
telnet://site address
```

For example, if you enter telnet://rs.internic.net, you are connected to the InterNIC domain name registration database site. The external Telnet program is displayed in a separate window. You can log in to the InterNIC database by entering whois. On other public Telnet systems, you log in to the system with a username and password, which are usually displayed on the log-in screen.

Sorry, no e-mail today

You can't use Mosaic to work directly with your e-mail. Instead, you have to Telnet to a site that offers e-mail, and use that e-mail program. For example, if you have a UNIX-based account at a service provider, you can Telnet to that site, log in, and use your e-mail program. But chances are, you'll want to use the Windows-based e-mail package that comes with your TCP/IP software.

Part III
Power Surfing

The 5th Wave — By Rich Tennant

"EXCUSE ME — IS ANYONE HERE NOT TALKING ABOUT MULTIMEDIA COMPUTING?"

In This Part...

*N*ow you're surfing the Web and building your own personal inventory of favorite sites. But wait, there's more. In fact, the best is yet to come. This part shows you how to customize your Mosaic surfboard and enter the exciting multimedia side of the World-Wide Web. We take you into the mosaic.ini initialization file and show you how to make a number of improvements to Mosaic, including changing the background color, turning off the automatic loading of the default Web document, and changing the number of documents stored in memory.

Then, you're off on the ultimate cyberdelic ride into the multimedia realm of the Web. We tell you how to get several multimedia programs and set them up to work with Mosaic. With these programs in place, you can view pictures and videos, play sounds, and view PostScript files. The World-Wide Web is teaming with multimedia files that are free for the picking.

Chapter 7

Customizing Your Mosaic Surfboard

● ●

In This Chapter

▶ Enhancing performance by editing the Mosaic initialization file

▶ Adding your return e-mail address to Mosaic

▶ Changing the default home page

▶ Increasing the number of Web documents Mosaic can store in memory

▶ Specifying your network news and e-mail servers

▶ Modifying the appearance of hyperlinks

▶ Changing fonts in Web documents

● ●

*W*hen you installed Mosaic, you copied the Mosaic initialization file, mosaic.ini, into your Windows directory. Mosaic.ini is a text file that Mosaic uses for storing program settings. When you launch Mosaic, the program finds and reads the mosaic.ini file.

You can select many of Mosaic's customization options using menu options and dialog boxes rather than editing the mosaic.ini file directly. However, many other customization changes require editing the mosaic.ini file. You can easily open the mosaic.ini file using the Notepad application, which is a Windows accessory. Editing the mosaic.ini file is surprisingly easy, and it gives you a strong sense of control over your Mosaic surfboard.

Making the Mosaic.ini File Easily Accessible

You can get to the mosaic.ini file in several ways. For example, you can open the Windows File Manager, navigate to the Windows directory, and double-click the mosaic.ini file. However, for the easiest access to mosaic.ini, you can make this file a Notepad icon in the group window that contains the Mosaic program. This way, the mosaic.ini file is always easily accessible whenever you need to make changes. You simply double-click the Mosaic Notepad icon, and then make your changes.

You'll be working with the mosaic.ini file throughout the next few chapters, so save yourself some time by taking a few moments to set it up as a Notepad icon.

Before you edit the mosaic.ini file that's stored in your Windows directory, make sure you have a backup copy of the file. You can keep the backup copy in your Mosaic directory. ■

Here's how you transform the mosaic.ini file into a Notepad file icon:

1. Open the group window that contains the Mosaic program icon. For example, if you have your Mosaic program in the group window for your TCP/IP software, open that window.

2. Open the Windows File Manager.

3. In File Manager, change to your Windows directory and find the mosaic.ini file.

4. Drag the mosaic.ini file to the group window you opened in the first step. The mosaic.ini file is now represented in the group window by the following Windows Notepad icon:

Mosaic

To open the mosaic.ini file, double-click the Mosaic Notepad icon that you just created. As shown in Figure 7-1, Windows launches the Notepad application and opens the mosaic.ini file.

To keep things organized, the mosaic.ini file contains various sections, such as [Main], [Viewers], and [Annotations]. These sections each contain a group of related settings.

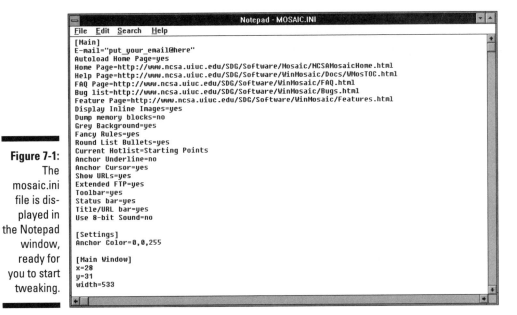

```
                    Notepad - MOSAIC.INI
 File  Edit  Search  Help
[Main]
E-mail="put_your_email@here"
Autoload Home Page=yes
Home Page=http://www.ncsa.uiuc.edu/SDG/Software/Mosaic/NCSAMosaicHome.html
Help Page=http://www.ncsa.uiuc.edu/SDG/Software/WinMosaic/Docs/WMosTOC.html
FAQ Page=http://www.ncsa.uiuc.edu/SDG/Software/WinMosaic/FAQ.html
Bug list=http://www.ncsa.uiuc.edu/SDG/Software/WinMosaic/Bugs.html
Feature Page=http://www.ncsa.uiuc.edu/SDG/Software/WinMosaic/Features.html
Display Inline Images=yes
Dump memory blocks=no
Grey Background=yes
Fancy Rules=yes
Round List Bullets=yes
Current Hotlist=Starting Points
Anchor Underline=no
Anchor Cursor=yes
Show URLs=yes
Extended FTP=yes
Toolbar=yes
Status bar=yes
Title/URL bar=yes
Use 8-bit Sound=no

[Settings]
Anchor Color=0,0,255

[Main Window]
x=28
y=31
width=533
```

Figure 7-1:
The
mosaic.ini
file is dis-
played in
the Notepad
window,
ready for
you to start
tweaking.

Jotting Down Your Changes in Notepad

Notepad is a text editor for working with small ASCII text files. Although Notepad isn't fancy, it allows you to edit the mosaic.ini file with minimal effort. Table 7-1 lists the basic commands for editing text in Notepad.

If you accidentally delete any selected text, you can recover the text by choosing Edit|Undo or pressing Ctrl-Z. ■

By default, Notepad doesn't use word wrap. As a result, long entries sometimes extend beyond the right side of the Notepad window. To tell Notepad that it should use word wrap, choose Edit|Wrap from the Notepad menu. Unfortunately, Notepad doesn't let you save the word-wrap setting. You may have to choose Edit|Wrap each time you edit the mosaic.ini file.

To print a copy of your mosaic.ini file, choose File|Print from the Notepad menu. Notepad displays the standard Windows Print dialog box for your printer.

Like other Windows applications, Notepad's File menu also includes Page Setup and Print Setup commands. When you choose these commands, Notepad displays the same setup dialog boxes that you use in any other Windows application.

Table 7-1: Basic Notepad text editing commands

Action	*How to do it*
Selecting text	Drag the cursor using the mouse, or hold down the Shift key while pressing the direction key that moves the cursor in the desired direction
Cutting selected text and placing it in the Windows clipboard	Choose Edit|Cut, or press Ctrl-X
Copying selected text into the Windows clipboard	Choose Edit|Copy, or press Ctrl-C
Pasting text from the Windows clipboard to the cursor location	Choose Edit|Paste, or press Ctrl-V
Deleting selected text without placing it in the Windows clipboard	Choose Edit|Delete, press the Delete key , or press the Backspace key
Undoing the last action	Choose Edit|Undo, or press Ctrl-Z

To save your changes to the mosaic.ini file, choose File | Save. When you choose this command, the mosaic.ini file remains open in the Notepad window. To exit Notepad, choose File | Exit. If you try to exit without saving your changes, Notepad displays a dialog box asking if you want to save them. Choose Yes to save your changes.

Adding Your E-Mail Address

The [Main] section of the mosaic.ini file includes an E-mail setting. If you enter your e-mail address in this setting, Mosaic can automatically add your return address to e-mail forms. As you'll see in Chapter 9, Mosaic also uses this entry when you create annotations for your Web documents.

The original entry in the mosaic.ini file is:

```
E-mail="put_your_email@here"
```

The edited entry should look something like this:

```
E-mail="dangell@bookware.com"
```

In other words, you simply insert your e-mail address following the equal sign in this entry.

Changing to a Different Default Home Page

By default, Mosaic automatically points to the NCSA Mosaic for Microsoft Windows home page when you launch Mosaic. You should change the default home page because the NCSA Mosaic for Microsoft Windows home page on NCSA's Web server is one of the busiest places in the Web universe. Waiting to get this document each time you launch Mosaic is a waste of time.

You can change this default setting to any home page you want by editing the Home Page field in the [Main] section of mosaic.ini. The original entry is:

```
Home Page=http://www.ncsa.uiuc.edu/SDG/Software/Mosaic/HomePage.html
```

You can change this setting to any URL address you want. For example, the following entry lets you start your Web surfing with the EINet Galaxy page, which provides access to hundreds of Web sites by topic:

```
Home Page=http://galaxy.einet.net
```

 When choosing your default home page, find a site that points to other Web sites or provides updates of new Web resources. See Part VI for other sites you might want to use as a default home page. ▪

Turning Off Home Page Autoloading

You don't have to load a default home page every time you launch Mosaic. The following entry in the [Main] section of mosaic.ini tells Mosaic that it should automatically connect to a home page when you launch the program:

```
Autoload Home Page=yes
```

If you don't want to see a home page when you launch Mosaic, you should change this entry to:

```
Autoload Home Page=no
```

With the Autoload feature turned off, no home page is displayed when you launch Mosaic. However, you're still ready to start surfing the Web.

Turning Off the Grey Background

By default, Mosaic displays documents with a grey background. Figure 7-2 shows a Web document with the default grey background.

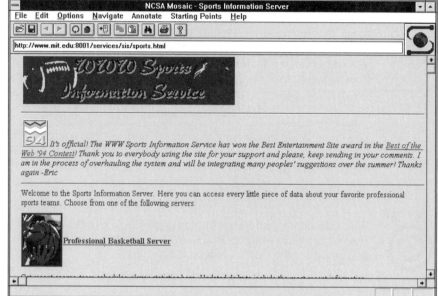

Figure 7-2:
The WWW
Sports
Information
Service
Web docu-
ment in
default grey.

As shown in Figure 7-3, you can turn off the grey and display documents with a white background. Web documents can be easier to read with the white background. However, some inline graphics blend in better with the grey background.

The background color is determined by a setting in the [Main] section of mosaic.ini. As mentioned, the default setting tells Mosaic to display the grey background:

```
Grey Background=yes
```

The following setting turns off the grey background:

```
Grey Background=no
```

In case you didn't notice, we turned off the grey background before we cre-ated the figures for this book. We like the white background. ∎

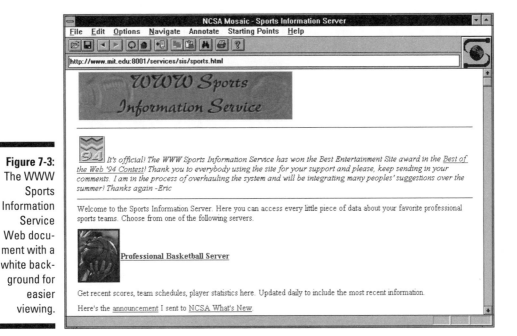

Figure 7-3:
The WWW
Sports
Information
Service
Web docu-
ment with a
white back-
ground for
easier
viewing.

Changing Mosaic's Document Caching

As you ride to different Web sites, a specified number of documents from your current Mosaic session are stored in your computer's memory. Storing information in memory, or *caching*, speeds up the process of revisiting Web documents that you've displayed during the current session. Without caching, Mosaic has to repeat the processing of downloading a document from a Web site each time you return to that document. However, the more Web documents you have cached, the more memory is used up, which can slow down your computer's performance.

By default, Mosaic caches two documents. The default entries in the [Document Caching] section of mosaic.ini are as follows:

```
[Document Caching]
Type=Number
Number=2
```

Don't change the Type=Number setting. If you have enough memory, you can increase the setting in the Number entry. However, you shouldn't cache more than five documents.

Displaying too many Web documents eats up memory and slows down your system's performance. If Mosaic runs out of memory, the only solution is to exit Mosaic and Windows, and then restart both programs to get a clean memory slate. ▪

Specifying Network News and Mail Servers

To use Mosaic with network news and e-mail, you need to connect to your service provider's network news and mail servers. When you set up an IP account, a service provider usually gives you the IP addresses for its network news and mail servers.

The [Services] section of mosaic.ini contains entries that tell Mosaic which servers it should use for network news and mail. The default settings are as follows:

```
NNTP_Server="news.cso.uiuc.edu"
SMTP_Server="ftp.ncsa.uiuc.edu"
```

To change these settings, enter the domain name or IP address for your service provider's network news server in the NNTP_Server field, and enter the IP address or domain name for your service provider's mail server in the SMTP_Server field. For example:

```
NNTP_Server="nntp.netcom.com"
SMTP_Server="smtp.netcom.com"
```

Altering the Appearance of Hyperlinks

You can change the visual appearance of hyperlinks in two ways. You can control whether hyperlinks are underlined, and you can change the color that Mosaic uses for displaying hyperlinks. You might want to change the appearance of a hyperlink for the following reasons:

- ✔ You need to have the hyperlinks underlined because you're using a greyscale or monochrome monitor.
- ✔ It's difficult to see hyperlinks in their default blue color because you're using the grey background.

The following entry in the [Main] section of mosaic.ini tells Mosaic that hyperlinks should not be underlined:

```
Anchor Underline=no
```

By making the following change to this entry, you can tell Mosaic to underline hyperlinks:

```
Anchor Underline=yes
```

The Anchor Color setting in the [Settings] section of mosaic.ini lets you change the color of hyperlinks from the default blue. You specify the anchor color using a combination of RGB (red, green, and blue) values. The RGB values range from 0 to 255. The setting for the default dark blue color is:

```
Anchor Color=0,0,255
```

You can change the hyperlink color by editing the RGB values. Table 7-2 lists several color alternatives.

Table 7-2: A collection of colors and their RGB values

Color	RGB value
Red	128,0,0
Yellow	255,255,0
Green	0,128,0
Cyan	0,128,128
Pink	255,0,255

Changing Fonts in Your Web Documents

Because Mosaic creates Web documents on your computer, you can control the appearance of the text in your Web documents. For example, you might want to change the font, the font style, and the size of the font that's used in document headings or text paragraphs. Figure 7-4 shows a Web document that uses the default fonts. Figure 7-5 shows the same Web document after we gave it a font lift.

Figure 7-4:
The Elvis
Web docu-
ment as it
appears
with
Mosaic's
default
fonts.

Figure 7-5:
The Elvis
Web docu-
ment with a
font lift.

Each Web document contains various elements, including headings, lists, and plain-old text paragraphs. Mosaic lets you change the font, font style, or font size for any of these elements in a Web document. You can choose from any of the TrueType and PostScript fonts that are installed in Windows, and you can choose font sizes ranging all the way up to 72 points.

Be careful with changing your fonts. Fancy display fonts can cause havoc in your Web document. In addition, using PostScript fonts slows down the rendering of your Web document because the Adobe Type Manager also must draw the fonts. TrueType fonts render much faster than PostScript fonts. ■

The Options|Choose Font command lets you customize the appearance of the current Web document in Mosaic. When you choose the Options|Choose Font command, Mosaic displays a submenu of font styles. The items in this menu are the different types of text used in Web documents. Table 7-3 describes the options in this submenu.

Table 7-3: The Choose Font submenu of text formatting options

Option	*Description*
Normal	Paragraphs of text
Header 1 through Header 7	Section headers
Menu	Menu entries or list entries
Directory	Directory names and filenames
Address	An address entry, which is usually at the bottom of the document
Block Quote	Blocked quotations — that is, quotations that appear as indented text
Example	Short code samples
Preformatted	Any block of text that was formatted before being placed in a Web document
Listing	Lists, such as numbered or bulleted lists

Choosing any item in this submenu displays the Font dialog box shown in Figure 7-6. For the document element that you selected in the Choose Font submenu, this dialog box lets you replace the default font, font style, or font size with any font that's available in Windows. Table 7-4 lists the default font settings for the different types of text that are found in a Web document.

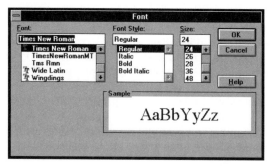

Figure 7-6: The Font dialog box lists the fonts, font styles, and font sizes that are available in Windows.

Table 7-4: Mosaic's default fonts, styles, and point sizes

Choose Font Menu Item	Font	Font Style	Font Size
Normal	Times New Roman	Regular	11
Heading 1	Times New Roman	Regular	24
Heading 2	Times New Roman	Regular	22
Heading 3	Times New Roman	Regular	18
Heading 4	Times New Roman	Regular	16
Heading 5	Times New Roman	Regular	14
Heading 6	Times New Roman	Regular	13
Heading 7	Times New Roman	Bold	12
Menu	Times New Roman	Regular	11
Directory	Century Gothic	Regular	18
Address	Times New Roman	Italic	11
Block Quote	Times New Roman	Regular	11
Example	Courier New	Regular	10
Preformatted	Courier New	Regular	9
Listing	Courier New	Regular	12

Unless you choose File I Save Preferences, your changes affect only the current document. If you choose File I Save Preferences, your changes become the standard fonts for all Web documents.

Numerous HTML commands are used to format Web documents. For example, a level-1 heading is <h1>, and a paragraph is <p>. You can't always tell which HTML command is behind a particular unit of text in a Web document. Chapter 11 provides more information on interpreting HTML codes. If you want to see the HTML codes used in the current document, you can try choosing File|Source Document from the Mosaic menu. However, this command doesn't always display the source document. ■

Here's how you change the fonts in a single Web document or for all Web documents:

1. Display a Web document in Mosaic.

2. Choose Options|Choose Font. Mosaic displays the submenu of Web document text formatting options.

3. Choose the type of text you want to change. For example, you might want to change the font that Mosaic uses for level-1 headings. Mosaic displays the Font dialog box.

4. Choose a new font, style, or size for the selected type of text.

5. Choose OK.

Moving On

The mosaic.ini editing skills you've gained in this chapter will come in handy as you continue your Mosaic power surfing. In the next chapter, we show you how to add multimedia capabilities to Mosaic by adding external programs to your Web surfing kit. Setting up these programs to work in conjunction with Mosaic requires some more tweaking of the mosaic.ini file, but it's worth the effort.

Chapter 8

Making Mosaic Multimedia

So far, you've only skimmed the text and inline graphics surface of the Web. Beyond simple text and pictures lies the cyberdelic, multimedia side of the Web. In this chapter, we show you how to obtain and install multimedia programs that work with Mosaic so you can surf the big ones.

The Web Surfer's Multimedia Toolkit

For most of your cyberdelic rides on the Web, you'll use a core set of multimedia programs that work with the most popular file formats. Together, these programs are a multimedia surfer's toolkit. These viewers and players are external to Mosaic — that is, they aren't part of the Mosaic program — but they work in conjunction with Mosaic.

After you've set up external viewers or players to work with Mosaic, you can click a hyperlink to transfer a file supported by any of these viewers or players. After the file is downloaded from the Web site to your computer, Mosaic automatically starts the appropriate application to let you display or play the contents of the file. You can also download the file to your system, and play it locally by using the external viewer or player by itself.

Multimedia is cool, but video and sound files are usually large beasts that take a while to download. If you're using a modem, be prepared to spend some time waiting for these files. Working with multimedia is a lot faster and smoother if you have an ISDN connection. Chapter 14 provides more information about ISDN connections.

All the programs we discuss in this chapter are certified by NCSA to work with Mosaic for Windows, and they're free for the downloading. Many other high-quality freeware, shareware, and commercial programs also work with Mosaic. ■

Where to Get Your Multimedia Programs

You can get the viewers and players that make up your Web surfer's multimedia toolkit from a variety of Web or FTP sites. Regardless of the site you use, you transfer files the same way, because they all appear in Mosaic as Web documents, with each file represented by a hyperlink.

The easiest way to get your multimedia programs is to point Mosaic to NCSA's External Viewer Information page, which is shown in Figure 8-1. You get there by entering the following address in Mosaic's URL box:

```
http://www.ncsa.uiuc.edu/SDG/Software/WinMosaic/viewers.html
```

Figure 8-1:
The NCSA
External
Viewer
Information
page is a
convenient
source for
your multi-
media
viewer and
player
programs.

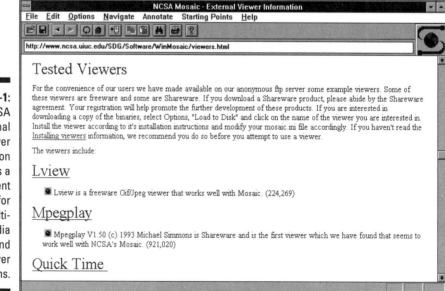

With the exception of the Drag and Zip compression program, you can download all your multimedia programs from this page. You can also access NCSA's External Viewer Information page from a hyperlink in the Mosaic for Microsoft Windows Home Page, which you can access by choosing Starting Points | Windows Mosaic Home Page.

The External Viewer Information page isn't the only site for these multimedia viewers and players. For example, you can point Mosaic to the NCSA's FTP server at ftp://ftp.ncsa.uiuc.edu, and then navigate to the PC/Mosaic/viewers directory. You can also access NCSA's FTP server through a hyperlink in the NCSA Windows Viewers page.

Other anonymous FTP servers offering these programs are:

```
ftp://ftp.cica.indiana.edu/pub/pc/win3
ftp://gatekeeper.dec.com/.f/micro/msdos/win3
ftp://wuarchive.wustl.edu/systems/ibmpc/win3
```

The directory structure after the win3 directory is the same for all of these sites. The viewers are stored in the /win3/mosaic/viewers directory. The compression utilities are stored in the /win3/util directory.

Another popular Windows FTP site is:

```
ftp://oak.oakland.edu/pub/msdos/windows3
```

This site's directory structure differs slightly from the previous sites. For example, the compression utilities are stored in the zip directory.

 When you are trying to connect to any of these FTP sites, Mosaic's error messages can be cryptic and misleading. Mosaic isn't always correct when it displays an error message. Before you write off any FTP site, try, try again. Mosaic often generates an error message because too many people are trying to connect to the site. ■

Exploding and Squishing Files the DZ Way

One of the most useful tools that you can have at your fingertips is a Windows compression program. Most programs and multimedia files are stored on the Internet as compressed files. Several compression programs are available, but Drag and Zip (DZ), a shareware program written by Dan Baumbach, is the most intuitive and easy to use compression program we've found. DZ is the first compression utility that's created to work from within Mosaic. In fact, it can automatically configure Mosaic, which means you don't have to manually edit Mosaic's initialization file (mosaic.ini). DZ also includes a feature that lets you view compressed files before you decompress them.

DZ works on the fly in conjunction with Mosaic, allowing you to decompress and store files while you're working in Mosaic. DZ also lets you decompress files that are stored in GZip (.gz), pack (.z), and compress (.Z) formats, which are standard compression formats for many files found on the Net.

DZ can quickly decompress files without using PKZIP, but you can save yourself a lot of time when compressing files by setting up DZ to compress the files using PKZIP. PKZIP has been refined over several years, so it's fast! You can drag and drop files onto the Drag and Zip icon, and DZ will automatically use the PKZIP program to compress the selected files.

Getting Drag and Zip

Here's how you can get your free copy of Drag and Zip:

1. Create a directory named c:\transfer. You can use this temporary directory when you're downloading files.

2. Start Mosaic and enter the following address in the URL text box (if you have a problem connecting, try one of the other sites we listed earlier in this chapter):

   `ftp://ftp.cica.indiana.edu/pub/pc/win3/util`

3. Scroll down the file list until you find the dz50.exe hyperlink. (The dz50.exe file is a compressed file that automatically decompresses when executed.)

4. Hold down the Shift key and click the dz50.exe hyperlink. The Save As dialog box is displayed.

5. Choose the c:\transfer directory to store the dz50.exe file, and press Enter. The selected file is downloaded to your computer, where it is stored in the c:\transfer directory.

6. Exit Mosaic and exit your Net connection.

Installing Drag and Zip in Windows

To install Drag and Zip in Windows:

1. Create a directory for the Drag and Zip program — for example, c:\dz.

2. Double-click the MS-DOS icon in the Main program group. The DOS prompt is displayed.

3. Move the dz50.exe file from the c:\transfer directory to the c:\dz directory by entering the following command at the DOS prompt:

```
move c:\transfer\dz50.exe c:\dz
```

4. Change to the c:\dz directory (the command for doing this is cd\dz), and enter dz50.exe. The Drag and Zip installation files are automatically extracted from dz50.exe.

5. To end your DOS session and return to Windows, enter the following command at the DOS prompt:

```
exit
```

6. Choose File|Run in the Program Manager window.

7. To start the setup program and open the Drag and Zip Installation dialog box, enter the following command in the Command Line text box, and choose OK:

```
c:\dz\dzsetup
```

8. Choose the Install Drag And Zip and Fileman Launcher option button. The Fileman Launcher option automatically launches DZ as an icon anytime you run the Windows File Manager. It also adds an Fmlaunch menu to the File Manager, which you can use to view files. Choose OK to continue the installation. A dialog box is displayed, asking you to enter the path you want to use for installing Drag and Zip.

9. You can accept the default path, c:\dz, by choosing OK, or you can enter another directory for storing Drag and Zip. If the directory doesn't exist, a dialog box is displayed, asking you to confirm that you want to create the directory. A status bar identifies the files that are being copied to your system. When the files are copied, a dialog box asks you to confirm that you want the Drag and Zip setup program to make changes to your win.ini file. These changes to win.ini associate the extensions .zip, .lha, and .gz with compression files that can be handled by the Drag and Zip program.

10. Choose the Add button. This option allows you to load files automatically in the Drag and Zip Viewer by double-clicking the name of the compressed file in the Windows File Manager. A dialog box asks if you want to use an external version of PKZIP and other external programs.

11. Choose Yes, enter the directory path in which PKZIP is installed (e.g., c:\pkzip), and choose OK.

When you double-click a filename ending with .zip in the Windows File Manager, the Drag and Zip program displays the Zip View window, which lists the names of the compressed files that are contained in the selected .zip file. The Zip View window is shown in Figure 8-2.

Figure 8-2:
The Zip
View win-
dow lists
the contents
of com-
pressed
files.

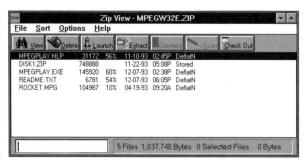

Setting up Drag and Zip to work with Mosaic

Using DZ in conjunction with the Windows File Manager is nice, but DZ really shines when you set it up to work automatically with Mosaic while you surf the Web. You can set up DZ so that it can work with compressed files directly from Mosaic. After setting up DZ to work with Mosaic, you can click a hyperlink to a compressed file and automatically open Drag and Zip's viewer window to display the compressed files. As a result, you can easily extract the files while working in Mosaic. This is a great time-saver. You can also click on a compressed file — for example, a readme text file — and see its contents. DZ also saves you time by automatically creating directories for decompressing files.

Here's how you set up DZ to work with Mosaic:

1. Double-click the Zip View icon.

2. Choose Options | Settings. As shown in Figure 8-3, the Zip View Settings dialog box is displayed.

3. Enter the directory in which the Mosaic program is installed — for example, c:\mosaic — in the WWW Browser text box. You can also use the Browse button to locate and choose the mosaic directory.

4. Click the OK button. Drag and Zip updates your mosaic.ini file so that the Drag and Zip program starts automatically when you click on the filename of a compressed file with the extension .zip.

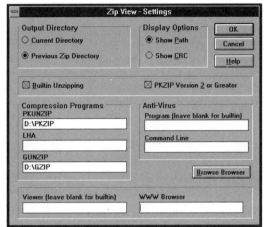

Figure 8-3:
The Zip
View Set-
tings dialog
box lets you
automati-
cally add DZ
to Mosaic.

Decompressing Files with Drag and Zip

With the Drag and Zip program installed, you'll never have to go to the DOS
prompt again to unzip files. You can use DZ to decompress files on the fly as
you download them using Mosaic, or you can decompress files in the Windows File Manager by double-clicking a filename with the .zip extension.

Here's how you use Drag and Zip to unzip a file:

1. Open the Drag and Zip window by clicking a hyperlink or double-clicking
   a zipped file in the File Manager.

2. Click the Extract button. As shown in Figure 8-4, DZ displays the Zip
   View dialog box, which allows you to specify the output directory for
   storing the decompressed files.

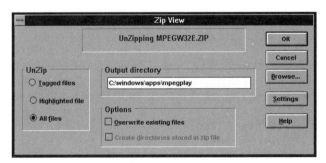

Figure 8-4: The Zip View dialog box lets you specify the output
directory for storing the decompressed files.

3. Enter the directory path for storing your decompressed files.

4. Click the All files button in the UnZip group, and choose OK. If a directory doesn't exist, DZ asks if you want to create it. Choose OK. DZ decompresses the files.

Lviewing Picture Files

Lview is a freeware picture file editor that lets you view and work with GIF and JPEG (or JPG) files. GIF and JPEG (Joint Photographic Experts Group) are the standard formats for graphics files on the Web. To run Lview, you need at least a 386 processor. It's recommended that you use a true-color Super VGA card.

GIF and JPEG are particularly useful formats because they include built-in compression. GIF uses the LZW (Lempel-Ziv-Welch) compression method, which is fast and efficient. JPEG uses a compression technique called lossy, which offers extraordinary compression of files.

Setting up Lview

The easiest way to get Lview is directly from NCSA's External Viewer Information page. You can download the compressed Lview program file to the transfer directory you created earlier in this chapter.

Here's how you get Lview and set it up:

1. Start Mosaic and connect to NCSA's External Viewer Information page by entering the following address in the URL text box (if you have a problem connecting, try one of the other sites listed earlier in this chapter):

   `http://www.ncsa.uiuc.edu/SDG/Software/WinMosaic/viewers.html`

2. Click the Lview hyperlink. The Zip View window is displayed with the list of files in the compressed lview31.zip file.

3. Click the Extract button. Drag and Zip displays the Zip View dialog box.

4. In the Output directory text box, enter c:\windows\apps\lview. If you want to use a directory other than this default directory, enter the directory path. If you don't use the default directory, you'll need to edit the [Viewers] section of the mosaic.ini file, as explained later in this section.

5. In the UnZip group, click the All files radio button, and choose OK. If the directory doesn't exist, Drag and Zip asks if you want to create the directory. Choose OK.

6. Choose File|Exit to close the Zip View window.

7. Open the program group in which you want to add the Lview icon, and drag the file c:\windows\apps\lview\lview31.exe from the File Manager window into the program group. The following icon is added to the program group:

Lview

If you didn't store the Lview program in the default drive and directory, you need to edit the mosaic.ini file. Open the mosaic.ini file by double-clicking the Mosaic Notepad icon that you created in Chapter 7. You need to change the following lines in the [Viewers] section of the file:

```
image/gif="c:\windows\apps\lview\lview31 %1s"
image/jpg="c:\windows\apps\lview\lview31 %1s"
```

Change these entries by entering the drive and directory in which the Lview program is stored:

```
image/gif="drive\directory path\lview31 %1s"
image/jpg="drive\directory path\lview31 %1s"
```

For example, if you stored Lview on your d: drive in the mosaic\apps\lview directory, you would enter the following:

```
image/gif="d:\mosaic\apps\lview\lview31 %1s"
image/jpg="d:\mosaic\apps\lview\lview31 %1s"
```

Displaying a picture in Lview

Working with Lview is easy. It all happens automatically whenever you click a hyperlink that points to a .gif, .jpeg, or .jpg file. When Mosaic receives the picture file, it launches the Lview program, which displays the file, as shown in Figure 8-5.

You can also download a file by holding down the Shift key and clicking the hyperlink that points to the file you want. Once you save the file on your system, you can open it with the Lview program.

Figure 8-5:
A Mona Lisa
picture file
displayed in
the Lview
program
window.

WAVing and WHAMing Sounds

Most of the sound files you'll encounter while surfing the Web will be in the Audio (au) format. Mosaic has built-in support for the Audio format, so you can play files in this format without a separate application. The other leading sound file formats are the Windows Waveform (WAV) format and the Apple/SGI AIFF format. Files in the AIFF format have names with the extensions .aiff or .aif. To work with WAV audio files, you can use the Sound Recorder applet that's automatically set up when you install Windows.

To play sound files, it's best to have a sound card. If you don't have a sound card, you might want to consider adding one to your system. Nowadays, it's easy to find a decent 16-bit sound card for around $100. WHAM (Waveform Hold and Modify) is a shareware program that plays sound files in the AU and AIFF format on systems with a Windows-supported sound card.

If you don't have a sound card, you can use the Microsoft speaker driver program to play sounds using your computer's speaker. Although the speaker's sound quality doesn't compare with a sound card, we'll show you how to download and set up the speaker driver program.

Setting up the WHAM sound player

Setting up the WHAM sound player is a bit more complicated than setting up Lview, because you need to edit the mosaic.ini file after you install the program. The Web is alive with the sound of music, and here are complete instructions for listening in:

1. Enter the following address in Mosaic's URL text box (if you have a problem connecting, try one of the other sites we listed earlier in this chapter):

   ```
   http://www.ncsa.uiuc.edu/SDG/Software/WinMosaic/viewers.html
   ```

2. Click the WHAM hyperlink, wham131.zip. The Zip View window is displayed.

3. Click the Extract button.

4. In the Output directory text box, enter c:\windows\apps\wham. If Windows is installed on a different drive or in a different directory, enter that path with the \wham subdirectory in the Output directory text box. For example, if Windows is installed on your d: drive, you should enter d:\windows\apps\wham in the Output directory text box.

5. Click the All files button in the UnZip group, and choose OK. If the directory doesn't exist, Drag and Zip asks if you want to create the directory. Choose OK.

6. Choose File|Exit to close the Zip View window.

7. Open the mosaic.ini file by double-clicking the Mosaic Notepad icon. You need to edit mosaic.ini so that Mosaic knows that it should launch the WHAM program for specific types of files.

8. First, you need to identify the types of files that work with the WHAM program. When you click on a file in one of these formats, Mosaic needs to launch the WHAM program. To define these file types, add the following lines to the end of the TYPE entries in the [Viewers] section of mosaic.ini:

   ```
   TYPE10="audio/au"
   TYPE11="audio/aif"
   TYPE12="audio/iff"
   TYPE13="audio/voc"
   ```

9. Next, you need to add entries that tell Mosaic where to find the WHAM program and launch it for any of the file formats identified in the previous step. Add the following lines after the TYPE entries in the [Viewers] section of mosaic.ini (if necessary, change the following entries to match the drive and directory in which Windows and the WHAM program are installed on your system):

   ```
   audio/au="c:\windows\apps\wham\wham %1s"
   audio/aif="c:\windows\apps\wham\wham %1s"
   audio/iff="c:\windows\apps\wham\wham %1s"
   audio/voc="c:\windows\apps\wham\wham %1s"
   ```

10. Finally, you need to identify the specific filename extensions that are used for the different file formats. Add the following lines to the end of the [Suffixes] section of mosaic.ini:

```
audio/au=.au,.audio
audio/aif=.aif,.aiff
audio/iff=.iff
audio/voc=.voc
```

11. Choose File | Save to save your changes to the mosaic.ini file, and choose File | Exit to close the Windows Notepad.

12. Open the program group in which you want to add the WHAM icon, and drag the file c:\windows\apps\wham\wham.exe from the File Manager window into the program group. The following icon is added to the group:

Playing sound files with WHAM

When you click a hyperlink that points to a file with the .au or .aif extension, Mosaic automatically loads the WHAM player after it receives the file. The WHAM player is shown in Figure 8-6.

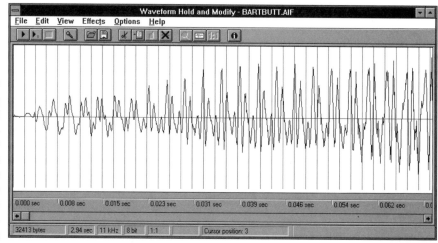

Figure 8-6:
The WHAM
Player auto-
matically
appears
with the
sound file
you
transferred.

You can download the sound file by holding down the Shift key and clicking the hyperlink that points to the file you want. Once you save the sound file on your system, you can open it with the WHAM program.

For the sound-card impaired

If you don't have a sound card, you can still play WAV files by using the Windows speaker driver. The speaker driver plays these files through your computer's speaker. This driver doesn't come with Windows, but it's available through NCSA's External Viewer Information page and from Microsoft's anonymous FTP site at the following address:

```
ftp://ftp.microsoft.com/Softlib/MSFILES
```

If a sound card driver is already installed on your system, don't install the Windows speaker driver. ■

The speaker driver's filename is speak.exe. Here's how you get Microsoft's speaker driver and set it up:

1. Enter the following address in Mosaic's URL text box:

   ```
   http://www.ncsa.uiuc.edu/SDG/Software/WinMosaic/viewers.html
   ```

2. Scroll down to the bottom of the page and click the license agreement hyperlink. Mosaic displays the license agreement page.

3. Hold down the Shift key and click the hyperlink named "here." Mosaic displays the Save As dialog box.

4. Select the c:\transfer directory path, and choose OK. Mosaic downloads the speak.exe file to the transfer directory on your computer. The speak.exe file actually contains several compressed files. To extract these files from speak.exe, you need to start a DOS session from within Windows.

5. Click the MS-DOS icon in the Main window. At the DOS prompt, type c:\transfer, and press Enter. Now that you're in the transfer directory, you can extract the files from speak.exe. Type speak, and press Enter. The speak.exe file explodes into several files. To end the DOS session and return to Windows, type exit, and press Enter.

6. Open the Control Panel in the Main program group and double-click the Drivers icon. As shown in Figure 8-7, Windows displays the Drivers dialog box.

7. Click the Add button. Windows displays the Add dialog box, with the Unlisted Or Updated Driver option highlighted.

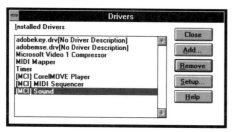

Figure 8-7: The Drivers dialog box lets you install program drivers for Windows.

8. Double-click Unlisted or Updated Driver, or click the OK button. Windows displays the Install Driver dialog box.

9. Type c:\transfer, and press Enter. Windows displays the Add Unlisted or Updated Driver box.

10. Click OK. As shown in Figure 8-8, Windows displays the PC-Speaker Setup dialog box. You use this dialog box to adjust playback speed and volume. The Test button plays the chime.wav file, which is stored in your Windows directory, and the Default button plays four tones in sequence.

11. Use the scroll bars to adjust the playback speed and volume. You can limit the sound duration to any value between one and ten seconds. Three seconds of sound — the default maximum duration — is sufficient for most purposes. By increasing the maximum duration of a sound, you reserve a larger sound buffer, which reduces the memory that's available for Mosaic.

12. When speaker.drv plays sounds, it disables your keyboard, your mouse, and any other devices that use your computer's interrupts. Using the

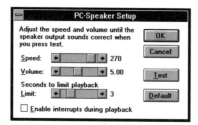

Figure 8-8: The PC-Speaker Setup dialog box lets you adjust settings for the Microsoft speaker program.

PC-speaker driver to replace the standard warning beep with the sounds contained in a WAV file might interfere with the operation of modem communications and applications software, which make extensive use of interrupts. To test the effect of enabling your computer's interrupts during playback, click the check box in the PC-Speaker Setup dialog box, and then click Test. If you hear distortion, disable interrupt testing by clicking the check box again.

13. Click OK to close the PC-Speaker Setup dialog box. Windows prompts you to restart Windows. Choose Restart Now. Windows installs drivers during its start-up process.

Let's Go to the Movies

Several video file formats are available on the Web. The three leading video file formats are Audio/Video Interleave (AVI), MPEG (MPG), and Quicktime (MOV). On the Web, however, you're more likely to find video files in the MPEG and QuickTime formats than in the AVI format.

To play AVI and Waveform (WAV) files (provided you have a sound card), Mosaic supports the Media Player that comes with Windows. To synchronize the audio and video portions of a movie, the AVI format interleaves video data with audio data within the same file. The AVI format accesses data from the hard disk without using great amounts of memory because only a few frames of video and a portion of audio are accessed at a time. AVI files are compressed to boost the quality and reduce the size of your video sequences.

MPEGing Motion Pictures

Mpegplay is a shareware program that lets you play MPEG video files. It includes push-button, VCR-like controls and a separate video window, which you can position anywhere on your screen. The MPEG standard, which was developed by the Motion Picture Experts Group, is a combined audio and video file format. MPEG compresses and decompresses images and audio sounds at the same speed, and its compression and decompression speeds are fast.

Setting up Mpegplay

It's easy to set up the MPEG video player. If you use the default directory settings, you don't need to edit the mosaic.ini file. The following steps explain how to set up the MPEG video player in the default directory:

1. Enter the following address in the URL text box:

```
http://www.ncsa.uiuc.edu/SDG/Software/WinMosaic/viewers.html
```

2. Click the MPEG hyperlink, mpeg32e.zip. The Zip View window is displayed.

3. Click the Extract button. Drag and Zip displays the Zip View dialog box.

4. In the Output directory text box, enter c:\windows\apps\mpegplay. If you use a directory other than this default directory, you'll need to edit the [Viewers] section of the mosaic.ini file, as explained later in this section.

5. Click the All files button in the UnZip group, and choose OK. If the directory doesn't exist, Drag and Zip asks if you want to create the directory. Choose OK.

6. Choose File|Exit to close the Zip View window.

7. Open the program group to which you want to add the Mpegplay icon. Drag the file c:\windows\apps\mpegplay\mpegplay.exe from the File Manager window into the program group. The following icon is added to the program group:

MPEG

Mpegplay

If you must use a different drive or directory to store the MPEG video player program, you need to edit the mosaic.ini file. Open the mosaic.ini file by double-clicking the Mosaic Notepad icon that you created in Chapter 7. You need to change the following line in the [Viewers] section of the file:

```
video/mpeg="c:\winapps\mpegplay\mpegplay %ls"
```

Change this entry by entering the drive and directory in which the MPEG video player program is stored:

```
video/mpeg="drive\directory path\mpegplay %ls"
```

For example, if you stored the MPEG video player program on the d: drive in the mosaic\apps\mpeg directory, you would enter the following:

```
video/mpeg="d:\mosaic\apps\mpeg\mpegplay %ls"
```

Playing MPEG videos

With Mpegplay installed, when you select a hyperlink to an MPEG video file, Mosaic displays Mpegplay, which is shown in Figure 8-9. You can also download a video file by holding down the Shift key and clicking the hyperlink that points to the file you want. Once you save a video file on your system, you can open it with Mpegplay. Keep in mind that Mpegplay slows down whenever you move the mouse.

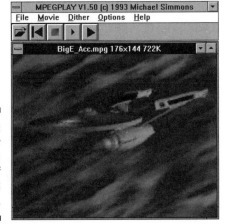

Figure 8-9:
Mpegplay
is displaying
a video of
the USS
Enterprise.

QuickTiming Movies

QuickTime is a popular Macintosh video format. Files using this format have the .mov filename extension because QuickTime is called the "movie" format. The QuickTime for Windows player is a program that lets you play Quick-Time videos using the Windows Media Player.

QuickTime movies may contain any combination of video, animation, audio, MIDI, text, and even interactive commands; each with different start and stop points. This sophisticated file format supports several compression-decompression schemes, such as Photo Compressor (JPEG) and Kodak Photo CD Compressor. The quality and performance of QuickTime movies is best on a system with a video card that can display 32,768 or more colors, and a sound card for playback of movies with sound. To work with QuickTime, you must be running DOS 5.0 or higher.

Setting up the QuickTime player

Because the QuickTime player is actually an extension of the Media Player program that comes with Windows, you'll need to make changes to both the win.ini file and the mosaic.ini file. Here's how you set up the QuickTime extension program, including all the necessary editing of .ini files:

1. Enter the following address in Mosaic's URL text box:

   ```
   http://www.ncsa.uiuc.edu/SDG/Software/WinMosaic/viewers.html
   ```

2. Click the QuickTime hyperlink. Mosaic displays the CUHK's QuickTime Mplayer Extensions page.

3. Click the qtw11.zip hyperlink. Mosaic displays the Zip View window, which lists the contents of the qtw11.zip file.

4. Click the Extract button. The Zip View dialog box is displayed.

5. In the Output directory text box, enter c:\windows\system. If you have installed Windows on a different drive, enter the correct drive and directory.

6. Click the All files button in the UnZip group, and choose OK. If the directory doesn't exist, Drag and Zip asks if you want to create the directory. Choose OK. All the compressed Quicktime (qt111.zip) files are decompressed in your c:\windows\system directory.

7. Choose File | Exit to close the Zip View window.

8. Double-click the sysedit.exe file in the c:\windows\system directory. As shown in Figure 8-10, Windows displays the System Configuration Editor window.

9. Click the WIN.INI title bar and add the following line to the end of the [Extensions] section:

   ```
   mov=mplayer.exe ^.mov
   ```

10. Add the following line to the end of the [mci extensions] section in the win.ini file:

    ```
    mov=QTWVideo
    ```

11. Click the SYSTEM.INI title bar and add the following line to the end of the [mci] section of the system.ini file:

    ```
    QTWVideo=mciqtw.drv
    ```

12. Save your changes to win.ini and system.ini by choosing File | Save. To close the System Configuration Editor, choose File | Exit from the menu bar.

13. Double-click the Mosaic Notepad icon to display the mosaic.ini file. You need to change the following line in the [Viewers] section of mosaic.ini:

```
video/quicktime="C:\WINAPPS\QTW\bin\player.exe %ls"
```

14. Change this entry to the following setting:

```
video/quicktime="c:\mplayer.exe %ls"
```

15. Choose File | Save to save your changes to the mosaic.ini file, and choose File | Exit to close the Windows Notepad.

16. Exit Windows, and then restart it. Your changes to the .ini files don't take effect until you restart Windows.

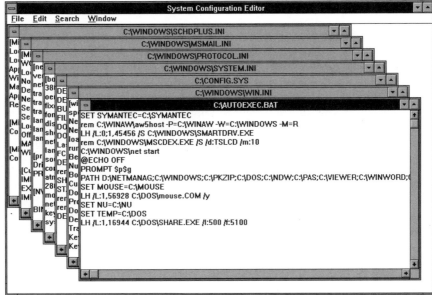

Figure 8-10: The System Configuration Editor window with all the Windows configuration files opened.

Playing a QuickTime movie

With the QuickTime player installed, when you click a hyperlink that points to a QuickTime movie (.mov) file, Mosaic automatically loads the QuickTime player after receiving the file. Figure 8-11 shows a QuickTime movie file in the QuickTime player. You can also download a QuickTime file by holding down the Shift key and clicking the hyperlink that points to the file. Once you save a QuickTime file on your system, you can open it with the Media Player.

Figure 8-11:
A frame of a
movie from
WIRED
magazine,
as displayed
by the
QuickTime
for
Windows
program.

Ghostviewing PostScript Files

Ghostview for Windows is a freeware program written by Russell Lang. Ghostview lets you view and print PostScript documents on any printer supported by Windows. Ghostview is actually a Windows graphical interface for a program called MS-Windows GhostScript. GhostScript is an interpreter for the PostScript page description language that's used by laser printers. The PostScript file format is a standard for desktop publishing.

Ghostview requires MS-Windows GhostScript 2.6 or later. GhostScript and Ghostview are sophisticated programs with lots of advanced features, but viewing and printing PostScript files is a breeze.

Setting up GhostScript and Ghostview

Here's how you set up GhostScript and Ghostview:

1. Launch Mosaic and enter the following address in the URL text box:

   `http://www.ncsa.uiuc.edu/SDG/Software/WinMosaic/viewers.html`

2. Click the GhostScript V2.6 hyperlink. Mosaic displays the PostScript Viewers for Windows page.

3. Click the GhostScript hyperlink. The Zip View window is displayed.

4. Click the Extract button. The Zip View dialog box is displayed.

5. In the Output directory text box, enter c:\gs.

6. Click the All Files button in the UnZip group, and choose OK. If the directory doesn't exist, Drag and Zip asks if you want to create the directory. Choose OK.

7. Choose File|Exit to close the Zip View window.

8. Click the Ghostview hyperlink in the PostScript Viewers for Windows page. The Zip View window is displayed.

9. Click the Extract button. The Zip View dialog box is displayed.

10. In the Output directory text box, enter c:\gsview. Click the All Files button in the UnZip group, and choose OK. If the directory doesn't exist, Drag and Zip asks if you want to create the directory. Choose OK

11. Choose File|Exit to close the Zip View window.

12. Open the File Manager and copy the gsview.exe and gsview.hlp files from the c:\gsview directory to the c:\gs directory.

13. Open the program group to which you want to add the Ghostview icon. Drag the file c:\gs\gsview.exe from the File Manager window into the program group. The following icon is added to the program group:

14. Double-click the Ghostview icon. The Ghostview for Windows window opens. Choose the GhostScript Command item from the Options menu. The Input dialog box is displayed, and the following entries may appear in the text box:

```
gs c:\gs\gswin.exe -Ic:\gs
gswin
```

15. Enter the following text in the command line text box:

```
c:\gs\gswin.exe -Ic:\gs
```

16. Choose OK. To close the Ghostview window, choose File|Exit.

17. Open the mosaic.ini file by double-clicking the Mosaic Notepad icon. You need to change the following line in the [Viewers] section of mosaic.ini:

```
application/postscript="c:\ghostview %ls"
```

18. Mosaic should launch Ghostview for Windows anytime you click on a PostScript file (.ps) hyperlink. To set this up, change the entry in the [Viewers] section of mosaic.ini to:

```
application/postscript="c:\gs\gsview %ls"
```

19. Choose File | Save to save your changes to the mosaic.ini file, and choose File | Exit to close the Windows Notepad.

Viewing a PostScript file

With Ghostview installed, when you click a hyperlink that points to a Post-Script file, the file is displayed in the Ghostview window. Figure 8-12 shows a sample Postscript document in the Ghostview window. You can also download a PostScript file by holding down the Shift key and clicking the hyperlink that points to the file. After saving the file on your system, you can open it with the Ghostview program.

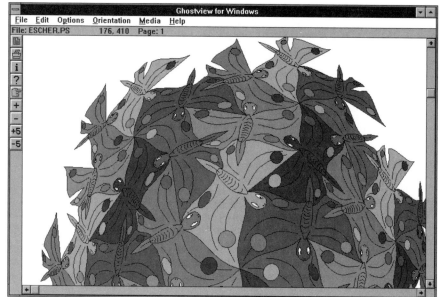

Figure 8-12: The Ghostview PostScript Viewer displaying an Escher Postscript image.

Moving On

By working with the core multimedia programs explained in this chapter, you'll experience a new, exhilarating level of Web surfing. But wait, there's more. In the next chapter, you learn more power-surfing techniques. For example, we tell you how to set up several other applications to work in conjunction with Mosaic, including a Telnet tool, the Windows Notepad, Word for Windows, and Abobe Acrobat.

Chapter 9

More Power-Surfing Techniques

• •

• •

*A*s you surf the Web, Mosaic lets you write notes to yourself or other users. These notes can appear as your own private hyperlink in a Web document or as a hyperlink that is available to a group of people connected to a server.

Mosaic saves personal annotations on your computer. Group annotations are stored on a network server. Annotation hyperlinks appear at the bottom of the Web page. Your personal annotations are available to you each time you access the document. Group annotations are available to members of a group when they connect to the Web document.

In addition to showing you how to work with annotations, this chapter shows you how to take complete control of your hotlists as well as how to set up Mosaic to work with a variety of applications.

Working with Personal Annotations

To add personal annotations to a Web document, you need to create a directory called c:\ncsa\annotate. This is the default path specified in the [Annotations] section of the mosaic.ini file. If you want to create your annotate directory in another location — for example, c:\mosaic\annotate — you need to edit the [Annotations] section of the mosaic.ini file.

Before you start annotating your surfing adventures, you also need to change the Default Title setting in the [Annotations] section of the mosaic.ini file. Mosaic uses the text from this setting as the hyperlink text. The default text is just a generic placeholder.

To list the author of an annotation, Mosaic uses the e-mail address entry in mosaic.ini. Make sure this entry in mosaic.ini contains your return e-mail address. The e-mail address is the first setting in the [Main] section of mosaic.ini. (Chapter 7 shows you how to add your e-mail address to mosaic.ini.) ■

The following steps describe how you change the default directory for storing your annotations, and the Default Title setting, which Mosaic uses as the text for your annotation hyperlinks:

1. Open the mosaic.ini file in the Windows Notepad application by double-clicking the Mosaic Notepad icon.

2. Find the [Annotations] section of mosaic.ini.

3. Change the default setting — Directory=c:\ncsa\annotate — to another directory. For example, the following entry sets c:\mosaic\annotate as the directory for storing annotations:

```
Directory=c:\mosaic\annotate
```

4. Replace the setting, Default Title="Personal Annotation by Mosaic User", with your hyperlink text. For example, you might enter something like Default Title="David's Notes".

5. Save your changes to mosaic.ini by choosing File I Save. Exit Notepad by choosing File I Exit.

The Zen of the Annotate window

When you choose Annotate I Annotate from the Mosaic menu bar, Mosaic displays the Annotate window, which is shown in Figure 9-1. If necessary, you can expand the Annotate window by clicking the maximize button in upper-right corner of the window. Table 9-1 describes the elements of the Annotate window.

The Annotate menu includes two dimmed items: Edit this annotation and Delete this annotation. These features aren't active in alpha version 7.0 of Mosaic. At this point, there's no real convenient way to edit or delete an annotation. ■

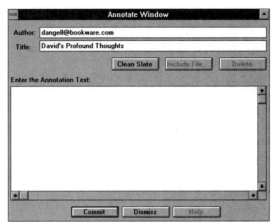

Figure 9-1:
The Anno-
tate window
lets you
enter your
profound
thoughts
about the
current
Web
document.

Table 9-1: The parts and pieces of the Annotate window

Control	*Description*
Author	Identifies the creator of the annotation. By default, this field displays your e-mail address, as defined in your mosaic.ini file.
Title	Lets you enter the text that becomes the hyperlink at the bottom of the Web document you're annotating. The default text comes from your mosaic.ini file.
Enter the Annotation Text	Lets you enter and edit the text of your annotation.
Clean Slate	Erases all the text in the Enter the Annotation Text area.
Include File	Inserts any text file that you specify into your annotation.
Delete	Deletes text that you've selected in the Enter the Annotation Text area.
Commit	Saves your annotation and exits the Annotate window.
Dismiss	Exits the Annotate window without saving your annotation.
Help	Accesses Help for working with the Annotate window.

Entering and editing text

The Enter the Annotation Text area in the Annotate window is a simple text editor. It doesn't include word wrapping, so you need to press Enter to end a line. Table 9-2 describes the common editing commands for working with text in the Annotate window. With the exception of the Clean Slate button, you need to select the text you want to change before entering any of these commands. You can select text by holding down the Shift key while you press any of the direction keys, or by dragging the cursor over the text using the mouse.

Table 9-2: Text editing commands used in the Annotate window

Command	Action
Ctrl-X	Cuts the selected text and places it in the Windows clipboard
Ctrl-C	Copies the selected text to the clipboard
Ctrl-V	Pastes text from the clipboard into the current cursor position
Del	Deletes the selected text
Delete button	Deletes the selected text
Clean Slate button	Deletes all the text in the Enter the Annotation Text area

Adding annotations as you surf

The Annotate window lets you put away your post-it notes and record your profound thoughts while you surf the Web. Mosaic lets you add multiple annotations to a Web document. Here's hoping that your nimble keystrokes can keep up with your thoughts.

Here's how you annotate a Web document:

1. Display the document you want to annotate.

2. Choose Annotate | Annotate from the Mosaic menu bar. Mosaic displays the Annotate window.

3. If you're satisfied with the default entries for Author and Title, you don't have to do anything with these fields. If you want to change either of these entries, click in the field you want to change and enter the text you want Mosaic to use for the author or title of the annotation.

4. Click in the Enter the Annotation Text area and type your annotation text.

5. Click the Commit button to save the annotation, or click the Dismiss button to close the Annotate window without recording your note.

Your annotation hyperlink appears only after you move to another Web document and then return to the annotated Web document. Remember, the annotation hyperlink appears at the bottom of the document. ■

Displaying annotations

As shown in Figure 9-2, when you display a Web document that includes annotations, the annotations appear as hyperlinks under the Personal Annotations header. Each annotation hyperlink includes a Title, followed by the day, date, and time it was created.

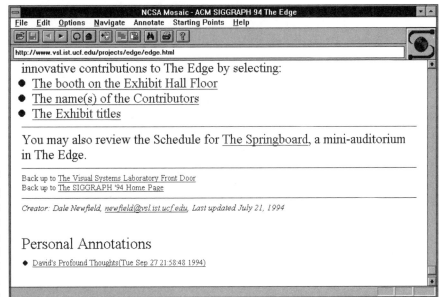

Figure 9-2:
An annotation appears as a hyperlink in a Web document.

Here's how you display an annotation that's already a hyperlink in a Web document:

1. Display the Web document to which you previously added an annotation. If the document is still available in your current session, you can return to the document by choosing Navigate I History or by using the navigation buttons on the button toolbar.

2. Move to the end of the Web document.

3. Click the annotation hyperlink. As shown in Figure 9-3, Mosaic displays the annotation as a Web document.

You can also load your annotations separately from Web documents. By doing so, you can make changes to a Web document's annotation without actually connecting to the Web site. To do this, choose File | Open Local File from the Mosaic menu bar. Mosaic displays the Mosaic Open dialog box. Navigate to the directory that you set up for storing your annotations, and choose any of the HTML documents. Mosaic assigns names to your personal annotations in sequential order starting with pan-1.htm, pan-2.htm, and so on. A log file in your annotation directory contains information that Mosaic uses to match an annotation to a specific Web document. Mosaic uses this information to display the annotation as a hyperlink in the appropriate Web document.

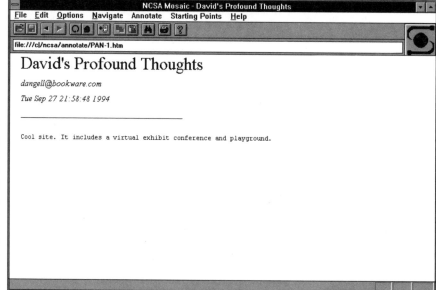

Figure 9-3: When you click an annotation's hyperlink, your annotation appears as a Web document.

Working with Group Annotations

Group annotations let you and other Mosaic users work with shared annotations that are stored on a network server. With a few exceptions, most of the tasks involved in creating, displaying, editing, and deleting group annotations are the same as those for personal annotations.

To work with group annotations, you need to change the Group Annotation Server setting in the [Annotations] section of the mosaic.ini file. This setting specifies the computer you want to use as an annotation server. This server is typically at your location, but it can be any server to which a group of people can connect remotely, such as a service provider's computer.

Here's how you change the Group Annotation Server setting:

1. Open the mosaic.ini file in Notepad by double-clicking the Mosaic Notepad icon.

2. Navigate to the [Annotations] section of mosaic.ini. You need to change the following setting:

   ```
   Group Annotation Server=hoohoo.ncsa.uiuc.edu:8001
   ```

3. Change the setting by entering the name of your server. For example, here's what the setting would look like if you're using a server named isdn.bookware.com:

   ```
   Group Annotation Server=isdn.bookware.com
   ```

4. Choose File | Save to save your changes to mosaic.ini. To exit Notepad, choose File | Exit.

Showing Group Annotations

To display group annotations in a Web document, choose Options | Show Group Annotations. Mosaic displays a check mark next to this menu item when it's toggled on. This option is inactive by default. Group annotations are available to members of your group any time they access the same Web document. You can't work with personal annotations and group annotations in the same document; it's one or the other.

Managing Your Hotlists with Mosaic.ini

The Navigate | Menu Editor command opens the Personal Menus dialog box, which lets you manage your hotlists without working directly in the mosaic.ini file. However, you can perform many hotlist tasks much faster by working directly in mosaic.ini. For example, instead of the tedious process of moving menu items one by one using the Personal Menus windows, you can move a group of items by simply cutting and pasting the entire group in mosaic.ini.

By working directly with mosaic.ini, you can also do several things that aren't possible with the Personal Menus dialog box. For example, you can rearrange submenus. You can also copy hotlist entries to a file and share them with other Mosaic users.

Before you start working with hotlist menus in the mosaic.ini file, make sure you have a backup of your latest mosaic.ini file. If something goes wrong, you can start over with the backup copy. ▨

Working with hotlist menus and menu items

Each hotlist menu in Mosaic has its own section in the mosaic.ini file. The hotlist menu sections in mosaic.ini are numbered sequentially, starting with [User Menu1], [User Menu2], [User Menu3], and so on.

Directly under each section header is the Menu_Name entry, which is the name of the menu as it appears in Mosaic. For example, the first entry in [User Menu1] is Menu_Name=Starting Points, which is the Starting Points menu. If the menu is a top-level menu — that is, a menu on the Mosaic menu bar — the entry Menu_Type=TOPLEVEL appears under the Menu_Name setting. Submenus don't include a Menu_Type entry. Figure 9-4 shows a top-level menu and a user menu in the mosaic.ini file.

```
                          Notepad - MOSAIC.INI
 File  Edit  Search  Help
[User Menu1]
Menu_Name=Starting Points
Menu_Type=TOPLEVEL
Item1=Starting Points Document,http://www.ncsa.uiuc.edu/SDG/Software/Mosaic/StartingPoints/Netw
Item2=NCSA Mosaic Demo Document,http://www.ncsa.uiuc.edu/demoweb/demo.html
Item3=NCSA Mosaic's 'What's New' Page,http://www.ncsa.uiuc.edu/SDG/Software/Mosaic/Docs/whats-n
Item4=NCSA Mosaic Home Page,http://www.ncsa.uiuc.edu/SDG/Software/Mosaic/NCSAMosaicHome.html
Item5=Windows Mosaic home page,http://www.ncsa.uiuc.edu/SDG/Software/WinMosaic/HomePage.html
Item6=MENU,User Menu2
Item7=MENU,User Menu3
Item8=MENU,User Menu4
Item9=MENU,User Menu5
Item10=MENU,User Menu6
Item11=MENU,User Menu7
Item12=MENU,User Menu8
Item13=MENU,User Menu9
Item14=MENU,User Menu10
Item15=MENU,User Menu11
Item15=MENU,User Menu12
Item16=Finger Gateway,http://cs.indiana.edu/finger/gateway
Item17=Whois Gateway,gopher://sipb.mit.edu:70/1B%3aInternet%20whois%20servers

[User Menu2]
Menu_Name=World Wide Web Info
Item1=Web Overview,http://info.cern.ch/hypertext/WWW/LineMode/Defaults/default.html
Item2=Web Project,http://info.cern.ch/hypertext/WWW/TheProject.html
Item3=Data Sources By Service,http://info.cern.ch/hypertext/DataSources/ByAccess.html
Item4=Information By Subject,http://info.cern.ch/hypertext/DataSources/bySubject/Overview.html
Item5=Web News,http://info.cern.ch/hypertext/WWW/News/9305.html
Item6=Web Servers Directory,http://info.cern.ch/hypertext/DataSources/WWW/Servers.html
```

Figure 9-4: A top-level menu and a user menu, as they appear in mosaic.ini.

The [User Menu] sections in mosaic.ini start with the top-level menu and its submenus, followed by the next top-level menu and its submenus. The menus are listed in the order they appear on the Mosaic menu bar from left to right. Any hotlist menus you've added to Mosaic appear at the end of the mosaic.ini file.

Menu items are numbered sequentially under a [User Menu] section, starting with Item1, Item2, and so on. Following the item number, each entry consists of an equal sign, the menu item title, a comma, and the URL address. For example, the following entry specifies that the third item in a menu is the Virtual Meetmarket:

    Item3=Virtual MeetMarket,http://wwa.com:1111/

As shown in the following example, instead of a URL address, the entry for a submenu points to another [User Menu] section:

    Item1=MENU,User Menu12

This entry tells Mosaic that Item1 is a submenu that's identified as [User Menu12]. Any items in this submenu are listed later in mosaic.ini under the [User Menu12] section header.

The [Hotlist] section of mosaic.ini is the Quicklist entry, which doesn't appear as a menu. Quicklist items are identified as URL0, URL1, and so on.

Moving and copying hotlist menus

To move, copy, and delete hotlist menus in the mosaic.ini file, you use standard text editing commands in Notepad. When you're modifying hotlist menus, remember that Mosaic arranges these menus according to the numbering of menu items and [User Menu] sections in mosaic.ini. You must ensure that the menu numbering reflects any changes you make in mosaic.ini.

Here's how you move or copy a hotlist menu:

1. Open the mosaic.ini file in Notepad by double-clicking the Mosaic Notepad icon.

2. Select the entire hotlist menu, from the [User Menu] section header through the last item in the menu.

3. If you want to move the menu, choose Edit|Cut or press Ctrl-X to cut the menu from its current position in the mosaic.ini file. If you want to copy the menu, choose Edit|Copy or press Ctrl-C.

4. Move the cursor to the position at which you want the menu to appear, and choose Edit | Paste or press Ctrl-V. The menu is inserted at the current cursor position.

5. Starting with the menu you just moved, renumber all the section headers down through the other menus in the top-level menu.

6. If any other menu contains an item that references the menu you just moved or copied, change that item's entry to reflect the new [User Menu] number for the menu you moved or copied.

7. Choose File | Save to save your changes to mosaic.ini, and choose File | Exit to exit the Notepad.

If you accidentally delete or cut a menu in the mosaic.ini file while you are using Notepad, choose Edit | Undo or press Ctrl-Z to undo the action. ▪

Deleting or renaming menus

To delete any submenu listed in mosaic.ini, select the menu header and all its items, and choose Edit | Delete or press the Delete key. Renumber all the menu headers, starting from the menu you just deleted. You also need to change the item in the menu that references the submenu you just deleted.

To rename a menu, you simply select the menu name in the Menu_Name setting and type in the new menu name. You don't have to change the item that references the menu because it's pointing to the user menu number, not the menu name.

Copying, moving, and deleting menu items

You copy, move, and delete menu items using the same editing commands you use for menus. But instead of renumbering menus, you must renumber the menu items sequentially so they appear correctly in the menu. If menu items are numbered incorrectly, the items after the last sequential menu item don't appear in the menu.

If you're moving menu items, try to put them in a block at the end of a menu. By doing so, you don't have to renumber any items already in the menu. If you're just moving one or two items, it's easier to use the Personal Menus dialog box. ▪

Adding a new hotlist menu and items

Instead of using the Personal Menus dialog box to add menu items one at a time, you can add a new hotlist menu or several hotlist items at the same time by using Notepad to work directly in mosaic.ini. The following paragraphs show you how to add a top-level menu, a submenu, or a hotlist item to the mosaic.ini file.

To add a top-level menu, move the cursor to a location before or after an existing top-level menu entry and all its submenus. Add the following lines to mosaic.ini (*n* represents the number of the new top-level menu):

```
[User Menun]
Menu_Name=your menu name
Menu_Type=TOPLEVEL
```

To add a submenu, you need to create a new [User Menu] section for the submenu, and you need to add an item to the top-level menu that is to contain your new submenu. Move the cursor to the position in mosaic.ini at which the submenu should appear in a top-level menu, relative to any existing submenus. Add the following lines to mosaic.ini (*n* represents the number of the new submenu):

```
[User Menun]
Menu_Name=your menu name
```

In the [User Menu] section for the top-level menu that is to contain your submenu, add the following entry (*MenuNumber* is a number indicating the position of the new submenu in the top-level menu):

```
ItemMenuNumber=MENU,User Menun
```

To add a menu item that points to a site, enter Item*MenuNumber*=*menu item name*, followed by a comma, and the URL address. For example:

```
Item1=Wacky Authors,http://www.bookware.com
```

Any time you make changes, be sure to renumber your menus (top-level menu or user submenu). If you don't, any menus after the misnumbering won't appear in your hotlists. ∎

Copying a hotlist and sharing it

One of the coolest things about editing the mosaic.ini file is that you can copy a hotlist menu and save it as a separate text file. After saving your hotlist as a file, you can share the file with other Mosaic users, who can add it to their hotlists.

Sharing hotlists can save a lot of time for you and your colleagues. Suppose you're working on a project and you've gathered a nice collection of related sites while surfing the Web. Instead of telling people all about your adventures, you can share your hotlist and let your co-workers see the sites for themselves.

You can share all your hotlists with other Mosaic users by simply giving them copies of your mosaic.ini file. Along with the hotlists, however, they'll get all your other Mosaic settings. ▪

Here's how you extract a hotlist from the mosaic.ini file:

1. Open mosaic.ini in Notepad. For every menu that you want to extract from the mosaic.ini file, select the entire hotlist menu or menus, from each [User Menu] section header through the last item in each menu.

2. To copy the selected text to the Windows clipboard, choose Edit | Copy or press Ctrl-C.

3. Choose File | New to open a new Notepad document.

4. To paste the hotlist menu from the clipboard into the new Notepad document, choose File | Paste or press Ctrl-V.

5. Choose File | Save. Notepad displays the Save as dialog box.

6. Select the directory in which you want to save the file, and enter a name for the file in the File Name field. Click the OK button to save the file.

7. Exit Notepad by choosing File | Exit.

Adding a hotlist copy to your mosaic.ini file

The flip-side of copying a hotlist to a file is adding the contents of a file to your hotlist. Here's how you add a hotlist file to your mosaic.ini file:

1. Double-click the Mosaic Notepad icon.

2. Choose File | Open. Notepad displays the Open dialog box.

3. Select the file containing the hotlist that you want to add to mosaic.ini, and choose OK. The selected file is opened in NotePad.

4. Copy the hotlist to the clipboard by selecting the text you want to copy — that is, the hotlist menu — and choosing Edit | Copy or pressing Ctrl-C.

5. Choose File | Open, select the mosaic.ini file in your Windows directory, and choose OK. Notepad opens your mosaic.ini file.

6. Move the cursor to the position where you want to insert the new User Menu in your mosaic.ini file.

7. Choose File | Paste or press Ctrl-V.

8. Starting with the menu you just copied, renumber all the menu headers for the user menus from this top-level menu.

9. Change the item in the top-level menu that references the menu you just copied.

10. If you want to give the hotlist a new name, edit the Menu_Name entry. Simply replace the existing name with the menu name you want to use. For example, if the original entry is Menu_Name=Dave's Faves, you might change it to Menu_Name=Other Home Pages.

Reach Out and Telnet Someone

To connect to some servers that include links to a Telnet site, Mosaic must use a Telnet program. You can use the Telnet program that comes with your TCP/IP software, or you can download a Telnet program and set it up for use with Mosaic.

Setting up your TCP/IP program's Telnet tool

In most cases, you can use the Telnet tool that comes with your TCP/IP software. By using the Telnet program that comes with your TCP/IP package, you avoid the trouble of downloading and decompressing a Telnet program.

Here's how you set up your Telnet tool for use with Mosaic:

1. Open the group window that contains your Internet tools. For example, if you're using NetManage Chameleon, double-click the Chameleon group.

2. Select the Telnet tool.

3. Choose File | Properties, make a note of the Command line entry, and choose Cancel. If you want to copy the text that you need to add to your mosaic.ini file, select the Command line entry and press Ctrl-C.

4. Double-click the Mosaic Notepad icon to open the mosaic.ini file. You need to change the following line in the [Viewers] section of mosaic.ini:

```
telnet="c:\trumpet\telw.exe"
```

5. Change this setting to the command line you noted in step 3. For example, if you use Chameleon, you might enter c:\netmanag\telnet.exe. If you copied the command line text from the Properties window, press Ctrl-V to paste the selected text.

6. Choose File|Save to save your changes, and then choose File|Exit.

When you click on a Telnet site, Mosaic will open your Telnet application. Figure 9-5 shows the Chameleon Telnet application.

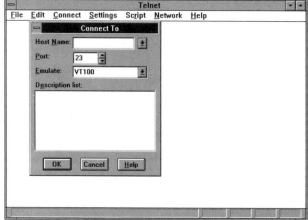

Figure 9-5:
The
Chameleon
Telnet
Viewer.

Setting up the TrumpTel program

If you don't have a Telnet application, you need to download one, decompress it, and modify your mosaic.ini file. Here's how you set up Mosaic to use the TrumpTel program:

1. Start Mosaic and enter the following address in the URL text box:

   `ftp://ftp.cica.indiana.edu/pub/pc/win3/winsock`

2. If you have a problem connecting, try one of the URLs mentioned in Chapter 8. For example, you might try the following URL:

   `ftp://wuarchive.wustl.edu/systems/ibmpc/win3/winsock`

3. Click the filename trumptel.zip. The Zip View window is displayed.

4. Click the Extract button. Drag and Zip displays the Zip View dialog box.

5. In the Output directory text box, enter c:\trumpet.

6. Click the All Files button, and choose OK. If the directory doesn't exist, Drag and Zip asks if you want to create it. Choose OK.

7. Choose File | Exit to close the Zip View window.

8. Double-click the Mosaic Notepad icon to open the mosaic.ini file. You need to change the following line in the [Viewers] section of the mosaic.ini file:

```
telnet="c:\trumpet\telw.exe"
```

9. Change this entry to:

```
telnet="c:\trumpet\trmptel.exe"
```

10. Choose File | Save, and then choose File | Exit.

11. Open the File Manager and drag the file c:\trumpet\trmptel.exe from the File Manager window into the program group that is to contain the icon for the TrumpTel Telnet tool. The following icon is added to the group:

Trmptel

When you click a Telnet site hyperlink, Mosaic opens the TrumpTel Telnet application, which is shown in Figure 9-6.

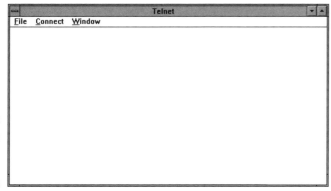

Figure 9-6:
TrumpTel
Windows.

Teaching Mosaic to Work with Other Useful Applications

You can set up Mosaic to launch any application. For example, you might tell Mosaic that any document files with the .doc extension should be loaded in Microsoft Word.

By default, text files are loaded in the Mosaic window. Unfortunately, you can't edit files directly in this window. As an alternative, you might want to specify that Mosaic should load all text files — that is, files with the .txt extension — in the Windows Notepad or another text editor of your choosing.

Notepad can't handle large text files. If a file is too large, you'll see an error message indicating that the file cannot be loaded. An alternative to Notepad is the WinEdit text editor. This shareware program is available from Wilson WindowWare at the following URL:

```
http://www.windowware.com/wilson/pages/winedit.html
```

One application that you're sure to find helpful when visiting sites on the Web is the Adobe Acrobat Reader. The Adobe Acrobat Reader lets users read files, regardless of which platforms are used to create and view the files. Adobe released a free version of this program in October 1994. You can download it by entering the following URL:

```
http://www.adobe.com
```

You can also get the file from Adobe. You'll find it in the /pub/adobe/Applications/Acrobat directory at the following site:

```
ftp://ftp.adobe.com
```

Because the Adobe Acrobat Portable Document Format (PDF) helps solve the problem of incompatibility between platforms, it is becoming increasingly popular on the Internet.

By adding several entries to your mosaic.ini file, you can set up Mosaic to support Microsoft Word, the Windows Notepad text editor, and the Adobe Acrobat Reader. After the last TYPE entry in the [Viewers] section of the mosaic.ini file, you need to add a TYPE entry for each application. For example, if the last TYPE entry is number 12, you would insert the following entries:

```
TYPE13="application/acrobat"
TYPE14="application/notepad"
TYPE15="application/winword"
```

Immediately after the last TYPE entry that you add to mosaic.ini, you need to identify the application that Mosaic should launch for each type of application you've just added. For example, to match the previous three TYPE entries, you would add the following entries:

```
application/acrobat="c:\acroread\acroread.exe %1s"
application/notepad="c:\windows\notepad.exe %1s"
application/winword="c:\winword\winword.exe %1s"
```

At the end of the [Suffixes] section, you need to add the filename extensions that you want Mosaic to associate with the three applications. For example, Adobe Acrobat Reader files end with the extension .pdf, text files typically end with the extension .txt, and Microsoft Word documents end with the extension .doc. As such, you would add the following entries to the end of the [Suffixes] section:

```
application/acrobat=.pdf
application/notepad=.txt
application/winword=.doc
```

When you click a hyperlink to a file that ends with one of these extensions, Mosaic will automatically launch the program you associated with the extension, with the file loaded in the application.

Part IV

Building Your Own Home Page for Fun and Profit

"Shoot, that's nothing! Watch me spin him!"

In This Part...

It's time to stake your claim in cyberspace by creating your own Web document. Adding your presence to the Internet via a Web document is surprisingly easy and affordable. This part covers the design and mechanics of building your own Web documents. We walk you through the fundamentals of working with HTML (HyperText Markup Language) to create Web documents. Once you create your document, we tell you how to get it published on the Internet.

Chapter 10

Serving Up Your Own Web Documents

. . . .

In This Chapter

▶ Defining the content of your Web presence

▶ Assembling the pieces of a Web document

▶ Understanding HTML documents

▶ Placing your Web document on a server

. . . .

*U*p to now, you've surfed the Web visiting one Web document after another. These documents are created by individuals, businesses, and other organizations as resources for Net users. You can stake an affordable claim in cyberspace for yourself, your business, or any organization. By creating your own Web document and renting space on a server, you can establish a presence on the Net that's available to millions of people. In this chapter, we present a blueprint for constructing your own Web document, and we show you how to make it available on the Net.

Establishing a Web Presence

The term *presence* can mean "the state of being," or "the ability to project an appearance of imposing kind." By creating a Web document, you establish your presence in cyberspace. A Web document is an exciting, powerful, and inexpensive way to present yourself, a business, or an organization to the millions of Net users. Establishing a Web presence is a multi-faceted process that involves the following steps:

➤ Defining the content of your Web presence. You need to determine what you want to provide as well as how you can package it as a service to people on the Web.

✔ Assembling the pieces of your Web presence. This step includes writing and copyediting text; creating or obtaining pictures, sounds, or video files; and assembling URLs for your hyperlinks.

✔ Creating the actual Web document. This step involves working with HTML commands, which you enter using an HTML editor or a text editor. We cover the details of creating your Web document using HTML commands in Chapter 11.

✔ Placing your Web document on a server, where it is available to Web users. This step involves working with companies that rent space on their servers.

Creating a Thumbnail of Your Web Document

Before you rush into putting all the pieces together, take some time to create thumbnail sketches of your Web presence. In other words, use a pen and paper to sketch possible designs for your Web document. Desktop publishers and graphic designers use thumbnails to generate ideas. Your thumbnail will act as a blueprint that helps you determine which items you need to assemble for your Web presence. By spending a little time on a thumbnail sketch, you can save a lot of time in the creation of your Web document.

It's the Content

Before you create your Web document, ask yourself a few questions. For example, how extensive do you want your presence to be? What are you going to say? What's your service to the Net community? Creating the Web document is the easy part; defining the content takes some thought and effort.

Web publishing options

Creating a Web document is on-line publishing. You can publish anything from a simple one-page Web document to a comprehensive, multi-page information center. The only limitations are your imagination, time, and cash. The biggest expense of publishing a Web document is the cost of placing the document on a server.

Publishing a one-page brochure is the easiest and least expensive option for establishing a Web presence. A basic Web document might include a few inline pictures, text, and hyperlinks to other Web resources (or other resources on the Net). The cost of placing such a Web document on a server can be as low as $25 per month.

A multi-page information center is a more sophisticated Web presence. However, these sites are also more expensive to place on a Web server. The cost of placing a multi-page Web information center on a server can be as low as $100 a month. You might establish this type of Web presence by creating:

- An on-line catalog that includes descriptive text, pictures of products, and icons. Web users can browse through your catalog, and place orders through your existing order fulfillment operation, such as an 800 telephone number.

- A resource center that focuses on a particular topic of interest. For example, your Web site might focus on culinary delights. The site could offer recipes, gourmet factoids, and links to related sites on the Web.

- Your own on-line newsletter or magazine. Almost anyone with a particular slant can create an on-line publication.

A *virtual storefront* goes beyond on-line publishing to include the capability to conduct on-line transactions using credit cards or secured accounts. This type of Web presence is a more complex and expensive endeavor that requires an infrastructure for handling the transactions. Establishing this type of Web presence is beyond the scope of this book. But many of techniques relevant to on-line publishing are important for establishing a virtual storefront. ■

Packaging your Web information as a resource

The Web is a great place for getting your message out. It's not an in-your-face medium like network news or e-mail, where mass postings or mailings typically elicit a flood of *flames* (irate e-mail or publicly posted messages) and negative publicity among Net users.

When defining the message you want to convey through your Web presence, try to take a content-based approach. In other words, you need to view your Web presence as a resource for the people and organizations that use the Net. As a digital community, the folks on the Net appreciate high-quality, carefully filtered information.

You should keep the following guidelines in mind when determining the content of your Web site:

- Attract Web users to your Web site by providing a useful or entertaining resource in addition to your own message.

> ✔ Keep your Web site fresh. One of the key tenets for maintaining a popular site is to keep it dynamic. If you create a site and then leave it alone, you defeat the true power of the Web.
>
> ✔ Make sure you're willing to commit the time and effort necessary to feed and care for your Web site. The bigger the site, the more it demands.

Watch out for copyrights

Copyright law applies to various types of human creations. Under federal law, copyright protection is automatically provided for original works of authorship in a tangible medium of expression, and created in the U.S. after January 1, 1978. The digitized material on the Web has this same copyright protection. E-mail, network newsgroup articles, programs, and files of all kinds are protected by copyright laws. Keep the following guidelines in mind when you're working with copied material:

> ✔ Copyright owners retain exclusive rights even when placing their work on the Net.
>
> ✔ The copyright owner doesn't need to publish a copyright notice with the work if the work was created in the U.S. after March 1989.
>
> ✔ The best way to avoid copyright problems is to never take anything and claim it as your own. Give credit where credit is due.
>
> ✔ By using hyperlinks to point users to an existing Web site, you can avoid having to copy anything from that site.

Gathering the Pieces

The key pieces of any Web document are text, inline images, hyperlinks, and external multimedia files. Before you start coding a Web document, you need to get your pieces together. In other words, you need to create the text, obtain or create GIF pictures for inline images, collect the URL addresses for your hyperlinks, and get any multimedia files you need.

The joy of text

The written word is an important part of your Web document. Don't skimp on the quality of your text. At many Web sites, the lack of attention to the textual message is all too obvious.

Here are some guidelines for creating the text for your Web document:

- ✔ Don't write advertising copy — that is, text that's full of hype and fluff.

- ✔ Target your text to the audience you want to attract.

- ✔ Have a copy editor review your text.

- ✔ Be aware that some extra thought is necessary when you're writing and organizing text for a hypertext environment. For example, longer documents are easier to work with and print than documents with an excessive number of hyperlinks.

- ✔ Make sure your text can stand on its own as a printed document. Even though a document can include hypertext links and pictures, a user who accesses a Web page should be able to grasp the context of the page as well as the information within the page without going to any links. Remember, if a Web user prints the document, the printed document includes only the text and pictures, not the hypertext information.

- ✔ Manage the size of your text blocks to make your Web document easy to read. Smaller blocks of text are easier to digest. Your documents can be long; they just need some white space to break up the text.

You can create your text in any text editor or word processor. If you use a word processor, such as Word for Windows, you'll need to save the file as a text file to bring it into a Web document. In Chapter 11, we tell you how to bring text into a Web document.

Assembling your files

After preparing the text, you need to get all the picture, video, sound, and other files that are going to be part of your Web presence. Any file that's not an inline image is an external file. Mosaic users can access external files from a Web document via hyperlinks. They can view or play these files using external programs that they've set up to work with Mosaic, or they can simply download the files.

As long as the files are in formats that are usable on the Web, it doesn't matter how you create these files. Table 10-1 lists the common file types on the Web.

You can create your own files using programs you already work with, such as desktop publishing programs that support GIF files. You can purchase commercial clip art packages, use clip art that comes with desktop publishing programs, or find free clip art on the Net.

Because they can be used as inline images — that is, the pictures that Mosaic users view directly in your Web document — GIF files are the most important files you need to assemble. By collecting a variety of GIF images, you can select just the right graphic elements for enhancing the visual appeal of your

Table 10-1: Common file types and their extensions

File type	Filename extension
Plain ASCII text with no formatting	.txt
Web document	.htm or .html (.htm is used on DOS and Windows systems)
Image	.gif
Sound	.wav, .voc, .aif, or .au
Picture	.jpg or .jpeg
Postscript	.ps
QuickTime movie (video)	.mov
MPEG video	.mpg or .mpeg

Web document. Stay tuned, in the next section, we tell you how to get some free GIF pictures on the Web.

You don't have to store large multimedia files at your Web site. You can create a hyperlink that points to the site that has the file you want to use. In addition to saving the time it would take to get the multimedia file, this approach saves you the cost of putting a large multimedia file on a server. ■

Getting GIF pictures on the Web

If you don't have any GIF clip art from commercial packages or your own creations, you can get GIF images on the Web. Numerous Web sites offer free images that you can use in your documents. You can find collections of decorative elements, such as bullets, icons, and lines, that let you enhance the appearance of your Web document beyond the defaults of HTML. You simply download these files to your system.

The following URL is a good site for grabbing some GIF bullets, icons, and lines:

```
http://colargol.edb.tih.no/~geirme/gizmos/gizmo.html
```

As shown in Figure 10-1, when you click the lines hyperlink, this site displays a Web page containing a nice collection of lines. If you see an image you want, just point to the corresponding hyperlink, hold down the Shift key, and click. The image is yours. Table 10-2 lists some other GIF file sites that offer full-size pictures, icons, bullets, and lines. We point you to even more sites for gathering files in Chapter 20.

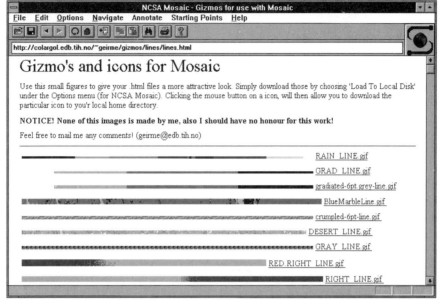

Table 10-2: Web sites that have GIF files

URL	Contents
http://white.nosc.mil/images.html	A gateway to an extensive collection of GIF files, including space, travel, medical, and other images. It also points to sites that offer icons, bullets, and other GIF files.
http://legendre.ucsd.edu/y/icons.html	A site that offers The Virtual Icon Collection, which includes access to GIF images, icons, bullets, lines, and other GIF files.
http://www-ns.rutgers.edu/doc-images/icons/	A page containing a collection of standard GIF bullet files.
http://ns2.rutgers.edu/doc-images/small_buttons/	A page containing a collection of standard GIF icons.
http://www.di.unipi.it/test/new/icons/icons1-6.html	A huge collection of icons in sheets.
http://akebono.stanford.edu/yahoo/computers/multimedia/pictures	A server named Yahoo, which offers a huge inventory of multimedia files.

Hyperlinks, hyperlinks, and more hyperlinks

Among the most useful features of Web documents are hyperlinks that connect to all kinds of information in different formats, anywhere on the Net. You can create hyperlinks to any of the following resources:

- Web documents.

- Parts of Web documents.

- FTP, Gopher, Telnet, network newsgroup, or WAIS sites. You create hyperlinks to these and other tools by using URLs in the same way you do for a Web document. The only difference is that you change the resource type from http:// to one of the tools listed in Table 10-3.

- Any files, including picture, video, and sound files.

Table 10-3: Pointing to other servers in hyperlinks

URL prefix	Points to
file://	A specific file on an anonymous FTP server, or a local file on your computer
ftp://	A directory on an anonymous FTP server
gopher://	A Gopher server
WAIS://	A WAIS server
news:	A specific network newsgroup
telnet://	A telnet server

You need to assemble the hotlists that you plan to use in your Web document. The easiest way to get URLs is by adding them to your Mosaic hotlist. In Chapter 11, we tell you how to get them directly from your mosaic.ini file.

Think before you link. Hypermedia provides a new generation of document design options and pitfalls that are not applicable in linear, paper-based documents. Don't overuse hyperlinks to the point of jarring a reader's concentration.

What Are HTML Documents?

The HyperText Markup Language (HTML) is the source code behind every Web document. The document containing the HTML codes is nothing more than a simple ASCII text file, referred to as a *source document* or an *HTML document*. It's this document — along with any inline images — that gets downloaded to Mosaic.

After receiving the HTML document and the inline images, Mosaic uses the HTML commands as instructions for constructing the Web document. These instructions define all the elements of the Web document, including the document title, section headers, character formatting, bulleted lists, inline images, and hypermedia links.

Figure 10-2 shows a typical Web document in its HTML form. Figure 10-3 shows the same document as it appears in Mosaic.

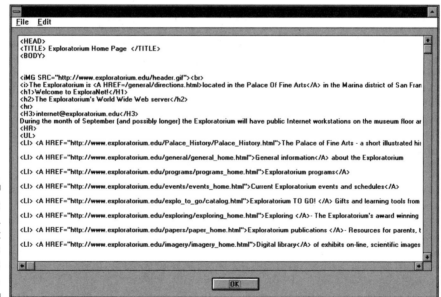

Figure 10-2:
An HTML document contains instructions for Mosaic.

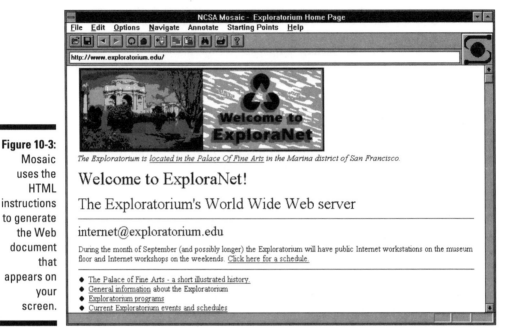

Figure 10-3:
Mosaic
uses the
HTML
instructions
to generate
the Web
document
that
appears on
your
screen.

Tools of the HTML Document Trade

You enter HTML commands in an ASCII text document, which you can create
with any text editor — for example, the Windows Notepad. However, a shareware or commercial HTML editor makes it even easier to create and edit
HTML documents. With most HTML editors, you can automatically launch
Mosaic and view your document while you're working on it — a very handy
feature.

HTML+: The next generation

A new generation of HTML, called HTML+, promises a number of enhancements that will allow you to create more sophisticated Web documents. HTML+ will include support for creating tables as well as other enhanced for-matting options. It will also include support for interactive forms for querying or updating information sources, and for e-mailing and faxing services.

The HTML Assistant for Windows is a shareware program developed by Howard Harawitz. This program offers an impressive array of features for creating and editing Web documents. It makes working with HTML documents easier and far less tedious than using a plain-old text editor. We show you how to get this program and use it in Chapter 11.

Putting Your Document on the Web

Many of the Web documents you've visited in your surfing safaris are stored on servers that are operated by server services. A server service is a company that sells space on their server.

Server service companies offer you an affordable avenue for publishing on the Web. They handle the expensive overhead of hardware and software systems, high-speed data lines, and the expertise involved in setting up and maintaining a server on the Net. You can think of a server service as a management company that operates a virtual mall. They take care of the technical details, and you just rent the space. Web users can either access your Web document through the server service's home page or they can move directly to your home page via its own URL address.

Shopping for a server service

With all the current interest in the Web, many new companies are offering server services. Companies that sell Net connections are also offering server space for rent. Services and pricing are all over the place, and there's no *Consumer Reports* to help you pick the right server service. However, your Web presence can be established inexpensively if you create your own Web document and shop around for a server service.

We get you on your way by providing a list of affordable server services in Chapter 16. But don't just take our word for it; do some more shopping on your own as you surf the Web. ▪

Here are some pointers to help you through the process of finding the right server service:

  ✔ To get a feel for the quality of a server service, check out its Web site. Are the documents well designed and professional?

  ✔ Make sure the server service accepts server-ready copy — that is, an HTML document.

- ✔ Find out whether the server service will help you monitor the results of your Web presence by tracking activity at your Web document. If so, find out how this is done.

- ✔ Ask about the volume of traffic at the Web site. These figures can give you an idea of the Web site's drawing power. Traffic can range from a few thousand hits to several hundred thousand hits a month.

- ✔ Find out how the server service is marketing its Web site, both on and off the Net. If your Web document is on their server, you stand to benefit from their promotions.

- ✔ Determine the sizes of the files for your Web document, including the HTML document, inline image files, and other multimedia files. This factor can affect your costs, because many server services charge according to the amount of space you require on their server.

- ✔ Find out how much the server service charges for posting an updated document and how fast they post your new documents.

- ✔ Find out what the server service charges for any support services required to support a Web server. These costs can be substantial, and are completely separate from the basic setup and monthly fees.

Putting your Web document on the Net as a file

You can also put your Web document on the Net as a file at an anonymous FTP site. Mosaic users can access your Web document by using Mosaic as an FTP client. For example, a Mosaic user might access the Web document by entering:

```
file://www.internex.net/planettrv/planet.html
```

Although this is an inexpensive option, it does require you to set up access to an FTP server, usually through your Net connection service. In addition, your Web document address will be different than the typical Web URL, which starts with http://.

Chapter 11

The Nuts and Bolts of Creating HTML Documents

. . . .

In This Chapter

▶ Getting the HTML Assistant program and setting it up

▶ Understanding the elements of HTML style

▶ Working with HTML tags

▶ Entering and formatting text in Web documents

▶ Adding inline images and hyperlinks to Web documents

. . . .

*Y*ou understand the pieces that are used to create your Web document; now it's time to put them all together. Creating a Web document is surprisingly easy. You simply create a text file that includes commands that tell Mosaic how to lay out your document and its components, such as text and pictures. This chapter shows you how to create an HTML document, which Mosaic uses to assemble the Web document that's displayed on a Mosaic user's screen. To make your life easier, we tell you how to obtain and use the HTML Assistant for Windows, a shareware program that lets you create your Web document in a friendlier environment than a plain text editor.

Hiring Your HTML Assistant

You can download the HTML Assistant for Windows from the developer's FTP site. Before you grab this program, make sure you have Drag and Zip installed, as explained in Chapter 8.

The HTML Assistant for Windows program is available at various sites on the Net, but it's often an older version. The version we use in this book is 1.0a, which is considerably different from earlier versions. ∎

The 5th Wave

By Rich Tennant

"Hey, I never saw a slow response time fixed with a paperweight before."

Here's how you download a copy of the HTML Assistant for Windows:

1. Launch Mosaic and enter the following address in the URL text box:

   ```
   ftp://ftp.cs.dal.ca/htmlasst
   ```

   You are connected to the FTP site at which the developer of HTML Assistant for Windows keeps the program. A list of file links is displayed.

2. Click the htmlasst.zip hyperlink. Drag and Zip displays the Zip View window, which lists the contents of the zip file you selected, htmlasst.zip.

3. Click the Extract button. Drag and Zip displays the Zip View dialog box.

4. In the Output directory text box, enter c:\htmlasst.

5. Click the All files button in the UnZip group, and choose OK. If the output directory doesn't exist, Drag and Zip asks if you want to create the directory. Choose OK.

6. Choose File | Exit to close the Zip View window.

7. Open the program group in which you want to add the icon for the HTML Assistant, and drag the file c:\htmlasst\htmlasst.exe from the File Manager window into the program group. Windows adds the following icon to the program group:

Htmlasst

Getting Started with HTML

Creating Web documents is a lot easier with the HTML Assistant than with a plain text editor such as Notepad. Before you start creating an HTML document, you need to launch the HTML Assistant and tweak a few settings.

You should create a separate directory for each HTML document. This is helpful because any GIF files that are used as inline images in a document must be stored in the same directory as the HTML document file. ■

Let's put your Assistant to work:

1. Double-click the Htmlasst icon. The About HTML Assistant dialog box is displayed. To open the HTML Assistant window, choose OK.

2. Choose File | New to open a new document window. You use this document window to enter your HTML codes for creating a Web document. This document is called a source, or HTML document.

3. Choose File | Save. HTML Assistant displays the Save As dialog box. By saving the document right from the start, you can take advantage of an Autosave feature, which we explain later in this section.

4. Enter the name of your source document in the File Name field, specify where you want the file stored, and choose OK.

5. Choose Options | Autosave file before test. This is a toggle option. To show that the option is active, HTML Assistant displays a check mark next to this menu item.

6. Choose File | Enter Test Program Name. HTML Assistant displays the Test program dialog box, which you use to specify Mosaic as your viewer for Web documents. In other words, Mosaic is the program HTML Assistant will use to let you test your Web documents as you create them.

7. Navigate to the directory containing your mosaic.exe file, which is usually c:\mosaic. Select the mosaic.exe file, and choose OK. HTML Assistant displays a dialog box asking if you want to save Mosaic as the test program. Choose Yes. As shown in Figure 11-1, the HTML Assistant program is ready for you to start working.

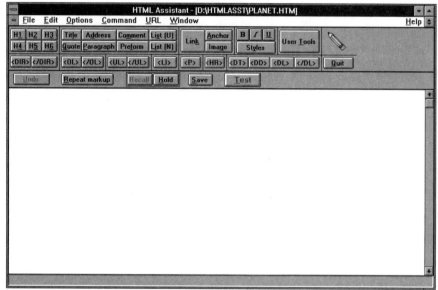

Figure 11-1:
The HTML
Assistant
program,
ready for
you to start
building
your Web
document.

Unfortunately, HTML Assistant doesn't let you save the Autosave setting beyond the current session. You need to choose Options|Autosave file before test each time you launch HTML Assistant to work on an HTML document. It's annoying, but you'll want to do it. ■

Tagging your HTML commands

HTML commands, which are called *tags*, tell Mosaic how to lay out the text in your Web document as well as how to make links to other resources. HTML tags consist of a less-than sign (<), the name of the tag, and a greater-than sign (>). For example, the tag <H1> identifies a top-level heading in a Web document.

Here are the key conventions for entering HTML tags:

✔ Tags usually come in pairs — for example, <TITLE></TITLE>. The ending tag is just like the starting tag, except a slash (/) precedes the tag name within the brackets. As with any rule, there are exceptions. For example, the paragraph tag, <P>, doesn't need a closing tag, </P>.

✔ HTML tags aren't case sensitive. The tag <title> is equivalent to <TITLE>. We use uppercase letters for the tags in this chapter simply to make it easy for you to recognize them.

The code of the Web

In an HTML document, tags and your text entries can get chaotic if you don't follow some coding style guidelines. Mosaic can read any HTML document as long as the tags are in the correct *syntax* — that is, the grammar of HTML. But what's easy for Mosaic to read isn't always easy for you to read as you work with an HTML document.

A simple Web document might include a document title, a level-one heading, a logo image, a heading, and two paragraphs of text. If you enter these tags with an eye to visually presenting the flow of HTML instructions in your document, the entry might appear like this:

```
<TITLE>Planet Travel Service/TITLE>
<H1>Planet Travel Service</H1>
<IMG SRC="GALAXY.GIF">

Tour Guides to the Stars<P>

Planet Travel Service is pleased to announce our special
space trekking packages. Leave the planet often.<P>

<UL>
<LI><A>To the Moon Alice="http://nasa.gov/moon.html"</A>
<LI><A>Venus:Planet of Love="http://nasa.gov/venus.html"</A>
</UL>

<ADDRESS>dangell@planettrv.com</ADDRESS>
```

If you ignore the elements of HTML style, the same HTML document might look like this:

```
<TITLE>Planet Travel Service/TITLE><H1>Planet Travel Service</H1>
<IMG SRC="GALAXY.GIF">Tour Guides to the Stars<P>Planet Travel
Service is pleased to announce our special space trekking
packages. Leave the planet often.<P><UL><LI><A>To the Moon Alice=
"http://nasa.gov/moon.html"</A><LI><A>Venus:Planet of Love=
"http://nasa.gov/venus.html"</A></UL><ADDRESS>dangell@planettrv.com
</ADDRESS>
```

Life's too short for trying to decipher this kind of HTML document. When creating HTML source documents, you should break up different formatting elements. You can add blank lines to break up tags into logical clusters that give you visual cues as to what's going on. These line breaks don't affect the Web document in Mosaic.

Important stuff! An HTML Assistant primer

HTML Assistant lets you click buttons to enter most of the tags you need for creating a Web document. Instead of manually typing tags, you can add them automatically by clicking the appropriate button at the top of the HTML Assistant window. You enter the tags first, and then add the text. For a pair of tags, position the cursor between the tags, and then enter your text.

Don't try to apply a tag by entering your text and then selecting it. If you select text and then click the button for a tag, HTML Assistant will delete the text and add just the tag. ∎

The Edit menu in the HTML Assistant includes standard Windows commands for copying, moving, and deleting text. It also includes commands for undoing the last action, and for searching and replacing text.

Each HTML document has its own window and toolbar that includes the Undo, Repeat markup, Recall, Hold, Save, and Test buttons. The Undo, Repeat markup, Save, and Test buttons are more convenient than using the corresponding commands in the HTML Assistant menus. The Repeat markup command lets you insert another instance of the command you just entered.

The Test button on the document window toolbar is the best button of all. It lets you automatically launch Mosaic to view the results of your HTML codes. Before you choose the Test button, make sure you save any changes you've made to the HTML document.

The best way to ensure that your changes are saved is by choosing Options | Autosave file before test each time you open the HTML Assistant. Otherwise, you have to remember to choose the Save button before you choose the Test button. If you don't remember to save your changes before choosing Test, HTML Assistant displays the ominous message in Figure 11-2, which warns you that Windows might crash if you precede — and it often will. If you see this message, choose Cancel and save your changes.

Before using HTML Assistant's Test button, make sure that you've turned off Mosaic's Autoload Home Page setting in your mosaic.ini file. (We showed you

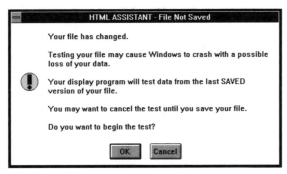

Figure 11-2: The File Not Saved message warns you of the dire consequences you face if you proceed with the test without saving your changes in HTML Assistant.

how to do this in Chapter 7.) Otherwise, you'll get the Failed DNS error message every time you launch Mosaic locally (without a connection) from HTML Assistant, as we explain later in this chapter. ■

If all goes well, after you choose the Test button, your Web document is displayed without any Mosaic error messages. The most common error message you may see informs you that Mosaic can't find the specified GIF file you're using for an inline image. We'll tell you more about this error message later in this chapter.

After viewing the document in Mosaic, choose File | Exit to close the Mosaic window. If you only reduce the Mosaic window to an icon, you'll run out of memory after a few tests in Mosaic, and HTML Assistant will display an out-of-memory error message.

Adding text to your HTML document

If your document contains more than a few sentences of text, you should create the text using a word processor or a text editor. If you have a choice, use a word processor with a spell checker.

After creating your text, you can use the standard Windows Copy and Paste commands to move text from your word processor to the HTML Assistant via the clipboard. To copy and paste your text, select the completed text in your word processor, and press Ctrl-C or choose the Edit | Copy command. In the HTML Assistant document window, position the cursor where you want the text, and press Ctrl-V or choose Edit | Paste. Then, you can add your tags.

HTML Assistant doesn't let you insert a text file into an HTML document. You must use the Windows clipboard to copy text and paste it into your HTML document. ■

General Structure Tags

The HTML, HEAD, and BODY tags are general document structuring tags. That is, they define the entire document's structure (HTML), the document heading (HEAD), and the body of the document (BODY). Currently, Mosaic and most other browsers don't use these tags, but their use may be more important in the future as Web browsers become more sophisticated. For now, the best strategy is to get in the habit of adding these tags to your documents.

Everything in an HTML document is nested between the <HTML> </HTML> tag. In other words, the first entry in any Web document is <HTML> and the last entry is </HTML>. This tag tells the Web browser that this is an HTML document and not some other type of document. To enter the HTML tag in HTML Assistant, select the text you want enclosed in the HTML tags and press Ctrl-T or choose Command | Mark Selected Text as HTML.

The <HEAD> tag is placed at the beginning of an HTML document, immediately after the <HTML> tag. The only important tag that you enclose in the <HEAD> tag is the <TITLE> tag (which we explain later). After the <TITLE> tag, you enter the </HEAD> tag. To enter the HEAD tags in HTML Assistant, select the text you want enclosed in the HEAD tags, and press Ctrl-D or choose Command | Mark Selected Text as HEAD.

The <BODY> tag is added to the beginning of the content of your document, immediately after the </HEAD> tag. At the end of your document — just before the </HTML> tag — you enter the </BODY> tag. To enter the BODY tags in HTML Assistant, select the text you want enclosed in the BODY tags, and press Ctrl-Y or choose Command | Selected Text as BODY.

The structure of the HTML, HEAD, and BODY tags is as follows:

```
<HTML>
<HEAD>
<TITLE>Title Text</TITLE>
</HEAD>
<BODY>
The body of your Web document
</BODY>
</HTML>
```

Playing Title Tag

Every HTML document should have a title. The document title appears in the title bar of the Mosaic window. It also appears as a menu item when a Mosaic user adds it to a hotlist. The words in a document title are also used as keywords by programs that search the Web or databases used by various Web sites to locate Web documents by subject.

Keep your Web document title concise, yet as descriptive as possible. A good rule of thumb is to keep titles within a half-dozen words or 64 characters in length. A long title is a nuisance for Mosaic users who want to add it as a hotlist entry.

The title tag has the following syntax:

```
<TITLE>Your Title Text</TITLE>
```

To enter a <TITLE> tag in HTML Assistant, position the cursor on the first line of the document, and click the Title button, which inserts <TITLE></TITLE>. Position the cursor between the two tags and enter your title text. For example, you might enter:

```
<TITLE>Planet Travel Service</TITLE>
```

Heading in the Right Direction

HTML has six levels of headings, numbered 1 through 6, with 1 being the top level. These headings include a larger font size than normal text, boldface text, and built-in spacing before and after the heading. Figure 11-3 shows the six heading levels of HTML as they appear in Mosaic. Mosaic users can change the fonts of these headings, as well as their styles and sizes. However, most users stick with the defaults.

The syntax of the heading tag is:

```
<Hn>Heading Text</Hn>
```

where *n* is the number of the heading (1-6). The first heading in each document is usually an <H1> heading. Don't use a heading more than one level below the heading that precedes it. For example, you shouldn't jump directly from an <H1> heading to an <H3> heading. Instead, an <H1> heading might be followed in a document by two or more <H2> headings. Each page in a multi-page document should begin with a header that orients the reader to the contents of that page.

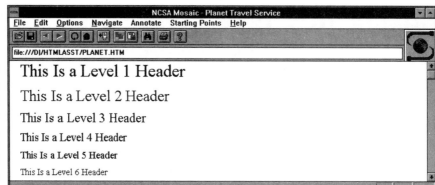

Figure 11-3:
The six
heading lev-
els of HTML
as they
appear in
Mosaic.

To insert a header in a document you're creating with HTML Assistant, choose the appropriate header button, H1, H2, H3, H4, H5, or H6. HTML Assistant inserts the selected tags — for example, <H1></H1> — in your document. Position the cursor between the two tags and enter your header text. For example, you might enter:

```
<H1>Tour Guides to the Stars</H1>
```

Defining Paragraphs

In HTML, the <P> paragraph tag lets you separate units of text that would otherwise flow together. You insert a paragraph tag in HTML Assistant by choosing the <P> button. Remember that the <P> tag is the exception to the tag pairs rule.

Mosaic handles a <P> paragraph tag by inserting a blank line after the text that is followed by a paragraph tag. Mosaic displays paragraph text in the Times New Roman, Regular, 11-point font.

Here's an example of a typical paragraph tag:

```
Mercury, the planet closest to the Sun, is off the beaten path.
This ancient planet offers lots of hiking adventures on its
heavily cratered surface. To add to your adventure, you'll
experience extreme temperatures and volatile gases from the
surface.<P>
```

Listing Your Good Points

HTML includes commands for creating several different types of lists, including unordered (bulleted) lists, ordered (numbered) lists, definition lists, and nested lists. Figure 11-4 shows a sample of each type of list as it appears in a Web document.

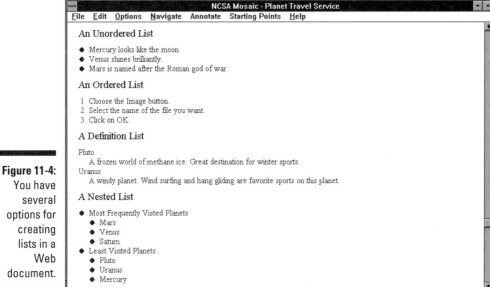

Figure 11-4: You have several options for creating lists in a Web document.

Creating unordered lists

In HTML, *unordered list* is just an awkward term for a bulleted list. To the Mosaic user, the list appears with default black bullets. An unordered list has the following syntax:

```
<UL>
<LI>List Item Text
<LI>List Item Text
<LI>List Item Text
</UL>
```

There are two ways to enter an unordered list in HTML Assistant. You can choose the List (U) button, which inserts the following tags:

```
<UL>
<LI>
</UL>
```

Or, you can add the individual tags one by one as you create the list by clicking the <UL>, </UL>, and <LI> buttons. The <DIR> and </DIR> tag buttons create the same type of list as the <UL> </UL> tag.

The <LI> items can contain multiple paragraphs. As shown in the following example, you just separate the paragraphs with <P> paragraph tags:

```
<UL>
<LI>Venus is the planet of love and beauty. It offers a shrouded,
greenhouse-effect getaway for lovers.<P>

There's lots to do on Venus, including inhaling carbon dioxide,
taking romantic walks on orange beaches, and experiencing crushing
atmospheric pressure.<P>

<LI>Mars is a popular destination that has it all.<P>

You can ride buggies across sand dunes and hills, feel lightheaded,
and be immersed in pink light by day and pale blue sunsets.<P>
</UL>
```

You can specify small GIF images, such as a pinpoint, as replacements for the default bullets. We show you how to change the bullet character later in this chapter. ■

Creating numbered lists

An ordered list is a numbered list. Its syntax is identical to an unordered list, except it uses the <OL> tag. List items use the same <LI> tag, and you can use multiple paragraphs for items in a numbered list. An ordered list has the following syntax:

```
<OL>
<LI>List Item Text
<LI>List Item Text
<LI>List Item Text
</OL>
```

Just like unordered lists, there are two ways to enter an ordered list in HTML Assistant. You can click the List (N) button, which inserts the following tags:

```
<OL>
<LI>
</OL>
```

Or, you can add the individual tags one by one as you create the list by clicking the <OL>, </OL>, and <LI> buttons.

Creating definition lists

A definition list gets its name because the list includes a term on one line, followed by its definition, which is indented on the next line. A definition list starts with the <DL> tag and ends with the </DL> tag. The term line uses the <DT> tag and the definition line uses the <DD> tag:

```
<DL>
<DT>Term Text
<DD>Definition Text
<DT>Term Text
<DD>Definition Text
</DL>
```

Like the other lists, the <DT> and <DD> entries can contain multiple paragraphs separated by <P> paragraph tags. To create definition lists in HTML Assistant, you use buttons for each individual tag. The buttons are: <DT>, <DD>, <DL>, and </DL>.

Creating nested lists

A nested list is a list within a list. You can create any mix of lists and nested lists, including ordered, unordered, and definition lists.

In the following nested list, notice that each list is enclosed within separate list tags and the entire nested list is enclosed within another set of list tags:

```
<UL>
<LI>Most Frequently Visited Planets
<UL>
<LI>Mars
<LI>Venus
<LI>Saturn
</UL>
<LI>Least Visited Planets
<UL>
<LI>Mercury
<LI>Pluto
<LI>Uranus
</UL>
</UL>
```

Looks Aren't Everything

HTML offers only three character-formatting options: bold, italic, and a typewriter (fixed-width) font. To tell Mosaic how to format text, you surround the text with the appropriate tag:

```
<B>Text You Want Boldfaced</B>
<I>Text You Want Italicized</I>
<TT>Text You Want to Appear as Typewriter Text</TT>
```

The text you want to format can be within another tag, such as a paragraph tag. In HTML Assistant, you use the <B> button for bold and the <I> button for italic. There's no <TT> tag button. To format text as typewriter text, click the Styles button, and choose the Fixed item from the menu that's displayed.

Can We Quote You on That?

The <blockquote> tag is similar to a paragraph tag, except it adds a line before and after the block of text. Like paragraph text, block quote text is displayed in the Times New Roman, Regular, 11-point font. The following example shows how you enter a block quote:

```
<BLOCKQUOTE>
Saturn, with its dazzling rings, is named after the Roman god of
agriculture. The rings of Saturn consist of dust- to boulder-size
icy particles. This planet offers all kinds of different
experiences, from joy riding through the rings to wind sailing in
gas storms.
</BLOCKQUOTE>
```

Let's get physical or logical

There are two types of character formatting options in HTML: physical and logical. Physical and logical formatting options produce the same result on the screen. This has to do with the Zen-like mantra of SGML (Standard Generalized Markup Language), in which document content is divorced from its presentation vehicle. Go ahead and use the physical tags — that is, the <B>, <I>, and <TT> tags. The equivalent logical character formatting tags — <EM>, <STRONG>, and <CITE>, respectively — aren't as easy to remember.

Addressing Yourself

The <ADDRESS> tag lets you highlight the author of the Web document or the site Webmaster. As shown in the following example, this tag usually includes a means of contacting the person, such as an e-mail address:

```
<ADDRESS>
dangell@planettrv.com
</ADDRESS>
```

The <ADDRESS> tag often appears at the bottom of a Web document. The output is displayed in Mosaic for Windows in the Times New Roman, Italic, 11-point font.

Forcing Line Breaks

The <BR> tag forces a line break with no extra space between lines. This tag lets you control the lengths of lines of text. The following example shows how you can use <BR> tags to force line breaks in an address listing:

```
Planet Travel Service<BR>
1739 Astro Drive<BR>
Rocket, CA 94040<BR>
Voice: (415) 326-8541<BR>
Fax: (415) 967-6083<BR>
E-Mail: info@planettrv.com<BR>
```

You Have to Draw the Line Somewhere

The <HR> tag produces a horizontal line the width of the browser window. There's no </HR> tag for a horizontal line. These lines act as visual aids in your Web document, breaking a document into parts. Figure 11-5 shows how horizontal lines can be used to visually organize the parts of a Web document.

As we explain later in this chapter, you can use GIF inline images to create horizontal lines that are more visually appealing than the lines created with the <HR> tag. ∎

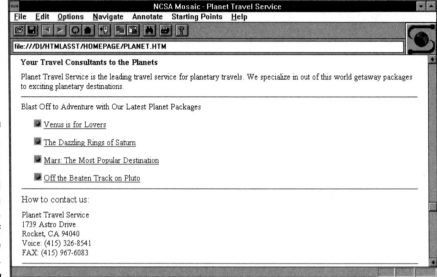

Figure 11-5:
Horizontal
lines add a
visual
dimension
to the orga-
nization of
your Web
document.

Adding Preformatted Text

The preformatted tag, <PRE>, lets you apply some limited layout formatting, such as spaces and tabs, to the text in your Web document. The big draw-back to using the <PRE> tag is that Mosaic omits the preformatted text when a user prints out a Web document from Mosaic. The following example shows a typical preformatted entry in an HTML document:

```
<PRE>
      Space Carrier Toll Free Numbers:

   Cosmic Express        (800)735-2268
   Pan Galaxy            (800)473-3060
   Warp Speed            (800)501-8659

</PRE>
```

Figure 11-6 shows what this preformatted text looks like in a Web document.

To insert preformatted text using HTML Assistant, choose the Preform but-ton, which inserts the <PRE></PRE> tags at the current cursor position. Posi-tion the cursor between the tags and press Enter to place them on separate lines.

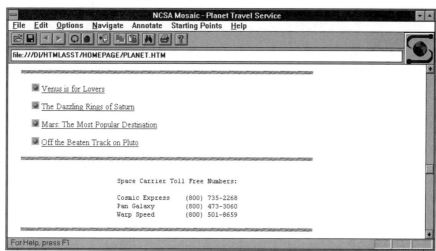

Before you enter the text with the <PRE> tag, you need to change to a fixed-width font so your text will line up properly. You can change fonts in HTML Assistant by choosing Options | Default font. You can move the text around using the Spacebar or the Tab key.

If you use a proportional font (most fonts in Windows are proportional), the text won't align properly because each character in a proportional font is a different width. For example, in a proportional font, the letter W takes up more space than the letter I. By definition, all characters in a fixed-width font take up the same amount of space. Courier New is a fixed-width font that comes with Windows.

Aren't These Characters Special?

The following special characters are used in HTML coding:

       ⟨   ⟩   &   "

Because these characters are part of HTML coding, they can't be entered directly as text. Instead, you need to use *escape sequences*, which let you fool Mosaic into displaying these characters as text. Table 11-1 lists the escape sequences for these characters.

Table 11-1: Escape sequences for special HTML characters

Character	Escape sequence
<	&lt;
>	&gt;
&	&amp;
"	&quote;

Keeping Your Comments to Yourself

The comment tag, <!----->, lets you insert comments that appear only in the HTML document. By using comments, you can add notes to the HTML document that can be helpful for anyone else who needs to work with the document. Choosing the Comment button inserts a <!----> tag. As shown in the following example, you enter your comment text between the brackets:

```
<!This GIF file came from the NASA site>
```

If you don't put the text between the brackets, your comment is displayed in the Web document. ■

Inserting Inline Images

An inline image is a picture that Mosaic displays within the Web document, and not in an external viewer. Although an external viewer isn't needed, the inline image is still a separate file that must be accessed by Mosaic. An inline image file is stored on the Web server, downloaded with the HTML document, and then rendered by Mosaic.

Downloading inline images takes time. If your Web document is full of graphics, Mosaic users will have to wait awhile for the files to be transferred from the Web server to their computers. This is particularly true for Mosaic users who are connecting to the Net with a modem. ■

The syntax for an inline image is:

```
<IMG SRC=image_URL>
```

where *image_URL* is the path or URL of the image file.

Here's how you use HTML Assistant to add an inline image:

1. Move the GIF files you want to use in your Web document into the same directory as the HTML document.

2. Click the Image button to display the Enter a URL for the Image dialog box, which is shown in Figure 11-7.

3. Click the Browse button. HTML Assistant displays the Select Name of Image File dialog box.

4. Find the GIF file you want to use as an inline image, select it in the File Name box, and choose OK. HTML Assistant displays the path of the file in the URL Text field in the Enter a URL for the Image dialog box.

5. Choose OK. HTML Assistant adds the completed inline image tag to your document. The new tag includes the full path for the GIF file you selected.

6. Delete the path in the tag that was just added to your HTML document, leaving only the GIF filename. For example, if the entry is C:\homepage\travel\saturn.gif, you would delete everything but the GIF filename, saturn.gif. Otherwise, the image doesn't appear when you launch Mosaic to display it.

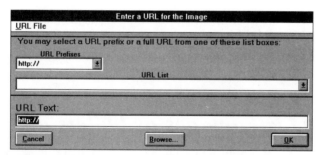

Figure 11-7: The Enter a URL for the Image dialog box lets you point to the GIF file you want to use as an inline image.

Putting your images in line

HTML offers only limited capabilities for positioning an inline image in your document relative to surrounding text. Figure 11-8 provides examples of the three options for placing an image in a Web document:

✔ The <IMG SRC=*image file*> tag, which is the default image tag, aligns adjacent text with the bottom of an image.

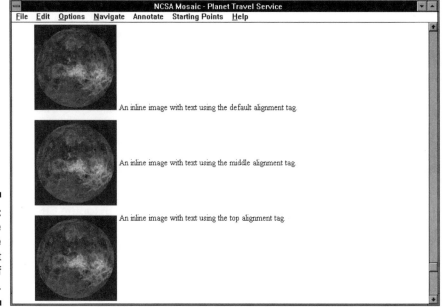

Figure 11-8:
The three
image
placement
options of
HTML.

✔ The <IMG ALIGN=MIDDLE SRC=*image file*> tag aligns the adjacent text with the center of the image.

✔ The <IMG ALIGN=TOP SRC=*image file*> tag aligns adjacent text with the top of the image.

Inserting GIF images as bullets and lines

You can use small GIF graphics instead of the default black bullets that Mosaic displays when you create an unordered list. By specifying a small GIF image in a list, you can insert colored bullets, pinpoints, or icons.

You can also use a GIF file instead of the default horizontal line from the <HR> tag. You simply add the GIF file to your document as you would any inline image. Chapter 10 explains how you can get some cool GIF bullet and line files from different Web sites. Figure 11-9 shows how the appearance of a Web document is enhanced by using GIF graphics as bullets and lines.

Here's how you add graphic bullets to a list:

1. Choose the <UL> tag and press Enter.

2. Click the <P> tag button.

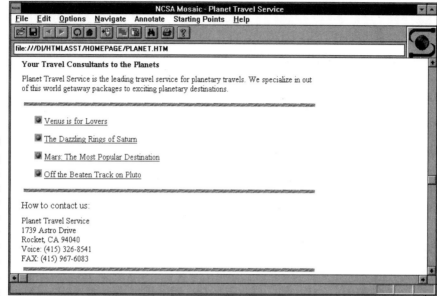

Figure 11-9:
You can use
GIF bullets
and lines to
spruce up
the presen-
tation of any
Web
document.

3. Click the Image button. HTML Assistant displays the Enter a URL for the Image dialog box.

4. Click the Browse button. HTML Assistant displays the Select Name of Image File dialog box.

5. Find the GIF file you want to use as an inline image, select it in the File Name box, and choose OK. The path of the file is displayed in the URL Text field in the Enter a URL for the Image dialog box.

6. Choose OK. HTML Assistant inserts the completed inline image tag in your document.

7. Delete everything but the filename from the path entry in this new tag.

8. Select the new bullet image tag, choose File I Copy, position the cursor on the next line in your document, and choose File I Paste or click the Repeat markup button. Repeat this step for each bullet you want to add to the document.

9. Choose <\UL> to close the list. After you've created the bullets, you can add text after them as you would for any list item. The next section tells you how to create hyperlinks from the text in your document.

Adding Hyperlinks to Your Document

By adding hyperlinks to your Web document, you let users connect to all kinds of information anywhere on the Net. You should keep the following guidelines in mind when you're adding hyperlinks to your document:

- ✔ Use descriptive text for your hyperlink. This helps Mosaic users quickly determine what's behind the hyperlink. Users typically focus on the highlighted text of a hyperlink. If you highlight descriptive text, users can easily find the links that are relevant to their purposes. If you only highlight a word like "here," the user must focus on the surrounding text to determine what's behind the link.

- ✔ Identify the size of the linked file. When you create a hyperlink to an external file, your hyperlink text should provide the Mosaic user with information about the size of the file. Multimedia files can be quite large, and a user who is connected to the Net with a modem will appreciate knowing how large the files are before deciding whether to download them.

Text and images in an HTML document are linked to other documents or images by HREFs (HyperText References). A hyperlink has the following basic form:

```
<A HREF="Resource URL">Hyperlink Anchor</A>
```

Resource URL is the URL address of the resource to which the hyperlink is connected. The *Hyperlink Anchor* is the text or image that the Mosaic user clicks to navigate to the hyperlinked resource. Mosaic highlights a graphic anchor with a blue border. A text anchor is displayed as underlined blue text. Figure 11-10 shows both types of hyperlinks as they might appear in a typical Web document.

Creating a hyperlink with a text anchor

In most cases, you use a text anchor with a hyperlink. By using a text anchor, you can add information about the link in the surrounding text.

Here's how you enter a hyperlink with a text anchor using HTML Assistant:

1. Click the Link button. As shown in Figure 11-11, HTML Assistant displays the Enter a URL Link dialog box.

2. To point to a Web document, enter the URL address in the URL Text field. Don't include the http:// prefix. To point to another type of server, such as FTP or Gopher, select the type of resource from the URL Prefixes list, and enter the URL address in the URL Text field.

Figure 11-10:
A graphic
anchor and
a text
anchor as
they appear
in a Web
document.

Graphic anchor   Text anchor

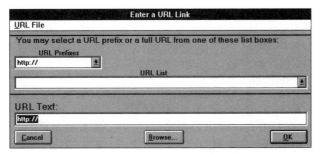

Figure 11-11: The Enter a URL Link dialog box lets you select the
Web document or other resource that is to be connected to your
hyperlink.

3. Choose OK. HTML Assistant inserts the <HREF> tag in your document.

4. Position the cursor between the opening and closing <HREF> tags —
that is, between <A HREF="..."> and </A> — and enter your anchor text.

Creating a hyperlink with a graphic anchor

The image you use for a graphic anchor is usually icon sized. Huge graphic anchors make your documents unnecessarily large.

Here's how you add a hyperlink with a graphic icon:

1. Choose the Link button. HTML Assistant displays the Enter a URL Link dialog box.

2. To point to a Web document, enter the URL address in the URL Text field. Don't include the http:// prefix. To point to another type of server, such as FTP or Gopher, select the type of resource from the URL Pre-fixes list, and enter the URL address in the URL Text field.

3. Choose OK. HTML Assistant inserts the <HREF> tag in your document.

4. Position the cursor between the opening and closing <HREF> tags — that is, between <A HREF="..."> and </A> — and enter your anchor text.

5. Click the Image button. HTML Assistant displays the Enter a URL for the Image dialog box.

6. Click the Browse button. HTML Assistant displays the Select Name of Image File dialog box, which is the same as the standard Windows Save As dialog box.

7. Find the GIF file you want to use as an inline image, select it in the File Name box, and choose OK. The path of the file is listed in the URL Text field in the Enter a URL for the Image dialog box.

8. Choose OK. HTML Assistant adds the completed inline image tag within your hyperlink tag.

Creating links to specific sections in other documents

You can use HTML to create a hyperlink that points to a particular section in another Web document. For example, suppose you want to set a link from a Web document named planets.htm to a specific section in a Web document named venus.htm. Here's how you do it:

1. Open the venus.htm document in HTML Assistant.

2. Choose the Anchor button. The HTML Assistant dialog box is displayed.

3. Enter the name you want to use for the anchor, and choose OK. An entry like <A NAME="Sights"></A> is entered into your HTML document.

4. Position the cursor between the <A NAME="Sights"> and </A> tags, and enter the text for the anchor to which your hyperlink will be connected.

5. Open the planet.htm document.

6. Choose the Link button. HTML Assistant displays the Enter a URL Link dialog box.

7. Enter the link to the anchor you created in the venus.htm document — for example, <A HREF="venus.htm#Sights">*Anchor Text*</A>. The # sign acts as a separator between the HTML document name and the anchor name. *Anchor Text* is the text that you want to display as a hyperlink in the Planet Web document.

8. Choose OK.

Using URLs from Your Mosaic.ini File

Entering URLs manually is tedious. All the URLs you need to work with are probably in your mosaic.ini file. HTML Assistant lets you create a list of the URLs in your mosaic.ini file that you can use any time you create a hyperlink.

If the URLs in your mosaic.ini file are larger than 32K, HTML Assistant truncates the list. If this happens, HTML Assistant displays an Out of String Space error message. Choose OK and continue. All the URLs before the 32K limit are captured. ■

Here's how you create a list of your Mosaic hotlist entries in HTML Assistant:

1. Press Ctrl-M or choose URL | Autoconvert File to HTML, and choose URLs in Mosaic.ini File. As shown in Figure 11-12, HTML Assistant displays the Select Mosaic Initialization File dialog box.

Figure 11-12: The Select Mosaic Initialization File dialog box.

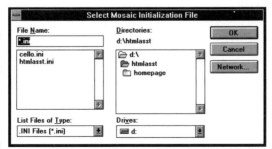

2. Select the mosaic.ini file in your Windows directory, and choose OK. As shown in Figure 11-13, HTML Assistant extracts a copy of your hotlist mosaic.ini entries and displays them in a document window. If HTML Assistant displays the error message, Out of String Space, choose OK and continue.

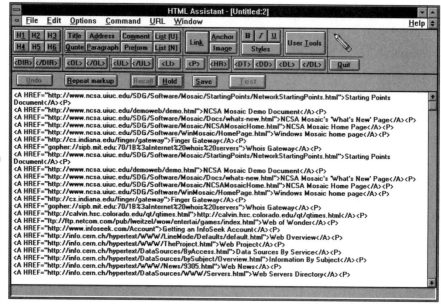

Figure 11-13:
The URLs from the mosaic.ini file in an HTML Assistant document.

3. Choose File | Save or click the Save button. HTML Assistant displays the Save As dialog box. Navigate to the directory in which you want to store the file, such as the directory containing the HTML Assistant program.

4. Enter a name for the file and replace the default .htm filename extension with .url. For example, you might enter mosaic.url. Choose OK.

5. Choose File | Close to close the file.

6. Click the Link button. HTML Assistant displays the Enter a URL Link dialog box.

7. Choose the Browse button. HTML Assistant displays the Select File Name dialog box.

8. Select the .URL Files (*.url) option in the List Files of Type list box.

9. Navigate to the directory containing your mosaic.url file, select the file in the File Name list, and choose OK.

10. Choose the Link button to open the Enter a URL Link dialog box.

11. Choose URL I Load URL List From File. The Select URL File dialog box is displayed.

12. Select the mosaic.url file, and choose OK.

The URLs from your mosaic.ini file are now available from the Enter a URL Link dialog box, which you open by clicking the Link button. To display the URLs, click the down-arrow button in the URL List box. The URLs from your mosaic.ini file are also available from the Enter a URL for the Image dialog box, which you open by clicking the Anchor button.

Let's Build a Web Document

OK, your head is swimming with all kinds of tags and design do's and don'ts. It's time to get your hands dirty and create a document using the HTML Assistant program. Just follow along as we show you, step-by-step, how to create our Planet Travel Service Web document. The document we're creating is shown in Figure 11-14.

Figure 11-14: The Planet Travel Service Web document shows you how easy it is to create Web documents.

Getting your GIF images

To create our imaginary Planet Travel Service home page, you need to do a few things. First, use the Windows File Manager to create a directory for storing your HTML document and the GIF images you'll be downloading. To keep things simple, create the directory c:\htmlasst\planet.

Next, you need to grab the GIF images we'll use to create this sample home page:

1. Connect to the Net, open Mosaic, and enter the following URL in the URL field:

   ```
   http://colargol.edb.tih.no/~geirme/gizmos/gizmo.html
   ```

2. Choose the Balls hyperlink. A page of small bullet images is displayed.

3. Point to the orangeball.gif link, hold down the Shift key, and click the left mouse button. The Save As dialog box is displayed. Choose the c:\htmlasst\planet directory, and choose OK.

4. Click the left-arrow button to return to the home page. Click the Lines hyperlink. A page of lines is displayed.

5. Point to the crumpled-6pt-line.gif link, hold down the Shift key, and click the left mouse button. The Save As dialog box is displayed. If necessary, navigate to the c:\htmlasst\planet directory, and choose OK.

6. Enter the following URL in Mosaic's URL field:

   ```
   http://white.nosc.mil/images.html
   ```

7. On the Web document that's displayed, scroll down to the Space Images group, and click The Solar System hyperlink.

8. Point to the Saturn hyperlink, hold down the Shift key, and click the left mouse button. The Save As dialog box is displayed. If necessary, navigate to the c:\htmlasst\planet directory, and choose OK.

Now that you've collected the GIF files we're going to use, you can exit Mosaic and your Net connection, and start building the HTML document.

Constructing the HTML document

You have all the graphic images you need to create your Web document. Here's how you create the Web document using the HTML Assistant for Windows program:

1. Double-click the Htmlasst icon, and click OK in the About HTML Assistant dialog box that's displayed. The HTML Assistant window is displayed.

2. Choose File|New. A document window is displayed in the HTML Assistant window. Click the maximize button to enlarge the document window to the full size of the HTML Assistant window.

3. Choose File|Save. The Save As dialog box is displayed. Enter the name of your HTML document in the File Name field. For this example, enter planet. Specify the c:\htmlasst\planet directory, and choose OK.

4. Choose Options|Autosave file before test. A check mark is displayed to the left of this menu item.

5. Click where you want to start in the document window. Remember, Mosaic doesn't care about how many blank lines you use or how many spaces you indent text. Mosaic only cares that your tags are correct.

6. Enter the following information in the HTML Assistant document window (you can use the buttons or type it in directly):

```
<HTML>
<HEAD>
<TITLE>Planet Travel Service</TITLE>
</HEAD>
<BODY>
<IMG SRC = "PLANET_S.GIF">
<H1>Welcome to Planet Travel Service</H1>
<IMG SRC = "CRUMPLED.GIF"><P>
Planet Travel Service is the leading interplanetary travel
service. We specialize in out of this<BR>world getaway packages.
Visit these exciting destinations.<P>
<UL>
<P><IMG SRC = "BALL_ORA.GIF"> <A HREF = "ftp:// netcom.com/pub/
billa/nineplanets/venus.html">Romantic Interludes on Venus</A>
<P><IMG SRC = "BALL_ORA.GIF"><A HREF = "ftp://netcom.com/pub/
billa/nineplanets/saturn.html">Dazzling Ring Adventures on
Saturn</A>
<P><IMG SRC = "BALL_ORA.GIF"><A HREF = "ftp://netcom.com/pub/
billa/nineplanets/mars.html">Great Family Fun on Mars</A>
</UL>
<IMG SRC = "CRUMPLED.GIF">
<H6>How to Contact Us</H6>
Planet Travel Service<BR>
1739 Astro Drive<BR>
Rocket Science, CA 94040<BR>
Voice: (800)326-8541<BR>
Fax: (415)967-8283<BR>
E-mail: info@planettrvl.com<BR>
<IMG SRC = "CRUMPLED.GIF">
<ADDRESS>imspacey@planettrvl.com</ADDRESS>
</BODY>
</HTML>
```

7. Click the Test button or choose File | Test. Mosaic is launched with your HTML document, which appears as a Web document in the Mosaic window.

8. Choose File | Exit in the Mosaic window to exit Mosaic and return to the HTML Assistant.

That's all there is to creating a Web document. With a bit of inspiration and a little Web surfing to collect ideas and inline images, you'll be ready to stake your claim on the World-Wide Web.

Part V

The Part of Tens

The 5th Wave   By Rich Tennant

"I TELL YA I'M STILL GETTING INTERFERENCE —
— COOKIE, RAGS? RAGS WANNA COOKIE? —
THERE IT GOES AGAIN."

In This Part...

*T*he following chapters contain tens upon tens of valuable resource nuggets that we've accumulated during our own Web surfing adventures. Much of this information enhances and supports topics covered earlier in this book. In this part, we tell you which TCP/IP packages, Mosaic clones, HTML editors, and other software goodies are available. We also provide an extensive listing of service providers offering IP connections and server services with which you can affordably publish your Web document on the Net. You'll find out how to establish an ISDN telecommunications connection, which lets you surf the Web at warp speed, and we'll give you some ideas for promoting your Web site.

Chapter 12

Ten Commercial TCP/IP Software Vendors

In This Chapter

▶ Checking out commercial TCP/IP software packages

▶ Finding more information about TCP/IP on the Net

---

*M*osaic requires TCP/IP software. TCP/IP software lets Windows speak the language of the Internet, which is the TCP/IP protocol. A number of companies offer TCP/IP packages that include a full suite of Internet tools, such as Gopher and FTP. This chapter points you to the leading TCP/IP software packages for Windows, and provides helpful guidelines for choosing the right package.

TCP/IP Software Options

Setting up your computer to communicate with the Net requires a combination of tools that come bundled in TCP/IP software. These tools include the Winsock.dll, the TCP/IP stack, and SLIP/PPP software. The easiest way to enable your computer to speak TCP/IP is by using one of the many available commercial TCP/IP software programs.

A growing number of service providers are offering TCP/IP programs for use exclusively with their service. However, most of these programs exclude you from working with Mosaic or other external programs. ■

Shopping for TCP/IP Packages

Commercial TCP/IP packages offer various combinations of Windows-based tools — for example, e-mail, Gopher, and FTP — for working with the Net. Because you'll probably use your IP account for other Net activities besides surfing the Web, you should make sure the TCP/IP program you choose offers the full complement of Net tools. A growing number of TCP/IP packages are including a Mosaic clone as one of their built-in tools.

Many of the commercial versions of Mosaic that are sold as stand-alone packages come with built-in TCP/IP. Chapter 15 provides a listing of companies that market commercial versions of Mosaic. ■

TCP/IP packages come in a variety of flavors for different computer systems and configurations. With many of these programs, you can choose from a stand-alone package (that is, a non-network version), a network version (e.g., for use with Windows for Workgroups), or a package with built-in NFS for networks connected to UNIX computers or routers. NFS, which stands for Network File System, is a UNIX networking system developed by Sun Microsystems. NFS lets you access drives and peripherals via TCP/IP across your network.

Stand-alone versions are usually the least expensive choice. You can use the stand-alone version of a TCP/IP package on a computer that's connected to a network as long as the computer has its own modem connection.

Here are the leading companies that publish commercial TCP/IP packages:

Beame & Whiteside, Ltd.
706 Hillsborough Street
Raleigh, NC 27603-1655
Voice: (800) 463-6637 or (919) 831-8989
Fax: (919) 831-8990
E-mail: sales@bws.com

Distinct Corp.
12901 Saratoga Avenue
P.O. Box 3410
Saratoga, CA 95070
Voice: (408) 366-8933
Fax: (408) 366-0153
E-mail: mktg@distinct.com

Frontier Technologies Corp.
10201 North Port Washington Road
Mequon, WI 53092
Sales: (800) 929-3054
Voice: (414) 241-4555
Fax: (414) 241-7084
E-mail: info@frontiertech.com
URL: www.Frontiertech.COM

FTP Software
2 High Street
North Andover, MA 01845
Voice: (800) 282-4387
Fax: (508) 794-4477
E-mail: info@ftp.com
URL: http://www.ftp.com

Intercon
950 Herndon Parkway, Suite 420
Herndon, VA 22070
Voice: (800) 468-7266 or (703) 709-5500
Fax: (703) 709-5555
E-mail: sales@intercon.com

Ipswitch, Inc.
669 Main Street, Suite 6
Wakefield, MA 01880
Voice: (617) 246-1150
Fax: (617) 245-2975
E-mail: info@ipswitch.com

NetManage, Inc.
10725 North De Anza Boulevard
Cupertino, CA 95014
Voice: (408) 973-7171
Fax: (408) 257-6405
E-mail: info@netmanage.com
URL: http://www.netmanage.com

O'Reilly and Associates, Inc.
103 Morris Street, Suite A
Sebastopol, CA 95472
Voice: (800) 777-9638 or (707) 829-0515
Fax: (707) 829-0104
E-mail: info@ora.com
URL: http://www.gnn.com

Spry, Inc.
316 Occidental Avenue South, Suite 200
Seattle, WA 98104
Voice: (800) 777-9638 or (206) 447-0300
Fax: (206) 447-9008
E-mail: info@spry.com
URL: http://www.spry.com

The Wollongong Group, Inc.
1129 San Antonio Road
P.O. Box 51860
Palo Alto, CA 94303
Voice: (800) 872-8649 or (415) 962-7100
In CA: (800) 962-8649
Fax: (415) 962-0286
E-mail: sales@twg.com

Getting More Information about TCP/IP Software

Information on TCP/IP and NFS (Network File System) software is available from the following World-Wide Web URLs:

- http://www.rtd.com/pcnfsfaq/faq.html
- http://www.cis.ohio-state.edu/hypertext/faq/usenet/ibmpc-tcp-ip/faq.html

You can also get information on TCP/IP from the following network newsgroups:

- comp.protocols.tcp-ip.ibmpc
- comp.protocols.nfs
- alt.winsock
- comp.sys.ibm.pc.hardware.networking

The following FTP sites contain up-to-date information on TCP/IP software:

Site	Directory
ftp.rtd.com	/pub/tcpip/pcnfsfaq.zip
ftp.netcom.com	/pub/mailcom/IBMTCP/ibmtcp.zip
sunsite.unc.edu	/micro/pc-stuff/ms-windows/winsock

Chapter 13

Tens upon Tens of Service Providers

....

In This Chapter

▶ Where to get an IP connection

▶ Where to get a list of service providers

....

Service providers sell connections to the Internet. To link your computer (which must be running TCP/IP software) to the Net, you establish an account with a service provider. This chapter provides a list of service providers that offer IP (Internet Protocol) accounts that allow you to work with Mosaic.

Service Providers Offering IP Connections

This section provides a listing of service providers that offer IP connections. Many of them offer nationwide service via local Point of Presence (POP) telephone numbers. The largest service providers are PSI, Netcom, AlterNet, and NovX. We worked with InterNex, PSI, Netcom, and Portal Communications throughout the development of this book.

You need to shop around carefully, because prices and services can vary substantially. When comparing prices, remember to factor any telecommunications costs into your calculations.

AlterNet
UUNET Technologies, Inc.
3110 Fairview Park Drive, Suite 570
Falls Church, VA 22042
Voice: (800) 488-6384 or (713) 204-8000
Fax: (703) 204-8001
E-mail: info@uunet.uu.net

BARRNET
Pine Hall, Room 115
Stanford University
Stanford, CA 94305
Voice: (415) 725-1790
Fax: (415) 723-0010
E-mail: info@nic.barrnet.net

Ccnet Communications
190 North Wiget Lane, Suite 291
Walnut Creek, CA 94598
Voice: (510) 988-0680
Fax: (510) 988-0689
E-mail: info@ccnet.com

CERFnet
California Education & Research Federation Network
P.O. Box 85608
San Diego, CA 92186-9784
Voice: (800) 876-2373 or (619) 455-3900
Fax: (619) 455-3990
E-mail: help@cerf.net

CICnet
2901 Hubbard Drive
Ann Arbor, MI 48105-2467
Voice: (800) 947-4754 or (313) 998-6703
Fax: (313) 998-6105
E-mail: info@cic.net

CNS Internet Express
1155 Kelly Johnson Boulevard, Suite 400
Colorado Springs, CO 80920
Voice: (800) 748-1200 or (719) 592-1240
Fax: (719) 592-1201
E-mail: info@cscns.com

Colorado SuperNet, Inc.
999 18th Street, Suite 2640
Denver, CO 80202
Voice: (303) 296-8202
Fax: (303) 296-8224
E-mail: info@csn.org

CRL
P.O. Box 326
Larkspur, CA 94977
Voice: (415) 381-2800
Fax: (415) 381-9578
E-mail: info@crl.com

CTS Network Services (CTSNET)
4444 Convoy Street, Suite 300
San Diego, CA 92111
Voice: (619) 637-3637
Fax: (619) 637-3630
E-mail: info@crash.cts.com

CyberGate, Inc.
662 South Military Trail
Deerfield Beach, FL 33442
Voice: (305) 428-4283
Fax: (305) 428-7977
E-mail: info@gate.net

DATABANK, Inc.
1473 Hwy. 40
Lawrence, KS 66044
Voice: (913) 842-6699
Fax: (913) 842-8518

Digital Express Group, Inc.
6006 Greenbelt Road, Suite 228
Greenbelt, MD 20770
Voice: (800) 969-9090 or (301) 220-2020
Fax: (301) 220-0477
E-mail: info@digex.net

Engineering International, Inc.
2313 Headingly NW
Albuquerque, NM 87107
Voice: (505) 343-1060
Fax: (505) 343-1061
Email: office@RT66.com

Global Enterprise Services
3 Independence Way
Princeton, NJ 08540
Voice: (800) 358-4437 or (609) 897-7300
Fax: (609) 897-7310
E-mail: info@jvnc.net

IDS World Network
3 Franklin Road
East Greenwich, RI 02818
Voice: (401) 884-7856
E-mail: sysadmin@ids.net

InterAccess
3345 Commercial Avenue
Northbrook, IL 60062
Voice: (800) 967-1580 or (708) 498-2542
Fax: (708) 498-3289
E-mail: info@interaccess.com

Internet Direct, Inc.
1366 East Thomas, #210
Phoenix, AZ 85014
Voice: (602) 274-0100
Fax: (602) 274-8518
E-mail: info@indirect.com

InterNex Information Services, Inc.
1050 Chestnut Street, Suite 202
Menlo Park, CA 94025
Voice: (415) 473-3060
Fax: (415) 473-3062
E-mail: info@internex.net

InterServ
NovX Systems Integration
316 Occidental Avenue South, Suite 406
Seattle, WA 98104
Voice: (800) 873-6689 or (206) 447-0800
Fax: (206) 447-9008
E-mail: info@novex.com

The Little Garden (TLG)
P.O. Box 410923
San Francisco, CA 94141-0923
Voice: (415) 487-1902
E-mail: info@tlg.org

Merit Network/MichNet
2901 Hubbard Pod G
Ann Arbor, MI 48105
Voice: (313) 764-9430
Fax: (313) 747-3185
E-mail: info@merit.edu

MIDnet
201 North 8th Street, Suite 421
Lincoln, NE 68588
Voice: (402) 472-7600
Fax: (402) 472-0240
E-mail: nic@mid.net

MRNet
511 11th Avenue South, Box 212
Minneapolis, MN 55415
Voice: (612) 342-2570
Fax: (612) 342-2873
E-mail: info@mr.net

MSEN, Inc.
320 Miller Avenue
Ann Arbor, MI 48103
Voice: (313) 998-4562
Fax: (313) 998-4563
E-mail: info@msen.com

MV Communications, Inc.
P.O. Box 4963
Manchester, NH 03108
Voice: (603) 429-2223
Fax: (603) 424-0386
E-mail: info@mv.mv.com

NEARNET
Internet Services Corp.
150 Cambridge Park Drive
Cambridge, MA 02140
Voice: (800) 632-7638 or (617) 873-8730
Fax: (617) 873-5620
E-mail: nearnet-join@near.net

NETCOM On-Line Communications Services, Inc.
3031 Tisch Way, 2nd Floor
San Jose, CA 95128
Voice: (800) 353-6600 or (408) 554-8649
Fax: (408) 241-9145
E-mail: info@netcom.com

NetIllinois
1840 Oak Avenue
Evanston, IL 60201
Voice: (708) 866-1825

NorthWestNet
15400 S.E. 30th Place, Suite 202
Bellevue, WA 98007
Voice: (206) 562-3000
Fax: (206) 562-3791

Northwest Nexus, Inc.
P.O. Box 40597
Bellevue, WA 98015
Voice: (206) 455-3505
Fax: (206) 455-4672
E-mail: info@halcyon.com

Nuance Network Services
904 Bob Wallace Avenue, Suite 119
Huntsville, AL 35801
Voice: (205) 533-4296
Fax: (205) 553-4296
E-mail: staff@nuance.com

OARnet
1224 Kinnear Road
Columbus, OH 43212
Voice: (614) 292-8100
Fax: (614) 292-7168
E-mail: nic@oar.net

Pathways
3220 Sacramento Street
San Francisco, CA 94115
Voice: (415) 929-4900
Fax: (415) 931-7931
E-mail: info@path.net

Performance Systems International, Inc. (PSI)
510 Huntmar Park Drive
Herndon, VA 12180
Voice: (800) 827-7482 or (703) 620-6551
Fax: (518) 283-8904
E-mail: info@psi.com

Phantom Access
1562 First Avenue, Suite 351
New York, NY 10028
Voice: (212) 989-2418
Fax: (212) 989-8648
E-mail: info@phantom.com

The Pipeline
150 Broadway
New York, NY 10038
Voice: (212) 267-3636
Fax: (212) 267-4280
E-mail: info@pipeline.com

Portal Communications Company
20863 Stevens Creek Boulevard, Suite 200
Cupertino, CA 95014
Voice: (408) 973-9111
Fax: (408) 725-1580
E-mail: info@portal.com

PREPnet
305 S. Craig Street, 2nd Floor
Pittsburgh, PA 15213
Voice: (412) 268-7870
Fax: (412) 268-7875
E-mail: prepnet@cmu.edu

South Coast Computing Services, Inc.
1811 Bering, Suite 100
Houston, TX 77057
Voice: (713) 917-5000 or (800) 770-8971
Fax: (713) 917-5005
E-mail: info@sccsi.com

Spectrum Online Services, Inc.
2860 S. Circle Drive, Suite 2202
Colorado Springs, CO 80906
Voice: (719) 576-6845
E-mail: jimw@sosi.com

SURAnet
8400 Baltimore Boulevard
College Park, MD 20740
Voice: (800) 787-2638 or (301) 982-4600
Fax: (301) 982-4605
E-mail: marketing@suranet.net

Systems Solutions
1254 Lorewood Grove Road
Middletown, DE 19709
Voice: (302) 378-1386
Fax: (302) 378-3871
E-mail: sharris@marlin.ssnet.com

Telerama Public Access Internet
P.O. Box 60024
Pittsburgh, PA 15211
Voice: (412) 481-3505
Fax: (412) 481-8568
E-mail: info@telerama.lm.com

Texas Metronet
860 Kinwest Parkway, Suite 179
Irving, TX 75063-3440
Voice: (214) 705-2900 or (817) 543-8756
Fax: (214) 401-2802
E-mail: info@metronet.com

Vnet Internet Access, Inc.
1206 Kenilwratch Avenue
P.O. Box 31474
Charlotte, NC 28231
Voice: (704) 334-3282
E-mail: info@vnet.net

Where to Get an Updated List of Service Providers

The Public Dialup Internet Access List, or PDIAL, is an updated list of Net service providers. Because service providers come and go, this list is constantly changing. You can get this list at the following FTP site:

```
rtfm.mit.edu:/pub/usenet/alt.internet.access.wanted/P"D"I"A"L"(P)
```

You can also get this list by sending an e-mail message to the following address:

```
info-deli-server@netcom.com
```

Make sure the Subject line of your e-mail message contains the phrase "Send PDIAL."

Chapter 14

Almost Ten Things You Should Know about ISDN Connections

● ●

In This Chapter

▶ Finding out whether ISDN is available in your area

▶ Determining your ISDN telecommunications charges

▶ Going stand-alone, by bus, or via digital modem

▶ Integrating ISDN into your existing analog equipment

● ●

*Y*ou'll love the power of ISDN, and, once you get used to it, you'll never go back. However, like almost everything that's connected with the Net, getting this power requires a journey through a maze.

Is ISDN Available in Your Area?

Most U.S. regional telephone companies expect that 85% to 95% of their lines will be capable of handling ISDN. However, implementation of ISDN is uneven and depends on your location. To find out whether ISDN is available in your area, you need to check with your local telephone company. However, getting information about ISDN can be a hit-or-miss proposition if you simply call the business office at your local telephone company. Table 14-1 lists sources of ISDN information available at regional telephone companies.

Another source of ISDN information is Bellcore, which is the research organization for the regional telephone companies. Bellcore provides a national ISDN information clearinghouse hotline at 800-992-4736.

Table 14-1: Obtaining ISDN information from regional telephone companies

Telephone company	Where to call
Ameritech	800-832-6328 provides access to a menu-driven, 24-hour voice/fax-back system
Bell Atlantic	800-570-4736 In NJ: 201-649-8775
BellSouth	800-858-9413
Cincinnati Bell	513-397-3282
GTE	800-888-8799 provides access to a menu-driven, 24-hour voice/fax-back system In CA: 800-483-5000 In FL: 800-483-5200 In OR and WA: 800-483-5100 In TX: 800-483-5400
NYNEX	800-438-4736
Pacific Bell	800-472-4736 provides access to a menu-driven, 24-hour voice/fax-back system 800-472-4736 contacts the ISDN marketing group
Rochester Telephone	716-777-1234
Southwestern Bell	Austin: 800-792-4736 Dallas: 214-268-1403 Houston: 713-567-4300
US West	Denver: 800-246-5226

Know Your Calling Charges

The first thing to consider about ISDN service is whether all your calls will be outside your local company's service area. If so, you should consider arranging for an ISDN direct-access line from a long-distance carrier. If any of your ISDN calls are within the local service area, you must use lines from your local-exchange carrier (LEC) — that is, your local telephone company.

ISDN is a usage-sensitive service. The more minutes you use and the farther your call, the more you pay. Although there are installation and monthly fees, the per-minute charges are usually the biggest cost. LEC pricing for telephone access comes from complex rules called tariffs, which are established

Behind the ISDN scenes

For the past 100 years, telephone service has used analog voice circuits between businesses and homes and the telephone company's central office. The central office, or CO, is the place where telephone circuits live. ISDN provides a digital link between businesses and homes and the CO. Inside the CO, a computerized switch accepts dialing instructions and interconnects local and long-distance circuits on demand. Availability of these digital circuits has been the biggest stumbling block for ISDN's wider acceptance.

The two leading digital switches at the telephone companies are the AT&T 5ESS and the Northern Telecom DMS-100. The major problem with ISDN is the differences at the CO. For example, ISDN service at Pac Bell differs from ISDN service at AT&T, which in turn differs from service at other telephone companies. Over time, more and more of these differences are fading away, resulting in a more integrated national ISDN system. Standardization is being implemented via the Bell Research Corporation (Bellcore), which is owned by the seven Baby Bells.

Transmissions via Inter-Exchange Carriers (IECs), such as AT&T, MCI, or Sprint can currently handle only 56Kbps, because each B-channel must also carry one-half of the D-channel information (8Kbps). In the meantime, the Baby Bells deliver the full 64Kbps for each channel within their local service area.

by both federal and state agencies. These telecommunications charges are separate from your service provider's charges.

The monthly service charges for ISDN service generally range from $20 to $60, plus taxes and surcharges. On top of the monthly service charge, you'll pay per-minute charges. Some telephone companies are offering ISDN residential services, which are considerably less expensive than business rates. For example, Pacific Bell charges $22.95 per month and one cent per minute for calls placed within the local calling area between 8AM and 5PM, Monday through Friday. After hours, the calls are free within the local calling area.

If you are on-line for more than two to three hours a day to the same location, you should consider using dedicated leased lines. As a rule of thumb, two to three hours is an average break-even point between dial-up and dedicated service; however, this varies according to local tariffs.

ISDN Service Providers

A growing number of service providers are offering ISDN connections. An example of an affordable ISDN connection to the Net is PSI's OnRamp service, which costs approximately $29 a month. PSI is a national service provider. InterNex, a service provider in Menlo Park, California, charges a $199 set-up fee for establishing your account (including your domain name registration), and a $29 monthly charge that includes 30 hours of free connection time.

 Because ISDN service is new, our advice is to shop around for the ISDN service provider that offers the best deal. Keep in mind that a growing number of national Internet service providers are offering ISDN service with local connections in many metropolitan areas. See Chapter 13 for a listing of service providers. ■

For a complete listing of service providers offering ISDN connections and a cornucopia of other information about ISDN, point Mosaic to the following URL:

```
http://alumni.caltech.edu/~dank/isdn/
```

The Two Flavors of ISDN Products

The equipment you need for establishing an ISDN connection comes in two basic flavors: stand-alone and bus. A stand-alone unit is a device that looks like an external modem. Stand-alone units usually connect to a LAN adapter card in your computer.

To use a standalone unit, you need a network operating system running on your computer. You can use a network system such as Windows for Workgroups, or you can use the networking capabilities that come with the network versions of most TCP/IP packages. Your computer doesn't need to be part of a network; it needs only to be able to communicate with the external ISDN device via the network adapter in your computer. The network adapter card acts as a high-speed communications port, in the same way that a serial port is used by your computer to communicate (at a slower rate) with a modem.

If you need to purchase a network card, you should get a card with a built-in RJ-45 port. If you already have a network card that doesn't have an RJ-45 port, you'll need a transceiver that lets you connect the AUI (Auxiliary Unit Interface) port on your network card to either an RJ-45 jack port or another AUI port, depending on the external device you're using. This adapter costs around $80. The bus or internal card option doesn't require a LAN adapter because the network functions are built in.

Get Built-in NT1

Avoid buying ISDN devices that don't include built-in NT1 devices. An NT1 device converts the two-wire ISDN circuit interface to four wires. Only two companies sell this device, and current prices for a stand-alone version are about $150. You'll also need to purchase a power supply device. This device plugs into a standard wall outlet, and brings power to the ISDN line. Unlike an analog telephone line, an ISDN line isn't powered by the telephone company. Fortunately, a growing number of ISDN equipment manufacturers are including this device in their equipment, which is as it should be.

Digital Modems (An Analog/Digital Twist)

Digital modems provide ISDN access and standard phone-line access, all in the same system. Only two digital modem products are currently available, but more are sure to follow. The IBM WaveRunner allows ISDN transmission speeds of up to only 64Kbps, and you need to purchase a separate NT1 terminator device. AccessWorks' QuickAccess Remote supports the full 128Kbps, and it comes with a built-in NT1 terminator.

IBM WaveRunner Digital Modem
IBM Direct
4111 Northside Parkway
Atlanta, GA 30327
Voice: (800) 426-2255
Faxback: (800) 426-4329

QuickAccess Remote
AccessWorks
670 North Beers Street
Building One, Floor One
Holmdel, NJ 07733
Voice: (908) 888-4570
Fax: (908) 888-4456

Leading ISDN Equipment Vendors

This section lists ISDN hardware that allows you to connect a computer to an ISDN line. Because ISDN is such a new service, you can expect to see a flood of new products. The good news on ISDN equipment is that prices on end-user equipment have decreased more than 50% over the past 5 years. We expect prices to fall even more as new and improved equipment becomes available.

External Units

Everyware 160
Everyware 400
Combinet
333 West El Camino Real
Sunnyvale, CA 94087
Voice (800) 967-6651 or (408) 522-9020
Fax: (408) 732-5479
E-mail: info@combinet.com or sales@combinet.com

Pipeline 50 ISDN
Ascend Communications, Inc.
1275 Harbor Bay Parkway
Alameda, CA 94502
Voice: (800) 621-9578 or (510) 769-6001
Fax: (510) 814-2300
E-mail: info@ascend.com

LANLine 5240i
Gandalf Technologies, Inc.
Cherry Hill Industrial Center-9
Cherry Hill, NJ 08003
Voice: (800) 426-3253 or (609) 461-8100
Fax: (609) 461-5186

Internal Cards

PC IMAC
PC IMAC/4
DigiBoard
6400 Flying Cloud Drive
Eden Prairie, MN 55344
Voice: (800) 344-4273 or (612) 943-9020
Fax: (612) 943-5398

Long Distance LAN Adapter E-101
Long Distance LAN Adapter E-201
Extension Technology Corp.
30 Hollis Street
Framingham, MA 01701
Voice: (800) 856-2672 or (508) 872-7748
Fax: (508) 872-7533

RemoteExpress ISDN LAN Adapter
RemoteExpress ISDN Bridge Pack
Intel Corp.
2200 Mission College Boulevard
P.O. Box 58119
Santa Clara, CA 95052
Voice: (800) 538-3373
Fax-back: (800) 458-6231

ISDN and Your Existing Telephones and Faxes

ISDN works with standard telephone lines. However, without special adapters or ISDN-ready equipment, you can't use analog equipment such as telephones, faxes, and modems over ISDN. Here are your ISDN options:

- ✔ ISDN as the only line to your office or business. For this option, all your telephones and fax machines must be ISDN ready, or they must be linked through a special terminal adapter. ISDN-ready telephones and faxes are currently too expensive, but this will change over time.

- ✔ ISDN as the only line, but with a digital modem. A digital modem lets you use both ISDN equipment and existing telephone or fax equipment. However, because you need to use one B-channel for analog communications, only one B-channel is available for digital communications.

- ✔ ISDN as a second line. This is often the least expensive alternative, and it lets you take advantage of ISDN's higher data transmission speeds while you continue to use existing analog lines for your current analog telephone and fax equipment.

Where to Get More ISDN Information

Several sites provide ISDN information. The following Web site is the best site for finding all kinds of ISDN information:

```
http://alumni.caltech.edu/~dank/isdn/
```

This site, which is maintained by Dan Kegel, provides links to various sources of ISDN information, including equipment vendors, service providers offering ISDN connections, and a lot more.

Bellcore, the research organization of the Baby Bells, provides a Web page for ISDN information at the following URL:

```
http://info.bellcore.com/ISDN/ISDN.html
```

Pacific Telephone, a leader in ISDN implementation, also maintains an ISDN Web page, which you'll find at the following URL:

```
http://www.pacbell.com/isdn/isdn_home.html
```

Chapter 15

Ten Assorted Mosaic Clones, HTML Editors, and Other Goodies

• •

In This Chapter

▶ Commercial and freeware versions of Mosaic

▶ HTML editors

▶ External viewers and other utilities you can add to your Mosaic toolkit

• •

*M*osaic is more than a program; it's a standard for working on the Web. Because of the popularity of Mosaic and the Web, a growing number of commercial versions of Mosaic, HTML editors, and other Web-related utilities are becoming available.

Sons and Daughters of Mosaic

Mosaic is the killer application of the '90s and many software publishers are jumping on the bandwagon by offering their own versions of Mosaic. Most of the commercial versions have the same look and feel as Mosaic, with a few more bells and whistles. The following sections list commercial versions of Mosaic that are already available or will be in the near future.

The developers of many of the TCP/IP programs listed in Chapter 12 are adding their own Mosaic clones to their suites of Net tools. For example, Net-Manage, Spry, and FTP Software are adding Mosaic clones to their TCP/IP packages. ■

Spyglass Mosaic

Spyglass licenses Mosaic to commercial firms, such as FTP Software, O'Reilly and Associates, and others. Spyglass doesn't sell Mosaic directly to end users. For more information, contact:

Spyglass, Inc.
1800 Woodfield Drive
Savoy, IL 61874
Voice: (217) 355-6000 or (800) 647-2201
Fax: (217) 355-8925
E-mail: info@spyglass.com
URL: http://www.spyglass.com/

Mosaic NetScape

This version of Mosaic comes from the company that recruited Marc
Andreessen, the developer of the original Mosaic program. This is one product to watch because it promises features optimized for 14.4 Kbps modems,
native JPEG support, enhanced memory caching, and more. Figure 15-1
shows the NetScape window.

For more information, contact:

Mosaic Communications
650 Castro Street, Suite 500
Mountain View, CA 94041
Voice: (415) 254-1900 or (800) net-site
Fax: (415) 254-2693
E-mail: info@mcom.com
URL: http://mosaic.mcom.com

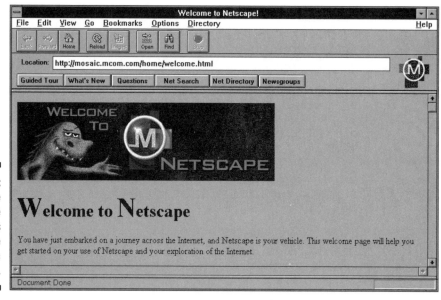

Figure 15-1:
The
Netscape
program is
one of the
best Mosaic
clones.

WinWeb (freeware)

WinWeb is one of the first Mosaic clones, and it runs smoothly. Figure 15-2 shows the WinWeb program window with its default ElNet Galaxy home page.

For more information, contact:

Enterprise Integration Technologies
459 Hamilton Avenue
Palo Alto, CA 94301
Site: ftp://ftp.einet.net/einet/pc/winweb/
File: winweb.zip

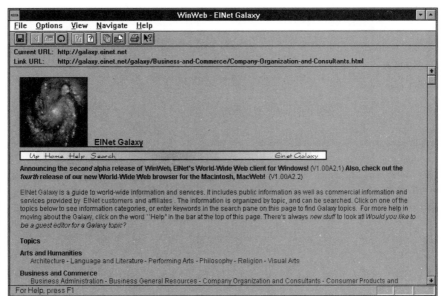

Figure 15-2:
WinWeb is
a smooth-
running
Mosaic
clone.

HTML Editors: Tools of the Web Document Building Trade

As we showed you in Chapter 11, you can simplify the creation of Web documents by using an HTML editor such as HTML Assistant. Various developers are planning to release new HTML editors, but numerous editors are already available.

For example, HTMLed is a useful program developed by I-Net Training and Consulting that's comparable to HTML Assistant. It also has a handy feature that lets you strip out all the tags from an HTML document, leaving only the text. Figure 15-3 shows the HTMLed program window.

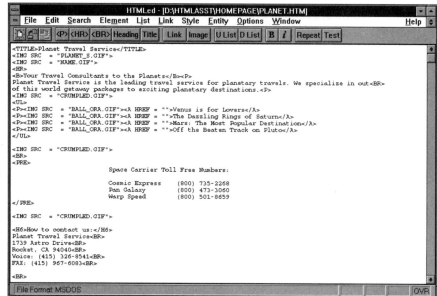

Figure 15-3:
HTMLed is a
useful
HTML editor
with some
handy
features.

The following HTML editor programs are already available:

HTMLed (shareware)
Site: ftp://ftp.ncsa.uiuc.edu/PC/Windows/Web/html/Windows
File: htmed09a.zip

HTML HyperEdit for Windows (shareware)
Author: Steve Hancock
E-mail: s.hancock@info.curtin.edu.au
Site: ftp://ftp.ncsa.uiuc.edu/PC/Windows/Web/html/Windows
File: hypedit.zip

HotMetal (shareware)
Site: ftp://ftp.ncsa.uiuc.edu/Web/html/Windows/HotMetal
Site: ftp://doc.ic.ac.uk/packages/WWW/ncsa
Site: ftp://gatekeeper.dec.com/net/infosys/Mosaic/contrib/SoftQuad
File: hotmetal.exe

Hotmetal Pro (commercial)
SoftQuad, Inc.
56 Aberfoyle Crescent, Suite 810
Toronto, Ontario, Canada M8X 2W4
Voice: (416) 239-4801
Fax: (416) 239-7105
E-mail: hotmetal@sq.com

More Mosaic External Viewers

We cover the essential external multimedia viewers and players in Chapter 8, but here are some other programs you might want to add to your collection of Mosaic viewers.

Adobe Acrobat Reader (freeware)
Adobe Acrobat Exchange
Adobe Acrobat Network Distiller

Adobe's Acrobat promises to become the standard for viewing shared documents. Adobe has opened up the architecture for Acrobat and is providing the Reader program for free. The Adobe Acrobat Exchange and Network Distiller programs are used for creating documents in Adobe's PDF format. You can get your free copy of Adobe Acrobat 2.0 for Windows at the following sites:

```
ftp://ftp.adobe.com/pub/adobe/Applications/Acrobat
http://www.adobe.com
```

For more information, contact:

Adobe Systems Incorporated
1585 Charleston Road
P.O. Box 7900
Mountain View, CA 94039-7900
Voice: (800) 862-3623 or (800) 833-6687
Fax: (415) 961-3769

Paint Shop Pro (shareware)

Paint Shop Pro is an image viewer, file format converter, image editor, and screen capture program. It displays, converts, edits, and prints images. It can open or convert files using any of these file formats: BMP, DIB, GIF, IMG, JAS, MAC, MSP, PIC, PCX, RAS, RLE, TGA, TIFF, and WPG. Paint Shop Pro lets you alter images, including rotating, resizing, resampling, and trimming. Paint Shop Pro also supports such functions as filter application, color adjustment, brightness and contrast adjustment, increasing and decreasing the color depth, gamma correction, and greyscaling. You can obtain a copy of Paint Shop Pro by downloading the file pspro20.zip from the following site:

```
ftp://oak.oakland.edu/pub/msdos/windows2/
```

For more information, contact:

JASC, Inc.
10901 Red Circle Drive, Suite 340
Minnetonka, MN 55343
Voice: (612) 930-9171
Fax: (612) 930-9172

Graphic Workshop for Windows (shareware)

Graphic Workshop for Windows lets you view, manipulate, and convert graphics files. It can read and convert between any of these file formats: ART, BMP, CUT, GEM, GIF, IFF, IMG, JPG, LBM, MAC, MSP, PIC, PCD, PCX, RLE, TGA, TIFF, and WPG. Graphic Workshop can start up in either Thumbnail mode or List Box mode. Thumbnail mode lets you can see small previews of each file in your current directory in addition to the filenames. You can obtain a copy of Graphic Workshop for Windows by downloading the file gwswn11k.zip from any of the following sites:

```
ftp://uunorth.north.net/pub/alchemy
http://uunorth.north.net:8000/alchemy/html/alchemy.html
```

For more information, contact:

Alchemy Mindworks, Inc.
P.O. Box 500
Beeton, Ontario LOG 1AO
Canada
Voice: (800) 263-1138 or (905) 936-9501
Fax: (905) 936-9502

Mosaic Utilities

Two utilities that you might want to check out are Set Mosaic and WinEdit. These programs provide useful features for working with the mosaic.ini file and other text files.

Set Mosaic (freeware)

Set Mosaic is a configuration utility created by Rod Potter that makes it easy to work with the mosaic.ini file. Set Mosaic is a Visual Basic program that provides a graphical interface for editing the mosaic.ini file. Figure 15-4 shows the Set Mosaic program window.

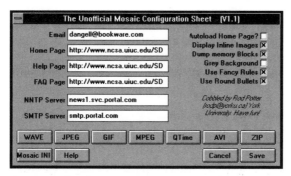

Figure 15-4: The Set Mosaic program window provides a visual interface for working with the mosaic.ini file.

You can obtain a copy of Set Mosaic by downloading the file smosaic.zip from the Web/PC/Mosaic/util/ directory at the following site:

```
ftp://ftp.ncsa.uiuc.edu/
```

WinEdit (shareware)

WinEdit is a Windows text editor program that offers more features and capabilities than the Notepad text editor that comes with Windows. For example, the WinEdit program lets you work with larger text files, and it supports word wrap. It also offers better printing capabilities than Notepad.

You can download a copy of WinEdit from the following site:

```
http://www.windowware.com/wilson/pages/winedit.html
```

For more information, contact:

Wilson WindowWare, Inc.
2701 California Ave. SW, Suite 212
Seattle, WA 98116
Voice: (206) 937-9335
Fax: (206) 935-7129
Sales: (800) 762-8383
Tech: (206) 935-9335
CompuServe forum: CIS:WINAPA
CompuServe E-mail: 76702,1072
Internet: ftp://ftp.www.windowware.com/WWWFTP/wilson

Chapter 16

A Lot More than Ten Affordable Server Services

● ●

In This Chapter

▶ Affordable server services
▶ Web document design services

● ●

Server services are companies that rent space on their servers for storing your HTML documents. Once your HTML document and any related files (such as inline image files) are stored on the server, any Mosaic user can access and view your Web document. Server service companies also offer other services, such as creating HTML documents. This chapter lists server service companies that you can contact for more information.

Serving Up Web Servers

Server services are springing up everywhere. Each offers different types of server services, and each has its own pricing scheme. In addition to independent server services, a growing number of service providers are also offering server services. Our best advice is to shop around. We've included URLs in the following listing of server services so you can check out their Web sites.

Automatrix, Inc.
P.O. Box 196
Rexford, NY 12148
Voice: (518) 372-5791 or (518) 877-7270
URL: http://www.automatrix.com

BizNet Technologies
Corporate Research Center
1872 Pratt Drive, Suite 1725
Blacksburg, VA 24062
Voice: (703) 231-7715
E-mail: biznet@bevnet
URL: http://www.biznet.com.blacksburg.va.us/index.html

Branch Information Services
2607 Patricia
Ann Arbor, MI 48103-2647
Voice: (313) 741-4442
Fax: (313) 995-1931
E-mail: branch-info@branch.com
URL: http://branch.com

Clark Internet Services, Inc.
10600 Route 108
Ellicott City, MD 21042
Voice: (800) 735-2258
Fax: (410) 730-9765
E-mail: info@clarknet
URL: http://www.clark.net

Computing Engineers
P.O. Box 285
Vernon Hills, IL 60061
Voice: (708) 367-1870
Fax: (708) 367-1872
URL: http://www.wwa.com

CTS Network Services
4444 Convoy Street, Suite 300
San Diego, CA 92111
Voice: (619) 637-3637
Fax: (619) 637-3630
E-mail: support@cts.com, info@cts.com, and webmaster@cts.com
URL: http://www.cts.com

Cyberspace Development
3700 Cloverleaf Drive
Boulder, CO 80304
Voice: (303) 938-8684
Fax: (303) 546-9667
E-mail: office@marketplace.com
URL: http://marketplace.com

Global City
P.O. Box 341556
Los Angeles, CA 90034
Voice: (310) 399-4349
Fax: (310) 396-5489
URL: http://kaleidoscope.bga.com/km/GCEnter.html

Global Electronic Marketing Service
200 Elmwood Davis Road, Suite 102
Liverpool, NY 13088
Voice: (315) 453-2035
URL: http://www.gems.com/index.html

Internet Marketing, Inc.
2162 NW Everett, Office #2
Portland, OR 97210
Voice: (503) 226-9128
Fax: (503) 224-1749
E-mail: advertiz@mcs.com
URL: http://venus.mcs.com/~advertiz/html/IntMarket.html

Internet Media Services
644 Emerson Street, Suite 21
Palo Alto, CA 94301
Voice: (415) 328-4638
Fax: (415) 328-4350
E-mail: info@netmedia.com
URL: http://netmedia.com

Internet Presence & Publishing Corp.
World Trade Center, Suite 1700
Norfolk, VA 23510
Voice: (800) 638-6155 or (804) 446-9060
Fax: (804) 446-9061
E-mail: info@tcp.ip.net
URL: http://www.shopkeeper.com/cgi-bin/shopkeeper

InterNex Information Services, Inc.
1050 Chestnut Street, Suite 201
Menlo Park, CA 94025
Voice: (415) 473-3060
Fax: (415) 473-3062
E-mail info: info@internex.net
E-mail sales: internex@internex.net
URL: http://www.internex.net

The Little Garden (TLG)
3004 16th Street, #201
San Francisco, CA 94103
Voice: (415) 487-1902
E-mail: info@tlg.org
URL: http://www.tlg.org

Metasystems Design Group, Inc.
2000 North 15th Street, Suite #103
Arlington, VA 22201
Voice: (703) 243-6622
Fax: (703) 841-9798
E-mail: info@tmn.com
URL: http://www.tmn.com

Multimedia Ink Designs
14544 High Pine Street
Poway, CA 92064
Voice: (619) 679-8317
Fax: (619) 679-1536
E-mail: rdegel@cts.com
URL: http://mmink.cts.com/mmink/mmi.html

NovX Systems Integration
316 Occidental Avenue South
Seattle, WA 98104
Voice: (800) 873-6689 or (206) 447-0800
Fax: (206) 447-9008
E-mail: info@novex.com
URL: http://www.interserv.com

Studio X
1270 Calle de Comercio #3
Santa Fe, NM 87505
Voice: (505) 438-0505
Fax: (505) 438-1816
E-mail: info@nets.com
URL: http://www.nets.com

Web Design Services

The following multimedia design companies offer Web document and site design and production services.

Bonsai Software
2582 Old First Street
Livermore, CA 94550-3155
Voice: (510) 606-5701
Fax: (510) 606-5702
E-mail: ksedgwic@bonsai.com

e-magination
931 Maplecrest
Lancaster, TX 75146
Voice: (214) 227-7822
Fax: (214) 227-6628
E-mail: info@e-magination.com

Free Range Media, Inc.
316 Occidental, Suite 406
Seattle, WA 98104
Voice: (206) 340-9305
Fax: (206) 442-9004
E-mail: info@freerange.com

Michele~Shine Media
1800 Market Street, Suite 204
San Francisco, CA 94103
Voice: (415) 621-0299
Fax: (415) 621-5023
E-mail: crmk@netcom.com
URL: http://www.internex.com/MSM/home.html

Virtual Advertising
606 N. 3rd, #1
Tacoma, WA 98403-2224
Voice: (206) 627-6827
Fax: (206) 627-7439
E-mail: arnold3a@halcyon.com
URL: http://www.shore.net/~adfx/top.html

Young Ideas
207 2nd Street, Suite B
Sausalito, CA 94965
Voice: (415) 331-3128
Fax: (415) 331-9620
E-mail: indy@bonsai.com

Chapter 17

Ten Plus One Ways to Promote Your Web Presence

. . . .

In This Chapter

▶ Promoting your Web site off the Net

▶ Getting publicity for your Web site in Net press

▶ Publicizing your Web site on the Net

. . . .

*I*t's one thing to create a Web presence, and it's another to let the Net community know you're in cyberspace. Getting the word out on the Net about your Web presence requires a concerted campaign. This chapter describes promotional options that are available to you both off and on the Net.

Promoting Your Web Presence off the Net

Every organization uses a variety of marketing and promotional tools, including business cards, display ads, radio spots, and TV commercials. These traditional marketing tools are useful for promoting your Web presence to people who are already using the Web. Net-literate people will appreciate knowing about your on-line service and what it offers.

As more people use your Net services, you can realize substantial savings by cutting back on traditional methods of marketing. For example, putting your newsletter on the Web saves printing and postage costs associated with a paper-based newsletter. Here are some ideas for promoting your Web presence:

 ✔ Give your customers the option of receiving information such as newsletters and new product announcements automatically via a Web presence.

✔ List your Web address on your business stationery.

✔ Promote your Web presence in your display, radio, or TV advertising.

✔ Include your Web address in all your direct mailings.

✔ Create an incentive for customers to make regular visits to your Web site. For example, you might offer a regularly updated newsletter or a listing of interesting sites.

Getting PR in the Net Press

By generating publicity for your Web presence, you increase your visibility on the Net and you gain credibility with other users on the Net. A number of paper-based publications covering the Net can be good sources of free publicity. For example, *Internet World*, *The Internet Letter*, and the *Internet Business Journal* are always looking for new and unique Web sites. Don't underestimate the value of promoting your server presence through these publications. They're frequently quoted in newsgroups and passed on via mailing lists to other Net users.

The amount of publicity your Web presence is likely to receive is related to the value it offers as a resource to the Net community. Focus your press information on what your server site is offering as a useful service.

The following are the leading Net publications. *BoardWatch Magazine*, *Internet World*, *ONLINE ACCESS*, and *WIRED* are available at newsstands (or by subscription).

Boardwatch Magazine
8500 W. Bowles Avenue, Suite 210
Littleton, CO 80123
Voice: (303) 973-6038
Fax: (303) 973-3731
E-mail: jack.rickard@boardwatch.com

Internet Business Journal
Strangelove Internet Enterprises, Inc.
208 Somerset Street East, Suite A
Ottawa, Ontario K1N 6V2
Canada
Voice: (613) 565-0982
Fax: (613) 569-4433
Email: mstrange@fhonorola.net

The Internet Letter
Net Week, Inc.
220 National Press Building
Washington, DC 20045
Voice: (202) 638-6020
Fax: (202) 638-6019
E-mail: info@netweek.com
URL: http://infosphere.com

Internet World
Mecklermedia Corporation
20 Ketchum Street
Westport, CT 06880
Voice: (203) 226-6967

Matrix News
Matrix Information and Directory Services
1106 Clayton Lane, Suite 500 West
Austin, TX 78723
Voice: (512) 451-7602
Fax: (512) 452-0127

ONLINE ACCESS
900 N. Franklin, Suite 310
Chicago, IL 60610
Voice: (312) 573-1700
Fax: (312) 573-0520
Internet e-mail: oamag.com

Open Systems Today
P.O. Box 1093
Skokie, IL 60076
Voice: (708) 647-6834
Fax: (708) 647-0226

WIRED
520 Third Street, 4th Floor
San Francisco, CA 94107
Voice: (415) 222-6200 or (800) SO-WIRED
Fax: (415) 222-6399
E-mail: info@wired.com
URL: http://www.hotwired.com

Promoting Your Web Presence through the Net

The Net provides an increasing number of no-cost options for promoting your Web presence. Several useful services can help you get the word out, including listserv mailings, network newsgroups, and various files that are maintained and distributed on the Internet.

Tell them what's happening through Net-Happenings

Net-Happenings is the most popular Net mailing list for announcing new products and services. People subscribe to Net-Happenings and receive constant updates via e-mail. It's a good source for you as a Web surfer because it's used to announce lots of new and improved Web sites.

You can subscribe to Net-Happenings by sending an e-mail message to the following address:

```
majordomo@is.internic.net
```

Leave the Subject: area blank, and enter the following text in the body of the message:

```
subscribe net-happenings
```

Once you subscribe, read different Net-Happenings postings to get an idea of how to structure your announcement. When you create your posting, send it as an e-mail message to the following address:

```
sackman@plains.nodak.edu
```

Here are some guidelines for writing an announcement for Net-Happenings:

- ✔ Keep announcements short, no longer than two screens or approximately 3,000 characters.
- ✔ Limit your announcement to a statement of the purpose and scope of your Web presence.
- ✔ Exclude promotional hype.
- ✔ Include contact information, such as a URL, phone and fax numbers, and any pertinent e-mail addresses, in addition to your server address.
- ✔ Don't include application forms, prices, or promotional information in the announcement.

Net-Happenings users can focus on topics in which they're interested by using keywords. When used with filter programs, keywords can also ensure that users receive only those messages in which they are interested. When creating your posting, tell the moderator, Gleason Sackman, which keyword you want to use. The moderator is the person who manages the mailing list. Common category keywords for Net-Happenings follow:

Keyword	Subject
WWW>	Generic Web announcement
NEWSLTR>	Newsletters
EJOUR>	Electronic journals
EMAG>	Electronic magazines, called *zines* for short
CONF-NA>	Conferences in North America
UPDATED>	Update of a previous posting

The Internet Mall

The Internet Mall is a monthly list of available commercial services on the Internet. This listing includes such categories as books, magazines, music, video, personal items, games, adult toys, computer hardware and software, research services, and travel. If you qualify, there is no charge for getting your server on this list. To be included on this list, a company must be on the Internet, it must have a salable product, and customers must be able to order the product directly through the Net, either by the Web or e-mail.

You can add your server presence to this list by sending an e-mail message to the following address:

```
taylor@netcom.com
```

This listing is maintained by Dave Taylor, who is responsible for the specific prose in each listing.

Registering at CERN

You should register your home page with the official list of Web servers at CERN. Point Mosaic to the following site, and follow the instructions that are displayed:

```
http://info.cern.ch/hypertext/DataSources/WWW/Servers.html
```

In many cases, your server service will register your home page for you.

Getting listed at NCSA's What's New Page

To have an announcement included in the NCSA What's New Page, you should attach your HTML-formatted document to an e-mail message that you send to the following address:

```
whats-new@ncsa.uiuc.edu
```

Keep your message concise and write it in the third person. The announcement will be added to the NCSA What's New Page, which is found at the following URL:

```
http://www.ncsa.uiuc.edu/SDG/Software/Mosaic/Docs/Whats-new.html
```

Registering a business Web presence

Open Market provides an extensive database of Web business sites at the URL site http://www.directory.net/, which is shown in Figure 17-1.

To display information about how to submit your announcement, click the How to Submit Listings hyperlink.

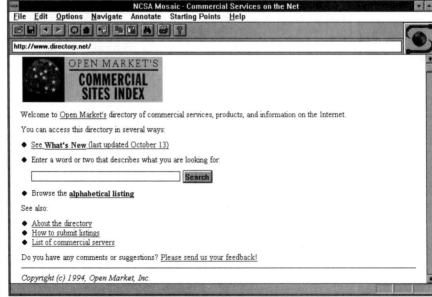

Figure 17-1: The Commercial Services on the Net home page is a popular place for listing your Web business presence.

Chapter 18

More than Ten Common Error Messages

Many of Mosaic's error messages include at least a brief text message that can give you a clue about what's going on. However, others don't give you any clue. Some error messages originate from sources other than Mosaic. For example, an error can come from the TCP/IP software you use in conjunction with Mosaic, or it might simply be a problem on the server to which you're trying to connect using Mosaic. The following sections list common error messages and provide suggestions for responding to these messages.

-10038

If you don't perform any actions at an FTP site for more than five minutes and then attempt to do something — for example, change directories — you may see this error message. Try reloading the FTP site.

-10048

Your TCP/IP program will display this error message if the service provider's DNS server is down and can't access the IP address of the server to which you're trying to make a connection. Try again. If you still can't make the connection, contact your service provider, or try it again at a later time.

-5

This message indicates that Mosaic has tried to download a file that doesn't exist or the specified filename isn't correct. Retry downloading the file.

Access not available

This message means you have tried to access a site or resource that is not available to you. Pack up your toys and go home.

Failed DNS lookup

This is one of the most common error messages you'll encounter, because it can be generated by a number of things. The Domain Name Service server (a database at your service provider's site that matches domain names to IP numbers) may have a problem matching the domain you've specified. Or, the document you're trying to access may be stored at a domain that is currently busy. Try again, and if it still doesn't work, try reconnecting to your service provider and relaunching Mosaic.

If the DNS is actually down, you'll get the error message -00048. If you see this message, contact your service provider. If the problem persists, try getting different DNS IP numbers from your service provider and entering them in your TCP/IP software program's configuration settings.

FTP login failed

This message lets you know the FTP site can't handle your attempted log-in. This frequently occurs when an FTP site is busy. Try again.

HTTP: Error response from server

This message indicates that the server is having some kind of problem. Retry the connection. If you still can't gain access, try again later.

HTTP: File/directory does not exist

You'll see this message if Mosaic is unable to locate the specified file or directory at the URL you entered. (By the way, HTTP stands for HyperText Transport Protocol.) Verify that the URL you entered is correct.

If you continue to get this error message, try moving up the path hierarchy a few steps. For example, let's say you're trying to access a document at the following URL:

```
http://www.bookware.com/books/recent/new.html
```

If the error message *HTTP: File/directory does not exist* is displayed, try shortening the path to something like http://www.bookware.com/books/, or just http://www.bookware.com/. Once you're at the site, you'll probably find the link you're looking for.

Lost FTP connection

This message means your connection to the FTP site was terminated for any number of reasons, such as a disruption in your telecommunications connection. Try again.

No link name specified

This message tells you that the link anchor you have selected doesn't have a URL specified in the HTML code. As a result, Mosaic doesn't know where to go to access the requested file. You can check the path of the hyperlink by moving the pointer over it, which displays the URL in the status bar. If you have the time, you can contact the site's Webmaster via e-mail about the problem.

Premature EOF

This message indicates that the end-of-the-file (EOF) marker has been reached unexpectedly, which most likely means the file is damaged or corrupted. Try downloading the file again. If you still get this message, the file is probably damaged on the server. You can send an e-mail message to the Webmaster to alert that person to the problem, or you can try to find the file at another site.

Socket errors

Your Windows TCP/IP program might display error messages like the following examples:

```
SOCKET:Connection has been aborted
SOCKET:Connection has been reset
SOCKET:Connection timed out
SOCKET:Host name is too long
SOCKET:Host is down
SOCKET:Host is unreachable
```

If you see a message you don't understand, check your TCP/IP software manual or contact the vendor.

Transfer cancelled

This message is displayed when Mosaic terminates a file transfer. This problem can occur for a number of reasons, including a bad telecommunications connection. This message is also displayed if you click the spinning Mosaic icon in the Mosaic window during a file transfer. Use your TCP/IP program to make sure your connection is still active. If your connection is working, reload the Web page and try the transfer again.

Part VI
The Web Surfer's Guide

The 5th Wave   By Rich Tennant

"IT HAPPENED AROUND THE TIME WE SUBSCRIBED TO AN ON-LINE SERVICE."

In This Part...

The Web is full of thousands of sites covering every topic imaginable. In this part, we provide an extensive, annotated guide to Web sites that we find useful, fun, interesting, and sometimes repulsive. We organize these sites into three main categories: starting points, business, and after-hours. Within each category, we organize the sites alphabetically. Because many of these sites act as gateways to other sites, you have access to thousands of sites using this surfer's guide. Have fun.

Chapter 19

Great Starting Points for Jumping into the Web

In This Chapter

▶ Connecting to giant, all-purpose directories of Web sites

▶ Finding sites with links to business and after-hours resources

*W*hether you're just surfing the Web to see what's out there or you're hunting for a specific site, there are plenty of good starting points. These sites, called *jumpstations*, act as hyperlink directories that point you to scores, hundreds, or even thousands of other Web sites. Several of these sites are mega-resources covering every topic imaginable, while others focus on a single topic, such as businesses on the Web or after-hours on the Net. At some sites, you can use both a database form with which you can search sites using keywords, and browsing hyperlinks that are organized into subtopics. Regardless of how you use them, jumpstations are a valuable resource for your Web surfing needs.

Commercial Services on the Net

http://www.directory.net/

The Commercial Services on the Net site provides a cornucopia of links to several hundred businesses on the Web. This site, formerly maintained by MIT, is now operated by OpenMarket, Inc. Figure 19-1 shows the Commercial Services on the Net home page. You can search for a specific site or browse an extensive alphabetical listing of businesses. Following the alphabetical listing of companies, you'll find a collection of hyperlinks to other business index sites. The site also includes a listing of server services that operate virtual malls or sell advertising space on the Web. Check the What's New link to see the latest additions. If you establish a Web presence for your business, you'll want to list it here. You can find out how to do this by clicking the How to Submit Listings hyperlink.

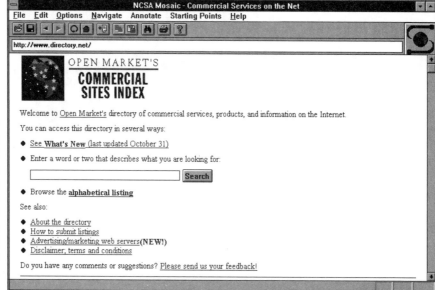

Computer and Communications Companies

http://www-atp.llnl.gov:80/atp/companies.html

Computer and Communications Companies focuses on companies and other organizations related to computers, networking, and telecommunications. It lists more than 800 companies under the Companies hyperlink. The Media link provides an extensive listing of industry publications, from the very technical to the avant-garde, such as *Wired*. This site also provides links to discussions, white papers, and other information resources on internetworking and telecommunications topics.

The Creative Internet

http://www.galcit.caltech.edu/~ta/creative.html

The Creative Internet site, which is shown in Figure 19-2, includes mostly entertainment links. The two big features of this site are The Complete TV Guide and The Ultimate Band List. Both include extensive links to sites

Figure 19-2:
The
Creative
Internet site
includes
two big
attractions,
the Com-
plete TV
Guide and
the Ultimate
Band List,
as well as
scores of
other enter-
taining
links.

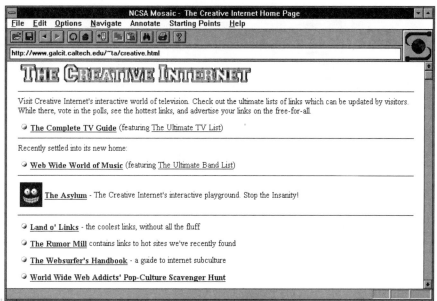

related to their topics. More links are available by clicking the Land o' Links hyperlink, including General, Computer, Music and Sound, Graphics, Cool Sites, and Entertainment. The Websurfer's Handbook includes the Top Ten Signs Your Home Page Is Not Cool and the Web-to-English Dictionary, which includes tongue-in-check definitions. For example, a barney page is a site or page designed only to capitalize on the current popularity of a subject on the Net.

CUI W3 Catalog

http://cui_www.unige.ch/w3catalog

As shown in Figure 19-3, the CUI W3 Catalog presents a form-based searching system for finding Web sites. You enter a search word in a text box, and click the Submit button. The W3 Catalog searches a database of over 10,000 Web resource entries. The search results are displayed as a report that contains brief abstracts for each site that matches your search word. You can go to these sites by clicking hyperlinks in the report.

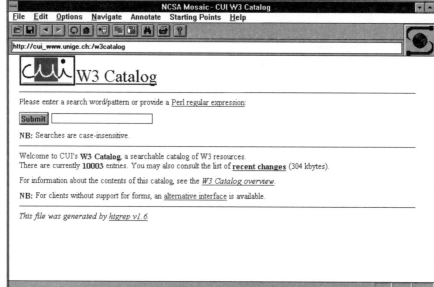

Figure 19-3:
The W3
Catalog lets
you search
a database
of more
than 10,000
Web
resources
using key-
words.

CyberSight

http://cybersight.com/cgi-bin/cs/s?main.gmml

The CyberSight site, which is shown in Figure 19-4, is pure entertainment, and lots of it. The sponsors, Internet Marketing, promote their site as "The Information Hotline for On-Line Hipsters." It's filled with plenty of links to after-hours hyperlinks. You can spend hours at this entertaining site, which presents information under the banners, Hot Stuff, Art, Fun, Noise, Electric Dinosaurs, Cybversive, Kitsch, and Leisure. Ongoing elections for favorite links keep this democratic site in a constant state of construction. The Randomizer includes a guide to film and video resources on the Net.

ElNet Galaxy

http://galaxy.einet.net

ElNet Galaxy is another mega-site of Web links, which you should definitely add to your hotlist. Figure 19-5 shows the ElNet Galaxy home page. ElNet is a commercial provider of network communication and information services, and they're part of MCC, a large high-tech R&D consortium. This site organizes hundreds of other sites into various broad topic areas, including Arts and Humanities, Business and Commerce, Community, Engineering and Technology, Government, Law, Leisure and Recreation, Medicine, Reference and

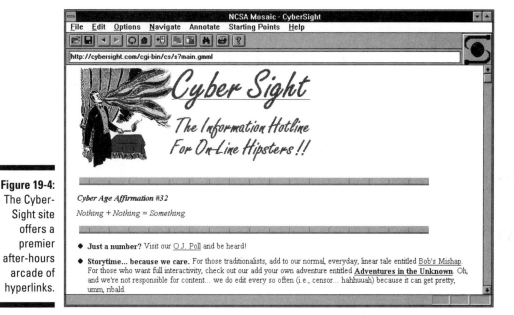

Figure 19-4:
The Cyber-
Sight site
offers a
premier
after-hours
arcade of
hyperlinks.

Figure 19-5:
The EINet
Galaxy site
is one of
the largest
jump-
stations on
the Web.

Interdisciplinary Information, Science, and Social Sciences. The EINet Galaxy site also includes a searching capability that lets you search for a specific site or sites based on a subject, including both Web and Gopher sites. The New Stuff link takes you to an update page.

FedWorld

http://www.fedworld.gov

FedWorld includes an A-to-Z subject listing of federal government sites on the Net. It's a government-funded project designed to provide a one-stop location for the public to locate, order, and receive U.S. government information. Fed-World is operated by the National Technical Information Service (NTIS).

The FineArt Forum

http://www.msstate.edu/Fineart_Online/art-resources.html

The FineArt Forum is a great springboard for jumping into the cyberspace art pool. It offers one of the most comprehensive collections of art-related links you'll find on the Net. The FineArt Forum includes an impressive listing of Events, General and Academic Resources, Electronic Art, Galleries and E-journals, and Individual Artists. The FineArt Forum is maintained by Jane Patterson at Willamette University in Salem, Oregon.

Games Domain

http://wcl-rs.bham.ac.uk/~djh/index.html

Lots of people play games on the Net. The Games Domain site is your ticket to all kinds of game information and links. It includes links to game-related USENET newsgroups, FAQs, and game company sites. The Games Related Home Pages hyperlink includes links to over 85 sites, from Air Warrior to Xsokoban.

Interesting Business Sites on the Web

http://www.rpi.edu/~okeefe/business.html

This site offers a more focused listing of businesses on the Web. Interesting Business Sites on the Web covers the most exciting uses of the Web as a teaching resource for conducting business. The general list of topics includes Pick of the Month, Large Name Companies, Small Companies, Financial Services, Advertising and Marketing, Legal Services, Publishing, Consulting Services, Virtual Malls, Event Information, Travel, Public Corporations, and Total Internet Providers. Each section includes a short briefing, and the links to other sites often include a sentence or two explaining why the site is interesting.

John Labovitz's e-zine-list

http://www.ora.com:8080/johnl/e-zine-list/

Zines — those small, do-it-yourself publications on every topic imaginable — have hit the Web, and this site lets you find them. John Labovitz's extensive list of e-zines includes over 170 links, which are organized alphabetically. This site also includes links to other sources of zine information on the Net.

Nonprofit Organizations on the Net

http://www.ai.mit.edu/people/ellens/non.html

The Web isn't just for profit-motivated organizations. A growing number of nonprofit organizations are adding their own Web sites. The Nonprofit Organizations on the Net site provides links to a variety of nonprofit groups. This site lists all types of organizations, from Amnesty International to the World Conservation Monitoring Center. The variety seems to know no political bounds. On the same page as the National Rifle Association, you'll find the Center to Prevent Handgun Violence. Each site listing includes a brief annotation. This site also offers a useful listing of financial information on nonprofit organizations.

Planet Earth

http://white.nosc.mil/pehp.html

The Planet Earth site, which is shown in Figure 19-6, is full of resource links for a wide variety of topics. This site's links are organized into Getting Started, Information Sources 1, World Region 1, Universities, Community, Government, Search Engines, Information Sources 2, World Region 2, Sciences, Multimedia, and San Diego. Search Engines is a useful link that takes you to a listing of sites that offer databases for finding resources. The Multimedia grouping offers links to lots of multimedia files.

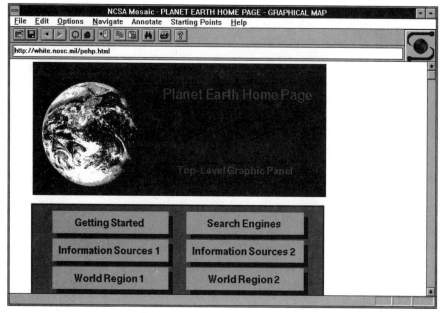

Figure 19-6:
The Planet
Earth jump-
station
offers a
wide assort-
ment of
useful links.

Thomas Ho's Favorite Electronic Commerce WWW Resources

http://biomed.nus.sg/people/commmenu.html

Thomas Ho's site offers numerous Net commerce links. His content list has an impressive array of topic headers, including Electronic Commerce Examples, Information Resources, General Articles, Company Lists, Electronic Storefronts, Industry Groups, Electronic Publishers, Financial and Professional Services, Emerging Services, Conferences & Training, Internet Mailing Lists, News, Jumpstations, User Groups, Research Groups, Teaching Resources, Repositories, and Government Services. All these topics and their links are on one very long Web document.

The Virtual Tourist

http://wings.buffalo.edu/world/

The Virtual Tourist helps you find information about different places by taking you to an extensive collection of Web servers around the globe. As shown in Figure 19-7, the home page presents you with a map of the world. Clicking on a particular region takes you to a listing of servers for that region. For

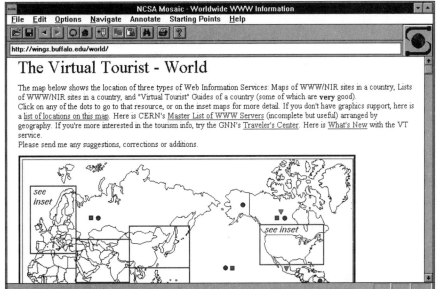

Figure 19-7:
The Virtual
Tourist pro-
vides links
to all kinds
of informa-
tion from
Web
servers
around the
world.

example, clicking on North America displays a more detailed map of North
America, where you can click on specific areas. For example, clicking on California takes you to a page of links clustered under a wide variety of headings,
including attractions, events, images, WWW resources, elections, and sports.
And, to make it complete for California, there are also surfing report and
earthquake update links.

What's Hot and Cool

http://kzsu.stanford.edu/uwi/reviews-1.html

The What's Hot and Cool site offers a solid collection of high-quality, mostly
after-hours Web site links. This site is part of The Web's Edge site, which
makes its home at Stanford University's KZSU Radio home page. A sampling
of site links includes Bits of OTIS, Strange Interactions, International Interactive Genetic Art, HyperDiscordia, Legos, Gravitar, My Brain Hurts, and Putrid
Afterthought. As shown in Figure 19-8, each site includes a brief annotation
and a thumbnail picture. If you're using a modem, you may want to turn off
the inline images feature in Mosaic because this site has a lot of images (one
thumbnail image with each site).

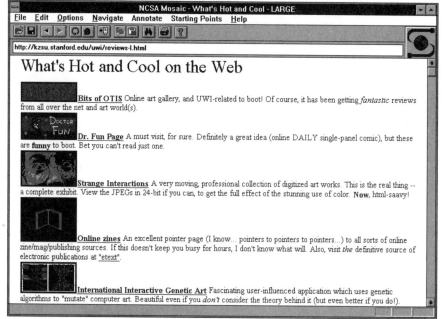

Figure 19-8:
The What's
Hot and
Cool site
delivers an
edited
collection of
mostly
after-hours
links.

What's New with NCSA Mosaic

http://www.ncsa.uiuc.edu/SD/Software/Mosaic/Docs/What's-new.html

Operated by the folks that developed Mosaic, the What's New with NCSA Mosaic site is a popular announcement board for new Web sites. They often provide a meaty description of the site along with the link to the site. They list all kinds of sites here, and they usually update this document a few times a week. By clicking on the archive of NCSA What's New pages, you can search updates going back two years, which is near the beginning of time in the Web universe.

The Whole Internet Catalog

http://nearnet.gnn.com/wic/index.html

Created by O'Reilly and Associates, the publishers of the popular book *The Whole Internet*, this site is a useful resource of links to a wide variety of sites. As shown in Figure 19-9, The Whole Internet Catalog site organizes links into the following categories: Arts & Humanities, Business, Current Affairs, Government & Politics, The Internet, Libraries, Reference & Education, Recreation, Science, and Technology. At the bottom of the screen is a text field in

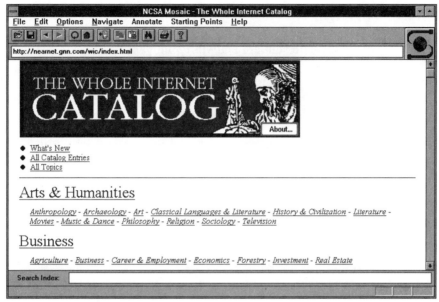

Figure 19-9:
The Whole
Internet
Catalog site
offers a
variety of
useful links.

which you can enter keywords to perform a search of Web sites. You can
check out the What's New page to see new additions.

World Wide Web of Sports

http://tns-www.lcs.mit.edu/cgi-bin/sports

The World Wide Web of Sports page is filled with a variety of sports links,
including Football, Basketball (NBA), Major League Baseball, Hockey (NHL),
Olympic Games, Soccer, Frisbee, Volleyball, Cycling, Rugby, Golf, Running,
Rowing, Skating, Cricket, and Tennis. A nice feature of this site is that you can
create a personalized sports page with only the links you want. Once you create your own sports page, you can add the site's URL to your hotlist.

The WWW Virtual Library

http://info.cern.ch/hypertext/DataSources/bySubject/Overview.html

From CERN, the developers of the World-Wide Web, The WWW Virtual
Library is a mega-resource of Web links. Links are organized by subject in an
A-to-Z format, with more than 70 subject headers. You can also browse the
listing by service type.

Yahoo

http://akebono.stanford.edu/~jerry/bin/yahoo

With more than 17,000 entries, Yahoo is possibly the best mega-jumpstation on the Web. Figure 19-10 shows the Yahoo home page. This is a cool site that is well organized and nicely presented. Its main topics include Art, Business, Computers, Economy, Education, Entertainment, Environment and Nature, Events, Government, Health, Humanities, Law, News, Politics, Reference, Regional Information, Science, Social Science, and Society and Culture. You can browse the links or search a database. As you browse, you'll find helpful guides along the way, including the number of entries in a topic, a new icon for a newly added topic, and a smiley face icon for cool sites. This site also offers What's New?, What's Popular?, and What's Cool? pages. Yahoo is a must-have addition to your hotlist.

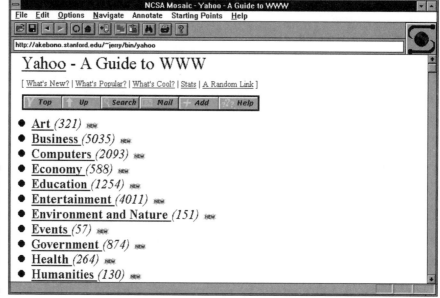

Figure 19-10:
The Yahoo server is possibly the largest jumpstation on the Web.

Chapter 20

Getting Down to Business

• •

In This Chapter

▶ Conducting on-line business research

▶ Getting multimedia files and other useful programs

▶ Performing on-line job searches

▶ Reading on-line publications

▶ Managing your investments

• •

*T*he number of businesses establishing a presence on the Web is growing by leaps and bounds. This chapter focuses on sites that offer hands-on, practical applications for business users. For example, AT&T provides an 800-number telephone directory. Because the Web is so new, many of these sites are under construction, with plans to offer even more services.

Adobe Systems, Inc.

http://www.adobe.com/

Adobe is the leading desktop publishing software company. They sell Post-Script, fonts, and desktop publishing programs. One of the best features of this site is that you can download the Adobe Acrobat Reader for free. This program lets you read a formatted document regardless of which computer system was used to create the document. The Adobe Systems site shown in Figure 20-1 includes company information, an on-line product catalog, and service and support information.

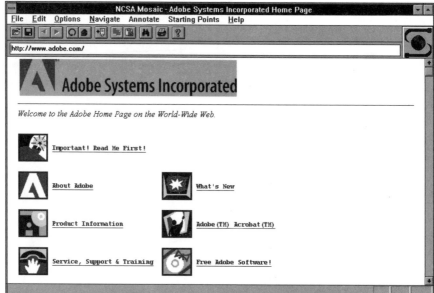

Figure 20-1:
The Adobe
site is a
desktop
publishing
resource
and a site to
get your
free copy
of Adobe
Acrobat
Reader.

AT&T 800 Directory

http://att.net/dir800

The AT&T 800 Directory site is a handy reference that lists all of the 800 numbers for AT&T. It's an on-line version of AT&T's printed 800 telephone directory. You can use this directory to find toll-free telephone numbers for almost every type of business or service in the United States. Figure 20-2 shows the home page for the AT&T 800 Directory. Simply click any link in the Browse by Category or Browse by Name areas to go to that part of the directory. AT&T plans to add a keyword search capability in the near future.

Bank of America

http://www.bankamerica.com/

Even banks are getting into cyberspace. The Bank of America is building a virtual bank on the Net. Over time, they plan to add more features for conducting on-line transactions. One nice feature currently available at this site is a listing of Bank of America's retail branches and ATM locations. You can see a listing of recent Bank of America announcements by clicking the News icon.

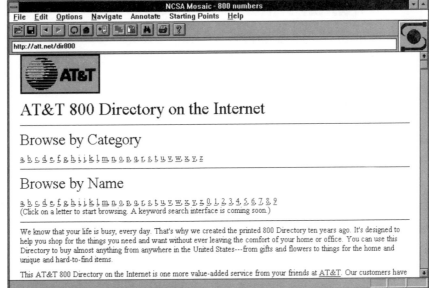

Figure 20-2:
The AT&T
800 Direc-
tory lets
your fingers
do the
walking via
the Web.

Boardwatch Magazine

http://www.boardwatch.com

Boardwatch Magazine deals with BBSs (bulletin board systems) and Net topics. This site offers a solid resource that doesn't scrimp on content. The
Boardwatch site includes on-line articles and excerpts from their newsstand
magazine for the last 12 months. eSoft's CEO, Alan Bryant, also provides a
collection of his favorite links here.

Book Publishers and Retailers Online

http://www.cs.cmu.edu:8001/Web/Booksellers.html

The Book Publishers and Retailers Online Web site acts as a gateway to the
publishing industry's growing presence in cyberspace. Links are organized
into the following general categories: General Interests, University, Technical,
Science Fiction, Fantasy and Horror, Alternative, On-line Books, Miscellaneous Specialty, Bookstores by e-mail, Publisher Catalogs, and Off-line Bookstores.

Branch Mall

http://branch.com:1080/

The Branch Mall is one of the pioneers in commerce on the Net. It started with the now-famous Grant's Florist & Greenhouse, which lets Web users order flowers on-line. The Branch Mall has since grown to include more than 60 businesses, and the Governor of the State of Michigan has a page here. This site offers affordable options for establishing a presence on the Web, and it shows you a good example of a successful virtual mall.

CareerMosaic

http://www.careermosaic.com/

CareerMosaic is an on-line, high-tech employment agency. It provides listings from an impressive array of employers, including Intel, Sun Microsystems, and Intuit. The site includes a variety of employment-related links, including an employment directory guide to North American markets, career conferences, and USENET jobs newsgroups. CareerMosaic also provides company profiles, a technical glossary, and Japanese phrases in sound files. Figure 20-3 shows the slick home page for this job-seeker's site.

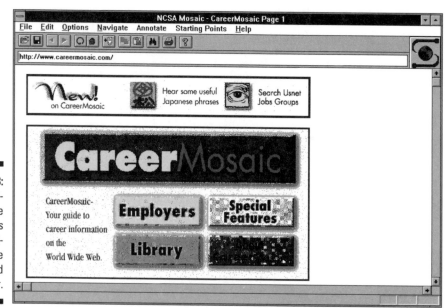

Figure 20-3: The Career-Mosaic site identifies opportunities for the Net-based job seeker.

CommerceNet

http://www.commerce.net/

CommerceNet is part of a project sponsored by a coalition of Silicon Valley high-tech and government organizations. It's a working model of an infrastructure for conducting electronic commerce. This site is worth watching to find out about new developments in commerce on the Web. For example, CommerceNet is creating a system for handling secured transactions via the Web. The CommerceNet Directories link provides access to a number of Net resources, such as a directory of Internet service providers and Internet consultants. The CommerceNet home page is shown in Figure 20-4.

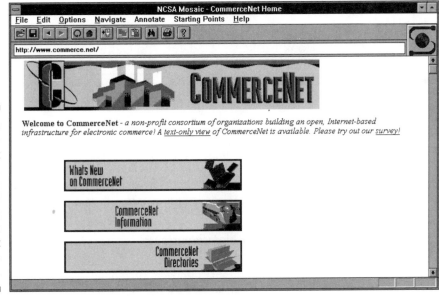

Figure 20-4: The CommerceNet site is a working model showing how to conduct commerce on the Web.

Computer Literacy Bookshops

http://www.clbooks.com

Computer Literacy Bookshops (CLB) specializes in technical books. The CLB Web site, which is shown in Figure 20-5, is a virtual library of technical book information. The best thing about this site is its huge book information database. You can search the database by title, author, or ISBN. Once the search is complete, you can select a title and display more information about the book, such as price, quantity in stock, and any reviews of the book. *New Book*

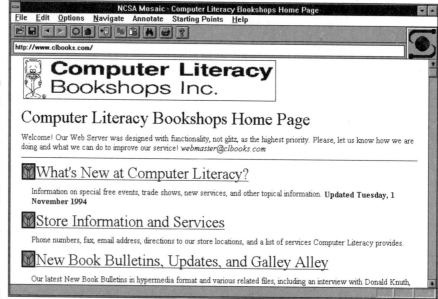

Figure 20-5:
The Computer
Literacy
Bookshops
Web site is
a great
resource for
computer
and other
technical
publications.

Bulletins is a CLB newsletter that is now available on-line. These bulletins include cover shots of books, and reviews by the CLB staff. This is a great site for finding out what's happening with computer books of all kinds.

Currency Converter

http://www.ora.com/cgi-bin/ora/currency

The Currency Converter is a program written by David Koblas that lets you compare the value of different countries' currencies. The Currency Converter home page lists the current week's exchange rates for countries listed alphabetically from Argentina to Venezuela. Choose the country that you want to use as the basis for comparison, and all the other currencies change to show the exchange rates against the base country's currency. The default base currency is the U.S. dollar.

Dan Kegal's ISDN Page

http://alumni.caltech.edu/~dank/isdn/

Dan Kegal's ISDN Page covers just about everything you might want to know about ISDN. This site is the most comprehensive source of information about

ISDN on the Net. It includes links to numerous types of related resources, including ISDN hardware vendors, telephone companies offering ISDN service, Internet service providers offering ISDN service, ISDN software and publications, and ISDN user groups. This site is a valuable resource for anyone considering the possibility of surfing the Web with ISDN.

Federal Express

http://www.fedex.com/

Federal Express, the leader in the overnight shipping business, has a new home page. Although the site is currently under construction, the customer service potential of this site for FedEx customers is exciting. The site currently offers information about a software program called Fedex Ship, which lets customers complete shipping transactions on-line. The FedEx site also presents some interesting factoids about Federal Express, such as sales, worldwide aircraft fleet, and service centers. We expect to see some useful developments at this site. Figure 20-6 shows the FedEx home page.

Figure 20-6:
The FedEx home page promises to make overnight delivery via Federal Express even faster and easier.

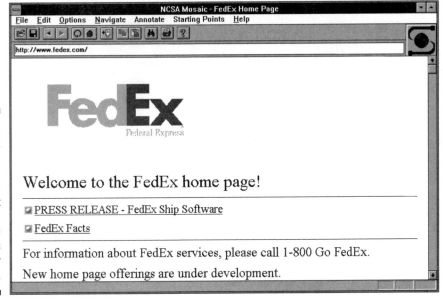

FTP Software

http://www.ftp.com/

FTP Software publishes a variety of TCP/IP software products, including a Windows TCP/IP package. This quality site includes information about the company and its products. You can also access a useful collection of technical support resources, and get information about their training services. Figure 20-7 shows the FTP Software home page.

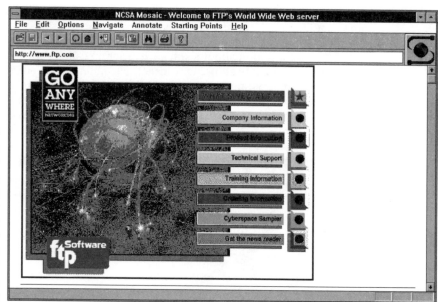

Figure 20-7: The FTP Software site is a resource for finding out about their Windows TCP/IP products.

Global Network Navigator

http://nearnet.gnn.com/GNNhome.html

Global Network Navigator (GNN) is one of the large virtual malls on the Web. It's provided by O'Reilly and Associates, the computer book publishers. From the GNN home page, you can access GNN NetNews, a weekly publication of Net news, and the quarterly GNN Magazine. The Whole Internet Catalog provides links to all sorts of Net resources. The GNN Business Pages connects you to businesses that rent Web server space at GNN. There's even a GNN Travel Center. You have to subscribe to GNN, but it's free.

Global Real Estate Guide

http://www.gems.com/realestate/index.html

The Global Real Estate Guide lets you browse or search through a huge database of more than 28,000 property listings. Properties are listed in the following categories: Residential, Commercial, Vacation, Luxury, Rental, and Services. The database includes properties in North America, the Pacific Rim, and other countries. This site also includes a database of real estate agents. The Global Real Estate Guide uses maps to direct you to specific regions. For example, the USA Map page breaks down the listings by state.

IBM

http://www.ibm.com/

Yes, Big Blue is on the Web. The International Business Machines site includes information about new developments at IBM. More important, the IBM site includes information about IBM products and how to connect to the right sales group within this giant computer company.

Index to Multimedia Information Sources

http://cui_www.unige.ch/OSG/MultimediaInfo

To help you keep abreast of developments in the multimedia industry, the Index to Multimedia Information Sources site provides a wealth of links to multimedia resources on the Net. The Multimedia Resources table of contents lists links to such resources as current events, media delivery services, newsgroups, digital galleries, publications, software, and companies.

Interactive Weather Browser

http://rs560.cl.msu.edu:80/weather/interactive.html

You're going on a trip and you want to check the weather? The Interactive Weather Browser is a near-real-time "Weather Channel" that lets you check the latest conditions using weather maps that are updated hourly at 5 minutes past the hour. Click any point on the map of North America, and you get the latest weather conditions for that location. You can also enter a station ID to get specific information about a location (they provide a directory of station IDs). The Interactive Weather Browser lets you change the conditions you want to monitor from numerous options.

Internet Better Business Bureau

http://ibd.ar.com/IBBB/IBBB.html

The Internet Better Business Bureau isn't a pretty site, but it does provide a useful service for consumers on the Net. This site includes an on-line complaint form that anyone can fill out to file a complaint against any business conducting virtual commerce on the Net. The complaint is then forwarded to the Better Business Bureau office for the area in which the business is located.

Internet Business Center

http://www.tig.com/IBC/

The Internet Business Center provides useful resources for learning more about conducting business on the Net. This site includes excerpts from the *Internet Letter* (a business-oriented newsletter), a white paper on Marketing on the Internet, and a Hot Sites link that provides a listing of business sites and services. The Valuable Stats link lists Net statistics of value to businesses. The Net Nuggets page includes links to such useful services as Net faxing. The Cool Posts page includes excerpts from newsgroups, mailing lists, and Web sites related to conducting business on the Net.

Internet Conference Calendar

http://www.automatrix.com/conferences/

The Internet Conference Calendar site is a valuable resource for finding out about upcoming conferences, courses, and workshops related to the Internet. It includes an impressive collection of links in the following categories: What's New, Calls for Papers, Conferences and Symposia, Expositions, Courses and Tutorials, Miscellaneous Gatherings, Conference Calendar Organized Geographically, and Other Conference Listings. This site offers hundreds of links. The Internet Conference Calendar includes a do-it-yourself event registration form, which lets you add your own announcement to the site.

Internet Credit Bureau

http://www.satelnet.org/credit/

The Internet Credit Bureau offers on-line credit reporting services. You can get credit information about any U.S. company or individual via the Net. You can also submit a request for the Internet Credit Bureau to search the Social Security number database. An on-line customer application form is available for setting up your account.

Internet Fax Server

http://town.hall.org/fax/faxsend-short.html

Sponsored by the Internet Phone Company, the Internet Fax Server lets you send a fax via the Net. You fill out an on-line form, enter the fax phone number, click a button, and off goes your fax. The current service area for sending faxes is extensive. To find out if you can send a fax to a particular phone number, you simply enter the number. The Internet Fax Server site is shown in Figure 20-8.

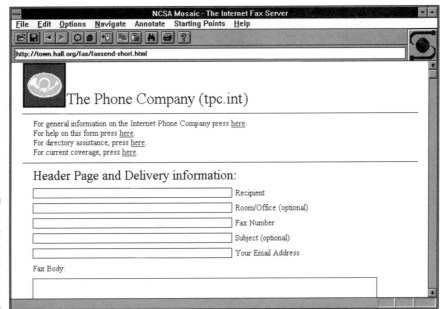

Figure 20-8:
The Internet
Fax Server
brings fax
capabilities
to the Net.

InterNIC

http://ds.internic.net/

Supported by the National Science Foundation (NSF), InterNIC provides several Internet services, including directory and database services, registration, and other information services. The Directory & Database Services link provides links to huge Internet databases that let you find users and other resources such as FAQs. The Registration Services link lets you search the InterNIC database of domain name registrations. The Information Services link provides links to all kinds of helpful information for Net users, such as information on getting connected to the Net.

Microsoft

http://www.microsoft.com:80/

The Microsoft site is the mothership of Windows resources. This site provides access to a bunch of Microsoft resources in such categories as Windows News, Sales Information, Software via Microsoft's FTP server, and Employment Opportunities. The KnowledgeBase link lets you access a database of information, including developer tools and Microsoft's software library. Figure 20-9 shows the Microsoft home page with its image map interface.

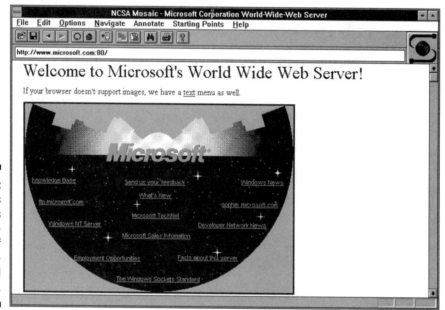

Figure 20-9: Microsoft's site offers a supermarket of Windows-related goodies.

Monster Board

http://www.monster.com

The Monster Board is a job posting service for companies in the northeast United States. Most of the jobs at this site are in the high-tech, health care, and biotechnology industries. It's sponsored by ADION, Inc., an advertising agency specializing in recruitment advertising. The big attraction is the jobs database, where you can search for jobs according to such variables as location, title, and industry. You can also check out company profiles for such firms as Fidelity Investments and Wellfleet.

Mosaic Communications

http://mosaic.mcom.com

Mosaic Communications is a Mosaic clone software company. What distinguishes Mosaic Communications from other commercial vendors of Mosaic clones is that this company hired the entire Mosaic development team from NCSA to develop their products. Mosaic Communications has created their own commercial Web browser called NetScape. They also sell Web server software. This site also points you to sites at which you can get a free copy of NetScape.

NetManage

http://www.netmanage.com/

NetManage is the leading Windows TCP/IP software vendor. The NetManage site, which is shown in Figure 20-10, includes a What's New page, product information, and company information. The Technical Support link takes you to a page of helpful technical tips, FAQs, and other information. The Internet Exploration link provides an extensive list of links for exploring the Web.

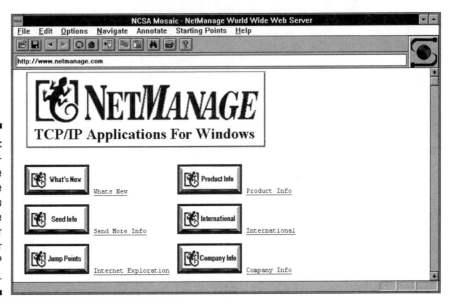

Figure 20-10: The Net-Manage Web site lets you learn more about their popular TCP/IP products.

Nolo Press

http://gnn.com/gnn/bus/nolo/

Nolo Press is a leading publisher of legal self-help books for individuals and businesses. The Nolo Press Web site shown in Figure 20-11 includes a combination of legal resources and an on-line catalog of the books they publish. The Legal Briefs link includes some useful articles, including "Copyrights in Cyberspace," "Can You Really Get a Patent Without a Lawyer," and "Law on the Internet." The Online catalog link provides a listing of Nolo's books along with descriptions. This site is great for finding books on a wide variety of business legal topics, including incorporation, patents, and trademarks.

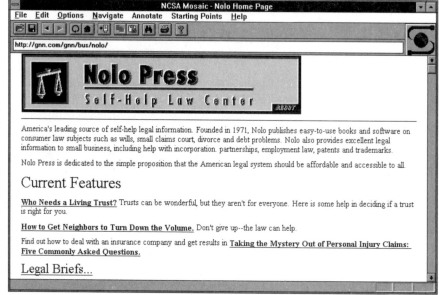

Figure 20-11: The Nolo Press Web site is a valuable resource for finding business self-help legal publications.

Novell

http://www.novell.com/

Novell is the leading PC networking software company, and their Web site is one of the better-designed sites. The Novell site delivers an extensive collection of customer services and product information, including product manuals. The Novell site also includes a technical support database, and software patches, updates, and drivers.

PC Magazine

http://zcias3.ziff.com/%7Epcmag/

PC Magazine, the largest circulation computer magazine, is now available on the Web. The PC Magazine site includes the table of contents for each issue, a list of the products reviewed, a column or two, and a piece on industry trends. Links at this site include Benchmark tests, which come from PC Magazine Labs and Ziff-Davis Benchmark Operations. This site also includes links to their favorite home pages.

PC Week Labs

http://www.ziff.com/~pcweek/

PC Week is a weekly newspaper about computer hardware and software. The PC Week Labs site provides up-to-date reviews, explanations of new technology, and the latest news in the computer industry. You can also search a database of articles. Some benchmark test results are available for downloading. The site includes selected reviews and columns from PC Week Labs and *NetWeek*, and Web-related articles. There are some excellent links, including PC Week Labs Best of the Web lists and PC Week Labs Cool Web Site of the Week. The PC Week Labs site also includes a local copy of NCSA's What's New on the Web.

Pizza Hut

http://www.pizzahut.com/

At last, you can order pizza in cyberspace! Just use Pizza Hut's Web site, which is shown in Figure 20-12. Using an on-line form, you enter your name, street address, and voice telephone number. The order is routed to the Pizza Hut nearest you. This site demonstrates the promise of using the Web as a worldwide ordering system. Try it out by ordering a large pizza with everything.

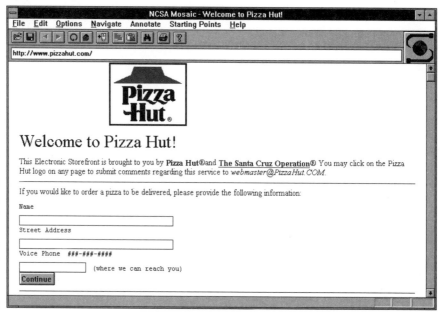

Quote.Com

http://www.quote.com/

Quote.Com is a membership-based stock trading and investment service. You can get stock quotes and related information based on your investment portfolio. This site offers the *Standard and Poor's Guide* on-line, newsletters, and other resources. Click More information to find out about registering for this service. The basic service package of $9.95 a month lets you get as many as 100 stock quotes a day, portfolio updates, and a lot more. You can even request warning alarms that are sent to you when a stock price goes above or below your specified range. Figure 20-13 shows the Quote.Com home page, in which each button in the grid points to part of their service package.

Rob's Multimedia Lab

http://www.acm.uiuc.edu:80/rml/

Rob's Multimedia Lab site is a treasure trove of links to thousands of multimedia resources. Sponsored by the Association for Computing Machinery (ACM), this site is a jumpstation to thousands of multimedia files. The Site

Figure 20-13:
The
Quote.Com
site brings
stock
trading and
other
investment
services to
the Web.

Seers Delight link points you to a huge listing of GIF files organized by topic. The Listen Up link connects you to a huge collection of sound file links. The Watch Your Step link points you to MPEG video files. Other multimedia site attractions include Smithsonian Sights, Fractals on the Move, Stellar Motion, At the Movies, Sound Off, Picture This, All Aboard (Trains), Climbing, Hang Gliding, Skydiving, Blues and Rock-n-Rock, Fantastic Fantasies, and ASCII Art Bazaar. Before you start building your Web document, check out this site for graphics, sound, and movie files.

SEC Database

http://town.hall.org/edgar/edgar.html

The Securities and Exchange Commission (SEC) database provides access to filings made by publicly held corporations to the SEC. These filings are available at no charge, and they're a valuable resource for objectively analyzing a company. The database allows you to obtain any 1994 filings to the SEC. By working with an easy-to-use WAIS database, you can get all kinds of useful forms for analyzing a business, including the 10K and 10Q forms.

Small Business Administration

http://www.sbaonline.sba.gov/

The Small Business Administration (SBA) site includes information about the SBA's programs and resources for starting, financing, and expanding small businesses. The site also lists the locations of the agency's 100 field offices, small business development centers, and small business institutes. Figure 20-14 shows the SBA home page.

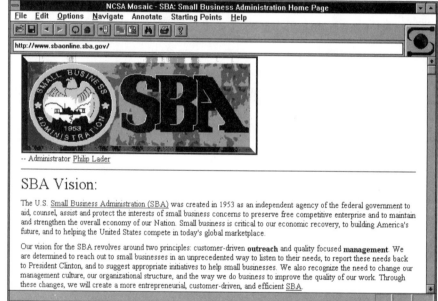

Figure 20-14: The SBA home page offers links to programs and other resources offered by this federal agency.

TravelWeb

http://www.travelweb.com/travel.html

The TravelWeb is sponsored by a hotel industry organization to promote its hotel and motel members in cyberspace. This site is still under construction, but it holds the promise of allowing Web users to check the availability of rooms and even book accommodations via the Web for most major hotel and motel chains. It will also provide electronic brochures for hotels, motels, inns, and resorts. Figure 20-15 shows the TravelWeb home page. Note the links at the top of the page that let you search a database of such lodging information as rooms, recreation facilities, and restaurants.

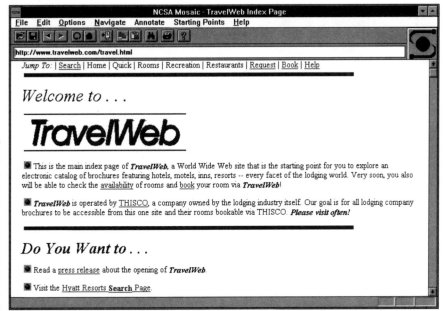

Figure 20-15: The Travel-Web site will soon be your one-stop source for booking hotel and motel rooms.

U.S. State Department Travel Warnings

http://www.stolaf.edu:80/network/travel-advisories.html

As the official line from the U.S. State Department, the main purpose of the Travel Warnings site is to provide on-line advisories for people traveling overseas. This site includes an extensive listing of countries from Afghanistan to Zimbabwe. For example, if you click on Libya, you'll find out that you shouldn't consider this country as a possible destination for your next get-away. This site also includes links to other travel-related information, such as maps, country flags, and the CIA World Factbook.

Wall Street Direct

http://www.cts.com:80/~wallst/

The Wall Street Direct site, which is shown in Figure 20-16, offers information, products, and services for investors. This site is sponsored by the *Wall Street Software Digest* and the *Traders' Catalog & Resource Guide*. It includes links to investment software, brokers, books, newsletters, and other investment resources for individual investors and traders. Wall Street Direct offers membership-based stock trading and investment services. You can sample a collection of software demos for analyzing stocks, bonds, and markets. Other

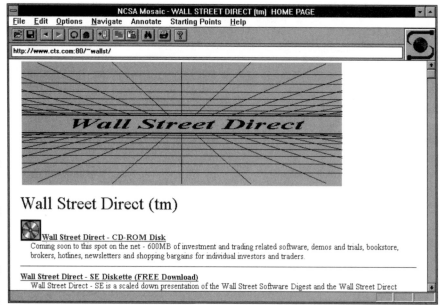

Figure 20-16:
The Wall
Street
Direct site
provides
resources
of interest
to investors.

resources include a listing of brokerage firms, a glossary of investment terms, and an on-line bookstore.

WWW Development

http://www.charm.net/~web/Vlib.html

The WWW Development site provides a one-stop resource for information about Web servers and tools for building Web documents. It includes hundreds of related links to HTML information, GIF images, HTML editors, and other types of Web resources. Before building your own Web document, you should check out this site, which is shown in Figure 20-17.

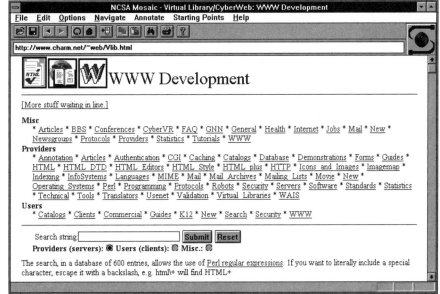

Figure 20-17: The WWW Development site is a rich vein of resources for building Web documents.

Chapter 21

The Web After-Hours

. . . .

In This Chapter

▶ Visiting virtual museums and digital art galleries

▶ Reading on-line publications

▶ Exploring music, humor, and other after-hours sites

. . . .

*T*he Web is a vast, cyberdelic playground that's full of after-hours activities. You can visit virtual museums and digital art galleries, read movie reviews and zines, or listen to music (everything from Elvis to opera). But wait, there's more. You can plan your next getaway, prepare gourmet meals from on-line recipes, or laugh at off-the-wall humor. Whatever your interests, the Web offers a dazzling array of entertaining, interesting, and provocative sites.

You should have your multimedia viewers ready before you start surfing the after-hours side of the Web. Many of the sites covered in this chapter include GIF and JPEG picture files, WAV and AU sound files, and MPEG and MOV files. See Chapter 8 for more information on installing the viewers that let you work with these files. ■

3W

http://www.3W.com:80/3W/index.html

Voted one of the ten best zine sites by *Wired* magazine, 3W is an exceptional guide to the Net. 3W is written clearly enough for the newbie, but it also includes information that will satisfy the experienced Web surfer. Check out the value-added pages, where each issue has a list of great links and files available via the Web. 3W also points to other interesting resources on the Net. This site also includes an interesting virtual reality experiment called the Virtual City.

The Amazing Fish Cam!

http://www.mcom.com/fishcam/fishcam.html

The fish cam is a classic form of nerd entertainment on the Net. A video camera is connected to a 90-gallon fish tank in order to create a virtual aquarium.
The tank includes one lionfish, one sailfin tang, two yellow-tail damselfish,
and two three-stripe damselfish. Images of the aquarium appear at regular
intervals at this Web site for your viewing pleasure. You'll need the Lview
program to view these pictures.

ANIMA

http://wimsey.com/anima/ANIMAhome.html

ANIMA (Arts Network for Integrated Media Applications) is a production of
Vancouver's WebWeavers. Figure 21-1 shows the ANIMA home page, where
you'll find a global collection of on-line art and related resources, including
pictures, video, audio, and other media. ANIMA's main links are all worth
exploring. ArtWorld is a rich multimedia cultural information service that
provides links to numerous impressive art sites. ATLAS provides information
resources that bridge the information gap between artists and technologists.
Spectrum is an on-line collection of arts and media publications, including

Figure 21-1:
ANIMA
offers an
impressive
collection of
media arts.

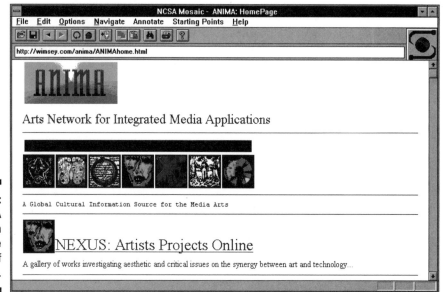

Front Magazine, *Media West Magazine*, and *Ctheory*. Nexus is an avant-garde forum for network art and literary projects.

Art Crimes

http://www.gatech.edu/desoto/graf/Index.Art_Crimes.html

The Art Crimes site presents a collection of graffiti from cities around the world. As the Webmaster states, it's "guerrilla art worth being arrested for." The pictures are elaborate, spray-painted pieces, fresh from the streets of such cities as Prague, Atlanta, and Los Angeles. Each city has its own page of thumbnails, which are links to the full-blown pictures. As you might expect, Los Angeles has one of the most extensive collections.

ArtServe

http://rubens.anu.edu.au

The Australian National University sponsors ArtServe, an academic art history site that includes a database of over 2,800 images of classical architecture and sculptures. One of the most interesting sites is called "Palace of Diocletian at Split. A Unique Structure from the Later Roman Empire." This site uses a "storybook" approach to test the Web's effectiveness for delivering book-length publications. ArtServe is largely the work of Webmaster and professor Michael Greenhalgh. A favorite research topic of Greenhalgh's is sculpture in Turkey, and this site includes a link to a short research paper on the subject. A link to the Canberra School of Art Gallery contains some impressive glass artworks.

ArtSource

http://www.uky.edu/Artsource/artsourcehome.html

ArtSource provides an extensive collection of links to art on the Net. The Art-Source site, which is shown in Figure 21-2, takes a broad view of art, covering media ranging from architecture to textile arts. You can even submit your own works to this site. ArtSource's main menu of links includes Art/Architecture, Art Journals, Electronic Exhibitions, Experimental Projects, Image Collections, and Museum Information. A What's New page keeps you up to date with new art-related sites on the Web.

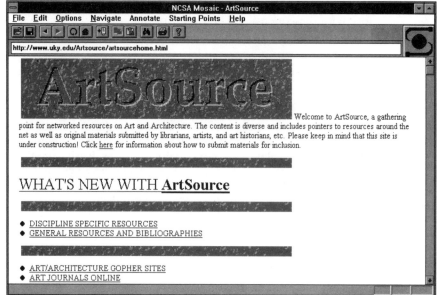

Figure 21-2:
ArtSource
includes an
extensive
collection of
links to art
and archi-
tecture
resources
on the Net.

The Asylum

http://www.galcit.caltech.edu/~ta/cgi-bin/asylhome-ta

The Asylum's guiding principle is "Idle minds are the Devil's playground." The Asylum is one such playground. Its main links include Graffiti Wall, Fiction Therapy Group, and Core Dump. The Graffiti Wall lets you add your name to a digital wall. The Asylum's Lite-Brite Gallery is a collection of Lite-Brite art links. Lite-Brite art uses pinpoint GIF images, which the artist arranges to create works of art, much as you might have done with the Lite-Brite toy.

Avid Explorer

http://www.explore.com

The Avid Explorer, which is shown in Figure 21-3, is a travel information center sponsored by Explore! Cruises & Expeditions, a full-service travel agency. This site is a good place for getting vacation ideas. The Special Packages link takes you to a listing of travel packages. The Cruising page links you to the different cruise line packages, as well as Windjammer and Clipper ship adventures. The Travel Forums page provides an extensive collection of links to other travel resources on the Net.

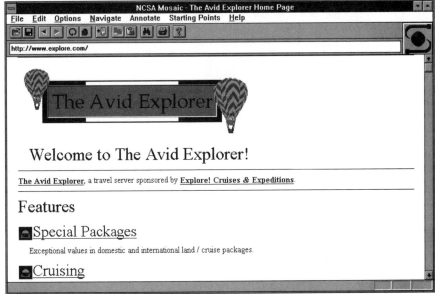

Figure 21-3:
The Avid
Explorer is a
great
resource to
help you
plan your
next
vacation.

Axcess Magazine

http://internex.net:80/axcess/

Axcess is an ultra-hip, graphics-intensive, Generation X zine that focuses on music, art, cyberculture, and style. It takes advantage of the Web's multimedia features. For example, an article often includes a sound clip of a reviewed song, or an animation review might contain a QuickTime clip from the movie. The articles for the Web version of Axcess come from the newsstand version of the magazine. This creative, state-of-the-art zine is definitely worth a look.

Barney's Page

http://www.galcit.caltech.edu/~ta/barney/barney.html

The site shown in Figure 21-4 isn't for kids. Barney's Page takes a sharp-fanged bite out of the great purple dinosaur. It includes pictures of Barney in dire circumstances, a Barney target, and Barney sound clips in the WAV format. This fun site also includes links to other Barney stuff on the Net, such as the Jihad to Destroy Barney on the Web. Other attractions include a Barney ASCII picture that delivers subliminal messages, and an Ask Dr. Barney advice column.

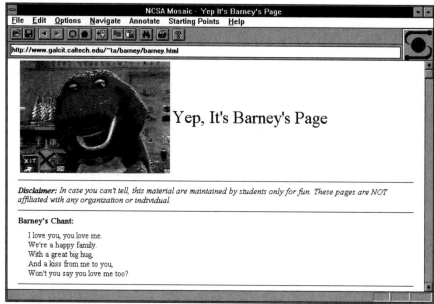

Figure 21-4:
Barney's
Page takes
humorous
bites out of
the latest
children's
superstar.

Beauty for Ashes

http://neuromancer.ucr.edu/~fetters/ashes.html

Beauty for Ashes blends photography with hypertext poetry. The Beauty for Ashes site was created by a group of Christian artists who believe, "art should be a reflection of the soul." There's an intriguing quality to the dark beauty of the photographs and poetry at this site. A special link called the White Rose honors a group of university students who defied the Nazi regime and were beheaded. One note of caution: this site includes huge inline graphics that can take a long time to download.

Beavis and Butt-Head

http://calvin.hsc.colorado.edu/

You should definitely check out the Beavis and Butt-Head site when the boss is on vacation. The Beavis and Butt-Head home page shown in Figure 21-5 is your gateway to finding out more than you ever wanted to know about this wacky duo. This site includes an extensive Beavis and Butt-Head FAQ (frequently asked questions) and the complete list of Beavis and Butt-Head

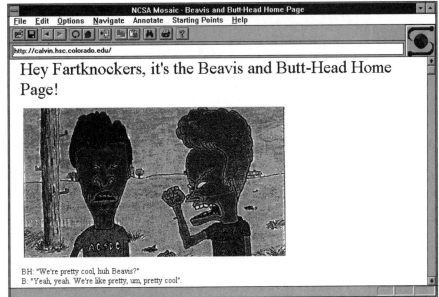

Figure 21-5:
The Beavis
and Butt-
Head home
page will
keep you
current on
the not-so-
dynamic
duo's
adventures.

episodes. There's also a large collection of QuickTime movie, sound, and picture files. However, you'll need access to a Macintosh computer to decompress these QuickTime movies because they're compressed using the
Macintosh Stuff-It program. Another drawback of these movies is their huge
(6-12 MB) files. This site also includes links to other Beavis and Butt-Head
resources on the Net.

The Best of Web

http://wings.buffalo.edu/contest/

The Best of the Web awards were presented at the First International World-
Wide Web Conference in Geneva. These awards are the result of over 5,000
votes cast in 13 categories. The categories include Best Overall Site, Best
Campus-Wide Information Site, Best Commercial Site, Best Educational Service, Educational, Professional, Entertainment, Navigational, Design, Best Use
of Interaction, Multiple Media, and Technical Merit. By clicking the 1994
Awards link, you can display a page containing links to the winning sites as
well as those that received honorable mentions. The World-Wide Web Hall of
Fame link recognizes the people who have made important contributions to
the Web. This is a great starting point to see what's possible on the Web.

bianca's SMUT-Shack

http://bianca.com/shack/index.html

bianca's SMUT-Shack is a highly interactive site built around a house metaphor. To help you navigate this site, you can use a map of the shack, a quick reference guide, or a text guide. bianca's SMUT-Shack lives up to its name with a bathroom that lets you write graffiti or discuss other bathroom duties. You can leave your love submissions to bianca at this site's altar. For a laugh, check out the Pantry for bianca's creative uses of duct tape. The Pantry also holds a collection of embarrassing record albums that you would never admit having in your collection, ranging from Abba to Wham. Besides the risqué, there are mainstream topics, such as the Movie room, where you can read bianca's movie reviews and reviews from other visitors, or you can leave your own reviews. The bookcase is a bizarre little collection, including excerpts from the *Official Boy Scout Handbook* and bianca's poetry.

bOING bOING

http://www.zeitgeist.net/public/Boing-boing/bbw3/boing.boing.html

bOING bOING magazine was launched in 1989 and entered cyberspace in 1992. bOING bOING started as a conference on The WELL, which is a popular chat system in northern California. This zine includes cutting-edge comics, as well as essays, art, and articles on technology. The tone is upbeat, fun, and irreverent, with a twist of the bizarre. The bOING bOING bazaar features high-tech gadgets, and there's also a section of zine reviews. bOING bOING also includes excerpts from *Beyond Cyberpunk* (the classic cyberculture e-text), and some exclusive on-line interviews.

Buena Vista Pictures

http://bvp.wdp.com/BVPM

Walt Disney is now in cyberspace. If your connection can handle large graphics and huge film clip files, grab some popcorn and go to the Buena Vista Pictures site. Clicking the Click here to enter the Movie Plex link takes you to the Buena Vista Movie Plex, which is shown in Figure 21-6. The Movie Plex lets you view QuickTime film clips of recent releases from Disney, Touchstone, and Hollywood Pictures. The Buena Vista Press Room displays press kits for current features along with the digital library.

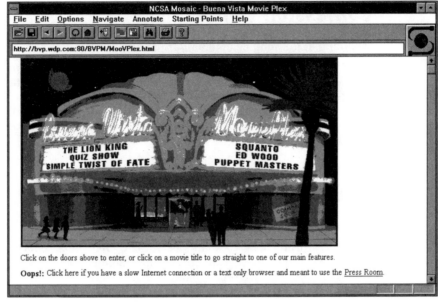

Figure 21-6:
The Buena
Vista Pic-
tures Web
site lets you
view clips
of the latest
Walt Disney
movies at
the Movie
Plex.

Cardiff's Movie Database Browser

http://www.cm.cf.ac.uk/Movies/

Cardiff's Movie Database Browser is a film-buff's heaven. This site provides a forms-based interface to a huge database of information on over 35,000 films and TV series. You can look up films or TV shows by title, actor, director, country of origin, production company, genre, certificate (rating), or by quotations. The database includes the complete archive of the rec.arts.movies newsgroup. Other attractions at this site include links to the top-40 films, academy award information, and celebrities' birthdays and deaths for the current date.

Chesley Bonestell Interactive Art Gallery

http://www.secapl.com/bonestell/top.html

Chesley Bonestell is well-known in the fields of architecture, motion picture illustration, and astronomical art. He worked on the Golden Gate Bridge, the Chrysler Building, and the special effects for *War of the Worlds*. He is best known for illustrating astronomical scenes. This site offers a great collection of his space illustrations, which include Earth, Mars, Jupiter, the Moon, and the Star Series. These images are GIF files. You need the Lview program to view them.

Confession Booth

http://anther.learning.cs.cmu.edu/priest.html

Billed as "Bringing the Net to its knees since 1994," this site is your virtual salvation. It's an interactive form for confessing your sins to a digital priest. This high-tech confession booth includes a checklist of common sins, and a text box for adding details. Click the Transmit Confession button and off your sins go into cyberspace. The default setting is to send your confession to God, a.k.a. the Root.

Cyber-Sleaze

http://metaverse.com/vibe/sleaze/index.shtml

Written by former MTV VJ Adam Curry, the Cyber-Sleaze report is a daily news update on the seamy side of the entertainment business. Figure 21-7 shows the Cyber-Sleaze report page, with links to daily reports organized by month. This entertaining, daily gossip sheet is the best part of the Vibe, which is the reincarnation of Curry's mtv.com site. Curry's mtv.com site was so popular on the Net that it got the attention of MTV as a hot piece of property. As a result, MTV sued Curry to get ownership of the mtv.com domain name.

Figure 21-7: Adam Curry's Cyber-Sleaze report keeps you up to date on the seamy side of the entertainment industry.

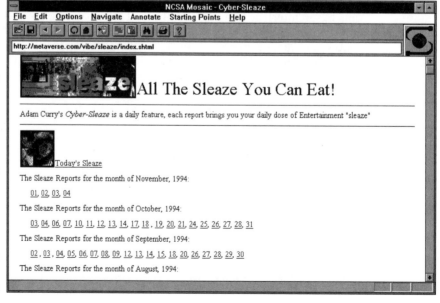

CyberArt

http://www.rpi.edu/~daniek2/

The CyberArt site is the result of the class on networking and technology at Rensselaer Polytechnic Institute, which is located in Troy, New York. This site includes student projects in art, hypertext, interactive animation, virtual space, and interactive network video. You'll find that this site delivers an in-your-face style of art.

Cyberkind

http://sunsite.unc.edu/shannon/ckind/title.html

CyberKind offers an interesting collection of fiction and non-fiction, poetry, and art writings. Structured like a traditional magazine, the Cyberkind zine, which is shown in Figure 21-8, includes feature stories, letters to the editor, and columns. The quality of writing is exceptionally high, despite the fact that the articles come from non-professional writers. An article published by Cyberkind that's frequently linked from other sites is "The Internet and the Writer" by Steven Elmer Baker. Cyberkind also includes a nice collection of links.

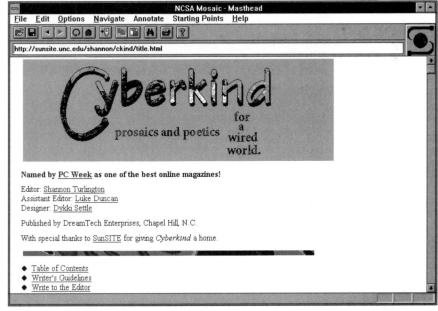

Figure 21-8: The Cyberkind zine is a quality digital publication that's definitely worth checking out.

Depth Probe

http://www.neo.com/DepthProbe/zine/index/home.html

Depth Probe is a collection of modern culture writings and links. It includes reviews of books, movies, and music. Other topics covered include upcoming events, newspapers and magazines, Net surfing news, random quotes, television, travel, and dreams. You can browse back issues sorted by topic and date. There's also a gallery of electronic art and a collection of interesting links.

Digital Journeys to Theme Parks

http://ziris.syr.edu/digjourney.html

Digital Journeys is an enormous, well-designed artistic forum. It's a collaborative art project sponsored by Syracuse University's Computer Graphics for the Arts Department. Digital Journeys themes include: Are We Alone?, Bands, Cybernetics, Dark Legends, Death Live, Digital Characters, Dreamers, Eye, Fantasy, Fashion, Pain, Revolution, Dinosaur Fever, Tattoos, TechnoGod, Virtual Self, UntoldVisions, and VisionQuest. Clicking an icon moves you to a theme page that includes stunning visuals related to the selected subject. Most of the thematic sites include one or more movies in QuickTime format. Anyone can contribute images, text, audio, or video files.

DOOM Gate

http://www.cedar.buffalo.edu/~kapis-p/doom/DoomGate.html

DOOM is a three-dimensional, virtual reality action game created by id Software. Since its introduction, DOOM has taken the Net gaming world by storm. The DOOM Gate site shown in Figure 21-9 includes links to an FTP site so you can download the shareware version of DOOM. (DOOM requires about 5MB of disk space after you decompress it.) In DOOM, you're a space marine relegated to working in a radioactive waste facility on Mars. You battle to reclaim a military base overrun by evil aliens. It's a ruthless, impressive, and state-of-the art game. Texture-mapped images and stunning sounds make the DOOM environment realistic. This site also links you to other DOOM Web servers, FTP sites, and forums. To read the DOOM FAQ, click the link to the alt.games.doom.newplayers newsgroup.

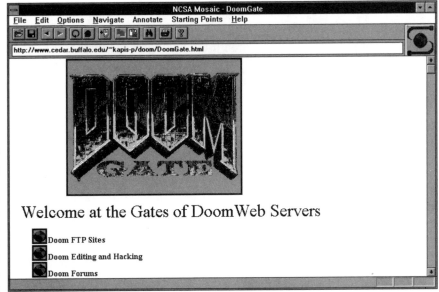

Figure 21-9:
The DOOM
Gate site is
your gate-
way to the
hottest
game on
the Net.

The Doors

http://www.vis.colostate.edu/~user1209/doors/

Jim Morrison isn't dead; he's in cyberspace at The Doors site. This slick site
includes song lyrics, pictures, newsgroup links, a Doors FAQ, and links to
other Doors-related resources. The lyrics and album cover shots for all The
Doors records are here. The Doors Collectors Magazine link shows shots of
Jim Morrison's grave site in the Pere Lachaise Cemetery, located in Paris.

Dr. Fun

http://sunsite.unc.edu/Dave/drfun.html

Dr. Fun is a single-panel cartoon created by David Farley that offers an amus-
ing Net diversion. Distributed every weekday, Dr. Fun images are high-quality
color graphics that you can download as JPEG images suitable for framing on
your fridge. You can also choose to look at back issues of the daily comic.

The Edge

http://www.vsl.ist.ucf.edu/projects/edge/edge.html

The Edge is an ongoing, virtual computer-graphics exhibition. The Exhibit Hall floor map lists the exhibits by codes that allow you to cross-reference related exhibits. Most exhibits are virtual reality (VR) experiments. Many exhibits change the point of perception of the participant, giving the user the experience of inhabiting a different world or a different body. For example, the NorthWater world draws you into the body of an arctic wolf. CyberFin simulates swimming with dolphins. Flogiston lets visitors experience the feeling of flying. One site lets participants virtually shrink to microscopic size and experience cell biology firsthand. Most of these exhibits include details about the techniques and computer technology used to create the VR experience. The Exhibit also includes a variety of interactive games that entertain while they educate. For example, Proyecto Xochicalco lets several networked users explore the accurately reconstructed environment of the Aztec/Mayan archeological site Xochicalco and take part in an ancient Aztec/Mayan ballgame.

The Electric Gallery

http://www.egallery.com/egallery/

The Electric Gallery shown in Figure 21-10 is a virtual art gallery in which various rooms each display three or four paintings, all of which are for sale. Along with each painting, you'll find its name, type, size, price, and other information. A couple of rooms contain the private collection of the site's Webmaster. Each artist's name is displayed as a link, so you can find out more about the artists and their paintings. There were eighteen rooms in the walking tour that we took.

Electronic Art Gallery

http://www.wimsey.com/Pixel_Pushers/

Pixel Pushers presents some of the premiere electronic artists in the world. All works in this exhibition are signed, limited-edition prints. These prints are offered for sale with a certificate of authenticity, and they can be purchased via e-mail. You can access works by the artist's name, which takes you to the artist's statement, biography, edition information, and a thumbnail inline (GIF) image. From there, a link displays a JPEG image of the art. If you can afford the bandwidth, you can download a handsome poster containing all of the GIF thumbnails. The Rogues' Gallery link presents live pictures from the

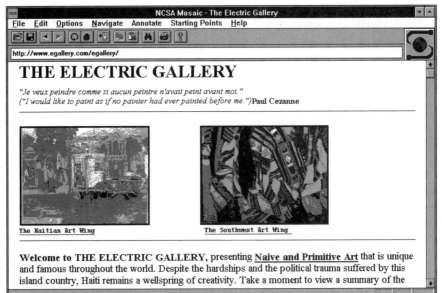

Figure 21-10:
The Electric
Gallery
includes a
nice collec-
tion of prim-
itive art.

opening festivities of the Electronic Art Gallery at Granville Island. You can
also drop a note in the Guest Book, and read what others have to say.

Elvis Aron Presley

http://sunsite.unc.edu/elvis/elvishom.html

It was only a matter of time until Elvis was sighted in cyberspace. At the Elvis
Aron Presley site, you can pay your respects to the King. This site lets you
take a tour of Graceland, view a collection of photographs from the Elvis
Exhibit, and play Elvis sound bites in AU and WAV formats.

The English Server

http://english-server.hss.cmu.edu

The English Server is a humanities resource run by students and staff at
Carnegie Mellon University. Figure 21-11 shows the English Server home page
with some of its impressive collection of topical links. This site includes links
covering a broad range of humanities disciplines, such as art, architecture,
drama, film, philosophy, poetry, and rhetoric.

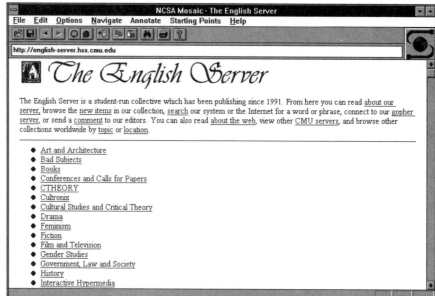

Figure 21-11:
The English
Server is a
must-visit
site for the
humanities.

Exploratorium

http://www.exploratorium.edu/

The source of ExploraNet is the Exploratorium, an interactive museum of science and art founded by Dr. Frank Oppenheimer and based in San Francisco. The ExploraNet follows the Exploratorium's philosophy of encouraging learning through personal experience. A link to the Digital Library includes images of Exploratorium exhibits and electronic versions of a few of the interactive exhibits. The images are JPEG format, and the files are usually smaller than 100K. You can check out the Exploratorium's quarterly magazine *Exploring*, which takes a look at science in the everyday world. The "Ask Us" link provides answers to such burning questions as "Do birds sneeze?" and "If you're in a vehicle traveling near the speed of light, what happens when you turn on the headlights?"

EXPO Ticket Office

http://sunsite.unc.edu/expo/ticket_office.html

EXPO is the starting gate for visiting some of the best expositions — called pavilions — on the Net. EXPO pavilions currently include the Vatican Exhibit, Soviet Archive Exhibit, 1492 Exhibit, Dead Sea Scrolls Exhibit, Paleontology

Exhibit, and the Splato Exhibit. There are three ways you can enter the pavilions: through the EXPO ticket office, from the EXPO Shuttle Bus link, or by clicking a hotspot on the EXPO terrain map. You can get more information about exhibits or get an exhibit catalog at the EXPO Bookstore. The EXPO shuttle bus page also includes links to other exhibits, such as the Dinosaur Exhibit. The Overview of Objects and Topics link shows an outline of the various exhibits, and offers direct access to all objects in the EXPO exhibits. All over the EXPO terrain, you'll find the EXPO Bulletin Board, which lets you enter comments about the exhibit.

French Ministry of Culture

http://dmf.culture.fr

The French Ministry of Culture is exporting French culture into cyberspace via their Web site, which is shown in Figure 21-12. The French Ministry of Culture's site is a great place for brushing up on your French and checking out French art, history, and culture. All the text at this site is in French, but the pictures are nice. Unfortunately, there's nothing on our favorite aspect of French culture, the cuisine.

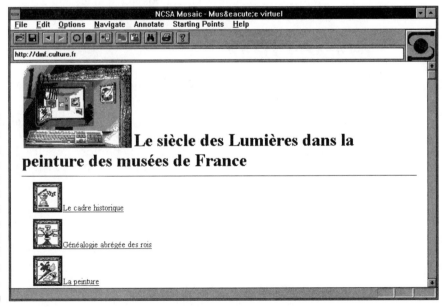

Figure 21-12:
You can brush up on French language and culture at the French Ministry of Culture's Web site.

Future Fantasy Bookstore

http://www.commerce.digital.com/palo-alto/FutureFantasy/home.html

The Future Fantasy Bookstore specializes in science fiction, fantasy, and mystery books. This site is a full-service, on-line bookstore. You can search their database of books by author, title, or publication date within the last 12 months. Once you've found the books you want, you can order them. You can check out their latest newsletter or browse back issues. They also announce upcoming author signings and other events.

General Hospital

http://ghwww.netcom.com/gh/gh.html

The General Hospital site offers everything you could ever want to know about this long-running soap opera. Ms. Purple, who is the maintainer of this site, lists GH's awards, behind-the-scenes info, character summaries, autographed pictures of the cast, the stars' birthdays, fan clubs, and scheduled personal appearances. More important, Ms. Purple dishes up daily summaries and weekly spoilers to help you catch up with the latest dramatic developments. The site also includes General Hospital comics and a top-ten list.

Grateful Dead

http://www.cs.cmu.edu:8001/afs/cs.cmu.edu/user/mleone/web/dead.html

The Grateful Dead site offers a feast of deadhead paraphernalia, including FAQs, tour dates, rumors, graphics, song lyrics, and sounds. The Song Lyrics link lets you check out a huge database of Dead lyrics. The Graphics link offers a rich collection of Dead Art, including photos, graphics, T-shirt designs, and, of course, tie-dyes. You can even download the Dancing Bear Screen Saver program from this site.

Hot, Hot, Hot

http://www.presence.com/H3/

Billed as a Culinary Headshop, the Hot, Hot, Hot site shown in Figure 21-13 offers an outstanding collection of hot sauces that you can order on-line. Using a visually vibrant catalog, this chili-head Mecca offers over 100 sauces with names like Ring of Fire, Pure Hell, and Dave's Insanity Sauce. You can search for sauces by heat level, origin, ingredients, or product name. There's

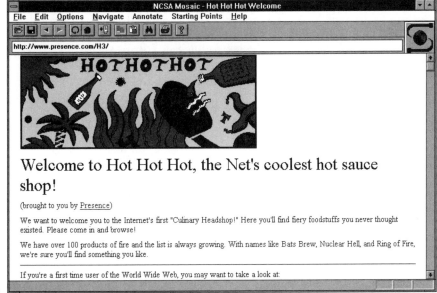

File   Edit   Options   Navigate   Annotate   Starting Points   Help

http://www.presence.com/H3/

Welcome to Hot Hot Hot, the Net's coolest hot sauce shop!

(brought to you by Presence)

We want to welcome you to the Internet's first "Culinary Headshop!" Here you'll find fiery foodstuffs you never thought existed. Please come in and browse!

We have over 100 products of fire and the list is always growing. With names like Bats Brew, Nuclear Hell, and Ring of Fire, we're sure you'll find something you like.

If you're a first time user of the World Wide Web, you may want to take a look at:

Figure 21-13:
If you're into spicy hot sauces, the Hot, Hot, Hot site is a cool place to visit.

an order button next to every item in the catalog, so you can immediately add items to your on-line order form.

HyperMedia Zines on the Net

http://www.acns.nwu.edu/ezines/

If you need help locating zines on the Net, you should connect with Hyper-Media Zines on the Net. The listing is broken down into Independent Publishers, Academic Publishers, and Commercial Publishers. Each zine includes a brief annotation. This site also includes links to related USENET newsgroups and other zine archives. The Independent Publishers link includes such zines as Bad Subjects, BLINK, Cyberkind, the Morpo Review, and PEZ.

International Teletimes

http://www.wimsey.com/teletimes.root/teletimes_home_page.html

Teletimes is a Canadian general-interest zine. It includes columns that are submitted by members of the Net community. The Cuisine column includes shared recipes and articles about food. An open column lets Net users submit short stories, poems, and creative essays. The News Room is a discussion forum presenting moderated debate. Teletimes also offers regular columns, such as Keepers of Light, a monthly piece by Kent Barret. This column covers specific photographers, photo galleries, and collections, with sample pictures. The wine enthusiast, Tom Davis, writes a wine column.

Internet Underground Music Archive

http://www.iuma.com/

The Internet Underground Music Archive (IUMA) presents music clips contributed by numerous unsigned bands. Figure 21-14 shows the home page for this great site. Started by Robert Lord and Jeff Patterson, students at the University of California at Santa Cruz, it's billed as the "Net's first free hi-fi music archive." IUMA applies the principles of free software to music distribution. From the main page, you can choose from three servers: East, West, or Europe. Once you're connected to a local server, you can choose from such topics as IUMA news and legal issues, or view the latest issue of the Seconds zine, which presents news and feature articles about obscure bands and virtual clubs. The home page also includes links to commercial record labels, such as Warner Brothers.

Figure 21-14: The Internet Underground Music Archive is chock-full of music.

J.P.'s Fishing Page

http://www.geo.mtu.edu/~jsuchosk/fish/fishpage

If you're hooked on flyfishing, the place to be is J.P.'s Fishing Page. This flyfishing site includes FAQs, fly information, pictures, links to newsgroups, and even home movies of flyfishing adventures. The Cool Stuff Nick's Doing link takes you to The Virtual FlyBox, which displays sample dry and wet flies and recipes for assembling flies. This site also includes fly hatch charts to pinpoint the best times for using specific flies. You'll also find links to flyfishing adventure sites in Arizona, New Mexico, Colorado, Northern California, and other places.

Jargon File

http://www.eps.mcgill.ca/jargon/jargon.html

As you spend time on the Web, you're undoubtedly going to bump into some hacker lingo that leaves you scratching your head. For help deciphering techno-slang, you should check out the Jargon File. The Jargon File is a comprehensive compendium of hacker slang in the public domain. This site does more than simply list definitions; it sheds light on many aspects of hacker tradition, folklore, and humor.

Jimmy Buffett

http://www.ils.nwu.edu/~april/buffett/buffett.html

The Jimmy Buffett home page shown in Figure 21-15 is a great place to get into some Caribbean Soul. This site gets you in the mood for kicking back and mixing some large tropical drinks. The Great Lyrics Compilation links serve up lots of Buffett's lyrics from all of his albums, including such hits as *Boats, Beaches, Bars, Ballads*; *Changes in Latitudes, Changes in Attitudes*; and *The Last Mango in Paris*. The North American Parrot Head Clubs link lists the cities, contact names, and phone numbers for Buffett fan clubs. The Images and Sounds links provide huge collections of files, including album covers and concert pictures, sound clips, and other imagery. You can get tour date information, read the *Coconut Modem* newsletter, and find an extensive collection of recipes for tropical drinks and key lime pie.

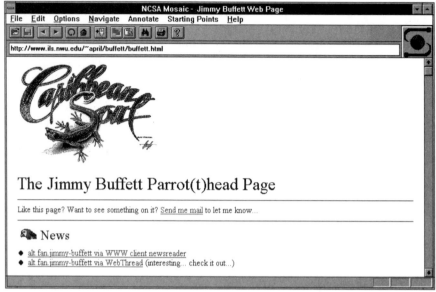

Figure 21-15:
The Jimmy
Buffett Web
page puts
you in a
Changes in
Latitudes,
Changes in
Attitudes
frame of
mind.

Justin's Links from the Underground

http://raptor.sccs.swarthmore.edu:80/jahall/index.html

Justin's Links from the Underground lives up to its motto, "when the going gets weird, the weird turn pro." This site includes such attractions as Web Worship, Spirituality, Mel's Godzilla Page, Nifty Net Nuggets, Top 50 Horney Geeks, and the Profanity and Insult Server. This alternative Web site lacks any socially redeeming qualities except pure entertainment.

Kaleidospace

http://kspace.com/

Kaleidospace is a virtual art gallery that promotes and sells the works of artists who would otherwise have difficulty reaching a mass audience. To showcase their work on Kaleidospace, artists pay a flat fee of about $50 per month. The Kaleidospace site is open to works from many types of artists, including graphic artists in traditional as well as electronic media, musicians, CD-ROM authors, writers, animators, filmmakers, artisans, and performers. Kaleidospace also promotes companies supplying resources for artists, such as film clips, sound patches, multimedia production software, and CD-ROM archives.

The Late Show with David Letterman

http://bingen.cs.csbsju.edu/letterman.html

Now you have a source for answers to all your questions about David Letterman and the Late Show. The number-one attraction of this site is its archive of the famous Top Ten lists, which you can view or download for each year dating back to 1987. Numerous picture files of Dave and Paul, and shots from selected vignettes are available in JPEG format. This site also includes links to sound clips, an FAQ, and the alt.fan.letterman newsgroup. You can also get the latest on Dave's upcoming guests.

Le WebLouvre

http://mistral.enst.fr:80/~pioch/louvre

Le WebLouvre deservedly won the Best of the Web '94 award for Best Use of Multiple Media. It has no official connection with the Louvre museum in Paris, but this French Web site contains a history of the Louvre and other French museums. The heart of this virtual museum is the Famous Paintings exhibition. Artworks are organized in three categories: Baroque (1600-1790), Revolution and Restoration (1740-1860), and Impressionism to Abstract Art (1860-1960). A glossary link defines painting styles, such as Baroque, Cubism, Dada, Expressionism, and Futurism. There's also an index of artists. This site is the work of Nicolas Pioch, who has become somewhat of a celebrity on the Net. For a bio of Nicolas, click the Nicolas Pioch icon at the bottom of each page.

Links in the Neighborhood

http://www.galcit.caltech.edu/~joe/links.html

From the co-creator of the Asylum, Madam Furry's Music Server, and Barney's Page, comes the Links in the Neighborhood Web site. This off-the-wall humor site includes the Top Ten Nancy Kerrigan Complaints about Disney World, Barney Meets the Gestapo, Mickey's mailbox, Disney Dollars, and The Madman Loose in Disney Land.

Literary Kicks

http://www.charm.net/~brooklyn/LitKicks.html

The Literary Kicks site is devoted to Beat writers, including Jack Kerouac, Allen Ginsberg, Neal Cassady, William S. Burroughs, and Gary Synder. This site includes information on films about Beats, films by Beats, and films based on Beat or Beat-related novels. The Recent Beat News link includes interesting Beat news and rumors.

Lonely Planet Books

http://nearnet.gnn.com:80/gnn/bus/lp/index.html

Lonely Planet Publications is the leading publisher of guidebooks for the independent traveler. LP guides and phrase books are travelers' bibles that are used by millions of global trekkers. The on-line Planet Talk newsletter includes field notes from travel book authors. The site also includes the Lonely Planet Story, a Book Sampler of the week, Mexico Guides, and Ordering Information.

The Marshmallow Peanut Circus

http://www.circus.com:80/

An eclectic source of fun and games, the Marshmallow Peanut Circus is an on-line extension of a geekhouse located in Santa Cruz, California. As you might have guessed, a geekhouse is a domicile for computer geeks. This house is painted screaming orange, and its residents occasionally announce parties at their Marshmallow Peanut Circus site. This site provides personal profiles of its inhabitants, including budda, carolee, and others. This geek site also lists present and past geekhouses, and provides all kinds of random links to other Net resources of interest.

Mother Jones

http://mojones.com/motherjones.html

Mother Jones is a magazine of investigative reporting. Like its paper-based counterpart, the objective of the on-line Mother Jones zine is to inspire action toward positive social change. The Mother Jones Web site is shown in Figure 21-16. Mother Jones supports the strong and growing Net activist network by acting as a catalyst for information about important issues. Readers' input, other relevant Net resources, and articles from *Mother Jones* magazine come together at this site. The link to Mother Jones Interactive Kiosks also presents information about non-profit organizations.

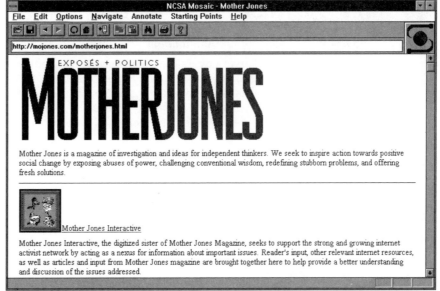

The Museum of Paleontology

http://ucmp1.berkeley.edu/museum.html

The University of California-Berkeley Museum of Paleontology server is an interactive natural history museum. At this site, you'll learn about phylogeny (evolutionary patterns), geological eras, and dinosaurs. Arrow buttons and scrolling menus at the bottom of each page let you quickly move to other parts of the museum. If the museum exhibits don't satisfy your thirst for pale-ontological knowledge, a searchable index lets you locate research papers for more information. The Museum of Paleontology was created by graduate students at the University of California, Berkeley.

Mystery Science Theater 3000

http://128.194.15.32/~dml601a/mst3k/mst3k.html

Mystery Science Theater 3000 is a popular TV cult show in which Joel Hodges and two robots named Crow and Servo make wisecracks while watching B-grade movies. This site provides links to video files, MST3K newsletters, program schedules, pictures, and sound files. The World Wide Web Sites link displays a page of other MST3K sites on the Net.

The Opera Schedule Server

http://www.fsz.bme.hu/opera/main.html

The Opera Schedule Server covers the opera scene on a global scale. It includes a database of programs offered by opera companies around the world, as well as information on opera houses. You can search the database by city, artist, title, or composer. A matrix of cities and dates lets you check out what's happening in opera for a given city and date.

OTIS

http://sunsite.unc.edu:80/otis/otis.html

OTIS is an acronym for Operative Term Is Simulate, which is an art community on the Net. Figure 21-17 shows the OTIS home page. OTIS has sponsored a number of collaborative projects under the flag of SYNERGY, and has set up e-mail forums for Net art discussions. A good example of a SYNERGY project was REVOLT. One person would create an image, another would manipulate the image, and a third person would finish the image. Probably the most famous SYNERGY project is ARCANA, in which Net artists collaboratively designed a deck of Tarot cards. Anyone can submit art to the OTIS project. Each artist has a page that includes everything from the artist's name to a full

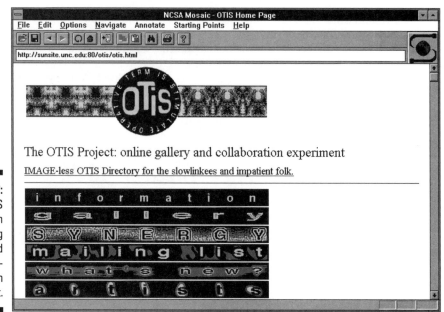

Figure 21-17:
The OTIS site is an interesting Net-based art collaboration project.

multimedia biography. The OTIS Web site has a related anonymous FTP site that contains numerous images and several of the collaborative projects in file form.

Over Coffee

http://www.infonet.net/showcase/coffee/

Over Coffee is a site for java devotees. The Coffee Reference Desk link overflows with cool links to coffee-related topics, including A Traveler's Guide to Coffee Houses, The Coffee Recipe Collection, Glossary of Coffee Terminology, and Coffee Trivia and Factoids. The Coffee Types and Varieties link provides information on the multitude of different coffees. For coffee shop owners and other coffee retailers, the Resources for Coffee Professionals link provides such information as *Coffee Talk Magazine* and wholesale coffee equipment resources. The Other Ports of Call link lists an extensive collection of java-related sites on the Net, including such notables as the Caffeine Homepage, Rothko: Queen Of Caffeine, Cyber Cafe Guide, and Mothercity Coffee.

QuarkWeb Nodes

http://alfred1.u.washington.edu:8080/~roland/quarkweb/quarkweb.html

QuarkWeb is a site that links unique, fun, and bizarre Web pages. QuarkWeb sites celebrate the fact that they are part of the exclusive network of nodes. Each node operates independently, so each site adds its own odd charm to the QuarkWeb. To qualify as QuarkWeb material, a site must offer something beyond the run-of-the-mill home page. Some of the sites in this realm are The Asylum, Schizophrenia Nervosa, The Dysfunctional Family Circus, and SPRAXLOID: Spraxlo's Illusions & Dreams.

Ranjit's HTTP playground

http://oz.sas.upenn.edu/

Ranjit's HTTP playground is loaded with an eclectic collection of links. Ranjit has a definite bent toward the realm of digital art. Check out the Playground Gallery Art link and the Everyone Loves a Hotlist link. The Tendrils of the Web link isn't always up to date, but it does include some interesting links. Many of the links on the main page point to useless, yet fun information. For example, Ranjit's lunch server lists what Ranjit had for lunch, as well as the Kinder Surprise Eggs, which includes pictures and descriptions of "the coolest candy in the universe."

Rei's Home Page

http://www.mit.edu:8001/afs/athena.mit.edu/user/r/e/rei/WWW/home.html

Rei's Home Page, which is shown in Figure 21-18, has links to anything that catches Rei's fancy. These links include his personal collection of fantasy images, art, bird images, and pet bird info, manga and anime stuff, yummy recipes, viola jokes, self defense, and an entrance to CyberMUD (Rei's random text adventure game). There are also links to some very popular Web sites, such as Cool Stuff on the Web, beer ratings, and Thomas Ho's list of Commercial Sites on the Web.

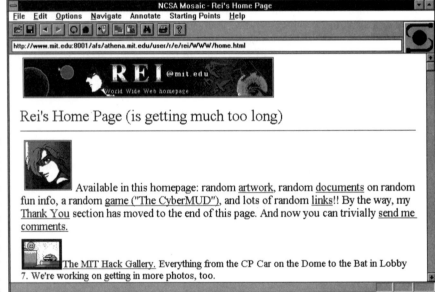

Figure 21-18:
Rei's Home
Page lets
you take a
random
walk
through a
huge collec-
tion of links.

RNN Home Page

http://www.pencom.com/rru.html

RNN stands for Roadkills-R-Us News Network. Not for the squeamish, this site bills itself as an Internet-based DisInformation Center. The RNN page includes such strange entries as roadkill recipes, links to the newsgroup talk.bizzare, the Obituary Page, and the Death of Rock 'n' Roll.

Rolling Stones

http://www.stones.com

Who says you can't teach old dogs new tricks? The Rolling Stones Web site projects the Stones into cyberspace. This site delivers all kinds of data and visuals on those popular, aging rockers, including their latest VooDoo Lounge tour. The site is filled with album covers, pictures of the boys in the band, interviews, and more.

ROUTE 66

http://www.cs.kuleuven.ac.be:80/~swa/route66/main.html

With an unfolding story about getting your kicks, the author of the Route 66 site is trying to relive the adventure of driving from Chicago to Santa Monica (Los Angeles), following as close as possible the remains of the historic Route 66. This site presents Route 66 factoids — for example, it's 2,448 miles long, crosses eight states, and officially opened in 1926. This site lists various Route 66 roadside attractions, organizations, and reference books. Some of the books referenced at this site include *Route 66: The Mother Road*, by Michael Wallis; *Route 66 Across New Mexico: A Wanderer's Guide*, by Jill Schneider; *Route 66 Postcards: Greetings from the Mother Road!*, by Michael and Suzanne Wallis; *Route 66 Travelers Guide*, by Tom Snyder; and the *Route 66 Cookbook*, by Marian Clark. This site also includes the lyrics to the Bobby Troupe song, "Get Your Kicks on Route 66."

Say Server

http://www_tios.cs.utwente.nl/say/

The Say Server won an honorable mention in the Technical Merit category in the Best of the Web awards. If you have a sound card, check out this unique, interactive sound site. Say Server lets you type text into a form and the server plays back the results on your computer.

Science Fiction Resource Guide

ftp://gandalf.rutgers.edu/pub/sfl/sf-resource.guide.html

A GNN Best of the Net award winner, the SFR Guide contains a mind-boggling amount of information on science fiction literature, film, TV, and criticism. The SFR site also includes long lists of links to bibliographies, sci-fi film and TV show sites, FAQs, sci-fi critical journals, conventions and awards, and other sci-fi archives on the Web.

Seinfeld Page

http://www.ifi.uio.no/~rubens/seinfeld/

The Seinfeld Page includes scripts, sound bites, and pictures grouped by episode or character for the popular Seinfeld sitcom. The Seinfeld index page shown in Figure 21-19 includes links to the alt.tv.seinfeld newsgroup, an episode guide, and links to other sites with Seinfeld stuff. Additional resources at this site include a Seinfeld FAQ, an episode guide, quotations, and an interview with Larry David, the creator of the show.

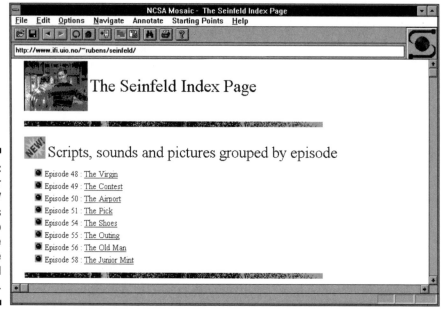

Figure 21-19:
The popular Seinfeld TV sitcom is beamed into cyberspace via the Seinfeld Web site.

Simon Gibbs' WWW Home Page

http://cui_www.unige.ch:80/OSG/Simon/

Simon Gibbs' home page is an image map that uses graphic symbols and words for links. The site has a techie bent, but non-techies also can find loads of interesting stuff. Clicking the Fonts link displays the Internet font browser, which lets you view hundreds of fonts on the Net. Clicking the Multimedia link displays a long list of multimedia information, such as FAQs, multimedia files, and links to other multimedia sites. Simon Gibbs' WWW Home Page is part of CUI, an interfaculty center for research and post-graduate teaching in Computer Science at the University of Geneva.

Snake Oil

http://fender.onramp.net/~analyst/snake/Snakeoil.html

The Snake Oil site skewers and roasts sanctimonious televangelists. The subtitle of this site is "Your Guide to Kooky Kontemporary Kristian Kulture." The site follows the exploits and lawsuits of such modern American evangelists as Robert Tilton and Benny Hinn and their accomplices. The grapevine link includes a collection of up-to-date hypermedia articles and anecdotes that expose pocketbook evangelists and their swindling crusades. Snake Oil is also available in hard copy by subscription.

Spiritual Consciousness on WWW

http://zeta.cs.adfa.oz.au/Spirit.html

Reach for enlightenment at the Spiritual Consciousness on WWW site, which is shown in Figure 21-20. This site offers the ultimate compendium of new age spiritualism. This site's links let you visit pages exploring astrology, alternative healing (Chakras and reflex zones), channeling and other out-of-body experiences, UFOs, alien cultures, yoga, and other spiritual topics. There are also links to journals and zines, mailing lists, and images, movies, and music that relate to new age spirituality and consciousness. This site also lets you perform a keyword search to find specific information.

Figure 21-20: The Spiritual Consciousness on WWW site is a great gateway to the spiritual side of the Net.

The Sports Information Server

http://www.mit.edu:8001/services/sis/sports.html

The Sports Information Server won the award for Best Entertainment site in
the Best of the Web awards. Sports fans can get the latest scoop on their
favorite teams and sports. The WWW Sports Information Server provides
links to the Professional Basketball, Professional Football, and Professional
Baseball servers. Get the latest scores and game schedules, the league stand-
ings as of the most recent games, and scores on all the season's games, with
statistics for every player. There are also links to the history of such awards
as Rookie of the Year and Most Valuable Player.

Sports Schedules as You Like 'Em

http://www.cs.rochester.edu/u/ferguson/schedules/

The sports schedule program provides a listing of schedules in either text or
calendar format. To get a schedule, choose the criteria for the schedule. For
example, you can choose to display schedules for all games, home games,
away games, or interdivision games. You can choose to display schedules for
any team or for all the teams in the National Hockey League, American
Hockey League, Major League Baseball, National Football League, Canadian
Football League, National Basketball Association, and the Australian Football
League. The site also includes a link to the source distribution list used by
the sports schedule program.

Star Trek

http://www.cosy.sbg.ac.at/rec/startrek/index.html

Star Trek travels the Net at warp speed. From the Star Trek site, you can
beam yourself down to the Star Trek newsgroup rec.arts.startrek.misc or
beam up to Star Trek pictures, sounds, quotations, stories, and parodies.
Nestled away at this site are episode guides, guides to Star Trek books,
comics, and much more. There are other diversionary links, such as how to
speak Klingonaase or play the Netrek game.

Star Trek: The Next Generation

http://www.ugcs.caltech.edu/~werdna/sttng/

Even the most demanding trekkie will be satisfied by the Star Trek: The Next Generation site. This impressive Web site includes an exhaustive hypermedia listing of episodes, with links to detailed summaries of every episode of Star Trek: The Next Generation. The cast link is exceptionally well done, with links specially tailored to each actor, such as the cast member's favorite episode and roles played. The Miscellaneous link presents links to press releases, pictures, animations, Star Trek FAQs, and an archive of postings to the rec.arts.startrek.info newsgroup. The site also includes a search facility.

Strange Interactions

http://amanda.physics.wisc.edu/show.html

Strange Interactions is a "Twilight Zone" art show created by John E. Jacobsen. John writes, "My work is an attempt to give a concrete aspect to the subconscious." The images at this site are surreal and ambiguous in meaning. They're typically figures — human or otherwise — faces, landscape elements, monolithic buildings, or technological constructions. John is a physicist/programmer who manages to sneak in time to create his dream-like art. You can click the thumbnails to view the JPEG files in 24-bit color, provided you have a display adapter that can handle them.

Tarot Reading

http://cad.ucla.edu:80/repository/useful/tarot.html

Tarot cards are a set of cards bearing allegorical representations that are used in fortune telling. The Tarot Reading site offers two readings. One is a short, personalized reading based on the current date, as shown in Figure 21-21. The other reading is called the Full Keltic Tarot reading. Clicking the Full Keltic Tarot reading link brings you to a Web page that you use to define who you are. A Keltic reading requires that the querent (that's you) choose a card from the minor arcana to represent yourself. You choose the card that most closely matches you, and you click it. The Tarot reader deals your cards for the current day, and tells you what they mean.

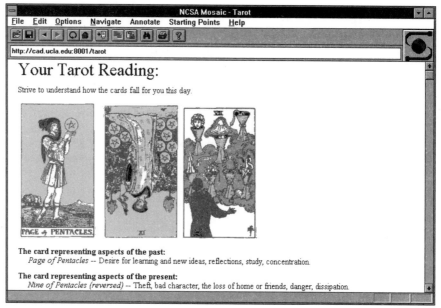

Figure 21-21:
The Tarot
Web site
helps you
keep
abreast of
future
develop-
ments.

Time, Inc.

http://www.timeinc.com/

The Time, Inc. site offers on-line versions of selected magazines and books from Time-Warner. You can check out the on-line version of *Time*, *Entertainment Weekly*, and *Vibe* magazines. *Time* magazine provides an on-line version of the current week's edition, as well as covers and tables of contents of back issues. The front page is the only graphic we found; most of the articles are text only. *Vibe* is a cool magazine of urban music, with sounds, forms, articles, and image map covers from previous issues. This site also includes a link to the Virtual Garden, which Time-Warner touts as being "the most comprehensive collection of consumer information on gardening available on-line."

Travels with Samantha

http://martigny.ai.mit.edu:80/samantha/travels-with-samantha.html

Travels with Samantha is a good example of storytelling on the Web. Written by Philip Greenspun, this book chronicles a summer he spent seeing North America. It promises, "You'll come face to face with examples of the stunning ethnic, scenic, and cultural richness of the continent." Philip takes you through the language war in Montreal, bored youths in the Midwest, and North Dakota Harley riders. This is a great travel story, complete with slides.

Trojan Room Coffee Machine

http://www.cl.cam.ac.uk/coffee/coffee.html

Thanks to the Trojan Room Coffee Machine site, you can check the status of a coffee pot located at the University of Cambridge in England. A special camera is trained on the pot, taking a picture every second. The pictures are digitized and made available to the server for your viewing. This is a more sophisticated upgrade of the nerd toy called the Internet Coke Machine, which lets you check the status of stock in a soda vending machine.

The Ultimate Band List

http://american.recordings.com/wwwofmusic/ubl.html

The Ultimate Band List site shown in Figure 21-22 contains over 1,000 links to almost 300 bands. This is one of the best sites for keeping up with music on the Net. It lists the bands by name, genre, or by resource. Bands are broken down into the following categories: Pop/Rock/Alternative, Metal/Hard,

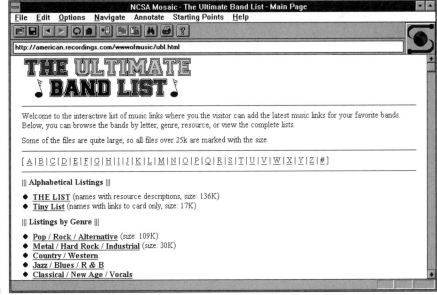

Figure 21-22:
The Ulti-
mate Band
List is a
gateway to
hundreds of
virtual band
sites on
the Net.

Rock/Industrial, Country/Western, Jazz/Blues/R&B, Classical/New Age/Vocals, and Dance/Techno/Rap. The Ultimate Band List also includes Band Updates.

The Ultimate TV List

http://www.galcit.caltech.edu/~ta/tv/utl.html

The Ultimate TV List site contains 225 links (mostly to Web pages) for more than 70 TV shows. It provides a listing of TV programs by name, genre, and resource type. The alphabetical list includes the name of the show and information about the show. The New Editions page lists new TV program links.

URoulette

http://kuhttp.cc.ukans.edu/cwis/organizations/kucia/uroulett/uroulette.html

Step right up and click on the floating roulette wheel, and you'll end up on a randomly selected Web page. This unique and often-linked site comes from Kansas University Campus Internet Association. Because the site selection is random, it's possible that the server or URL will not exist, which will result in a "Not found" error message. If you get a blank page, try choosing the Reload command.

The USENET Cookbook

http://alfred1.u.washington.edu:8080/cgi-bin/cookbook

The USENET Cookbook includes hundreds of recipes gleaned from the USENET newsgroup alt.gourmand. These recipes have been edited and organized into a huge collection of links, ranging from African Vegetable Stew to Zucchini Shreds with Ginger. Clicking a recipe link displays a recipe in text form, which you can print out using Mosaic. Bon appétit!

Verbiage

http://siva.cshl.org/~boutell/verbiage/index.html

Published bimonthly and edited by Thomas Boutell, *Verbiage* is a showcase for short fiction. *Verbiage* pays $10 for each published piece. Articles are between 100 words and 3,000 words in length. The zine encourages readers to comment on-line about the stories.

Waxweb

http://bug.village.virginia.edu/

Waxweb is the impressive hypermedia version of David Blair's film, "Wax or the Discovery of Television among the Bees." It consists of more than 900 pages of hypertext. Hypermedia portions of the document include the entire film embedded as 1,500 color stills, 500 MPEG video clips, and 2,000 AIFF audio clips, including the soundtrack in English, French, German, and Japanese. Waxweb also includes a unique authoring interface that allows users to make immediate, publicly visible hypermedia links to the main document.

Web Personals

http://www.netmedia.com/date/personals.html

The Web Personals site shown in Figure 21-23 is the best of the virtual matchmaking sites. It includes personal ads for all kinds of relationships, including Men Seeking Women, Women Seeking Men, Men Seeking Men, Women Seeking Women, Activity Partners, and Misc Romance. Like all dating services on the Net, the number of male ads overwhelms the number of female ads, which reflects the current demographics of the Web. You can even submit your own personal ad via an on-line form. Responses are sent to an e-mail address with a code for the ad. The message is then forwarded by the service.

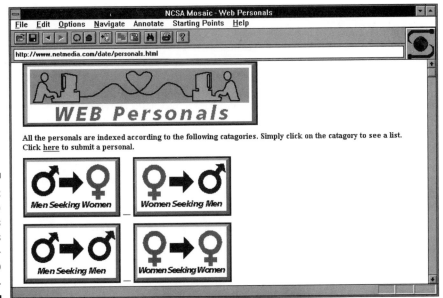

Figure 21-23:
The Web Personals site brings match-making to cyberspace.

The Web's Edge

http://kzsu.stanford.edu/uwi.html

The Web's Edge is not just an art and poetry site, it's also filled with links to odd stuff found inside and outside the computer world. One of the main attractions that comes out of the Web's Edge is Complement, a collection of strange art ranging from Dada/Fluxus-inspired art to small robotic art. The art used at this site is gathered at Noise-a-palooza, a noise and experimental music festival held in Ann Arbor, Michigan.

WebStars

http://guinan.gsfc.nasa.gov/WEBSTARS.html

You'll find everything you ever wanted to know about astronomy and astrophysics at WebStars. A huge image map includes links to a wide range of mostly scientific topics, including astronomy and astrophysics, cyberspace, data formats, virtual reality, and the Space Science Web Group (SSWG). NASA's High Energy Astrophysics Science Archive Research Center (HEASARC) sponsors the WebStars site.

WebWorld

http://sailfish.peregrine.com/ww/welcome.html

WebWorld is a cyberworld constructed entirely by the Net community. It contains over 100,000 objects on a hyperlink-filled globe. Click anywhere on the planet image and you're beamed down to that location. The world is shown in a 3-D perspective. At the top of your screen, there's a legend indicating where you are. To move around, click the direction labels or click an image. If you click a link, you're transported to wherever the link points. You can also click on a pyramid-shaped container. Containers might contain an entire virtual city or an area devoted to a specific subject. Clicking a container takes you inside it. Anyone can create structures that are linked to a home page. To begin a construction project, click the "Build" label at the bottom of the screen. Anything you build in WebWorld is yours to change.

Welcome to the White House

http://www.whitehouse.gov

The White House has gone interactive with the electronic citizens handbook shown in Figure 21-24. This site is designed to make government information

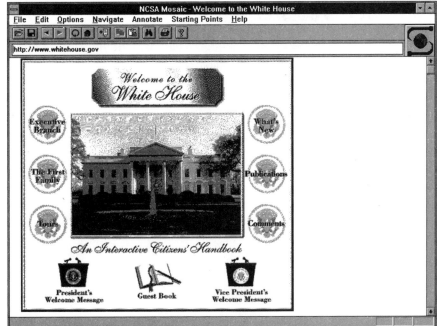

Figure 21-24:
You can pay
a virtual
visit to the
White
House via
the Wel-
come to the
White
House Web
site.

more accessible to citizens across the country. It includes detailed information about cabinet-level and independent agencies, information about the
President and Vice President and their families, and a subject-searchable
index of federal information. The White House site also provides a virtual
tour of the White House.

The WELL

http://www.well.com/

The WELL (Whole Earth 'Lectronic Link) has it roots firmly planted in cyberspace from its earliest days. Known for its conferences in the olden days of
ASCII text and mainframes, this group has gone on to the Web. The WELL is
divided into over 250 public and private discussion groups ranging from
cooking to virtual reality. This site tells you about many of these conferences
and how to get involved. The WELL community is made up of a diverse group
of professionals, artists, writers, lawyers, programmers, entrepreneurs, musi-
cians, and others. The Community page has some cool links set up by the
people of the WELL community.

Wine Home Page

http://augustus.csscr.washington.edu/personal/bigstar-mosaic/wine.html

The Wine Home Page is for wine lovers. As shown in Figure 21-25, it's a cool site with lots to do and view. The site includes an experimental, interactive Virtual Tasting Room link that lets you add tasting notes using forms. You can add your thoughts on wines, and view the thoughts of others. The Wine Home Page includes an archive of assorted tastings, tasting notes, wine reviews, and winery tasting room reviews. The Wine Net Newsletter includes extensive wine reviews from all over the globe. The Wine Home Page also includes links to other wine resources on the Net.

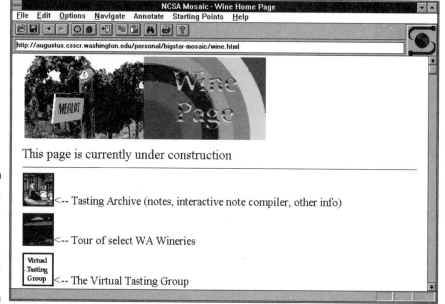

Figure 21-25:
The Wine
Home Page
gives you
a virtual
tasting of
wines.

WIRED/Roadside America Hypertour '94

http://www.wired.com:80/Hotwired/roadside/index.html

WIRED/Roadside America Hypertour '94 is a travel journal sponsored by *Wired* magazine. This cross-country, 7-day journey from New York to Los Angeles takes you to more than 50 weird places along the way. Text, photos, and QuickTime movies of sites augment this virtual trip across the U.S. The *Wired* crew visits such sites as the replica bomb crater in Boise City, Oklahoma, the stubby Stonehenge of Rolla, Missouri, and Phillipi, West Virginia's Mummies of the Insane.

WNUR-FM Jazz Information Server

http://www.acns.nwu.edu/jazz/

The WNUR-FM Jazz Information Server is packed with jazz information and links. You can search a database of contents or titles. You'll also find information on artists, jazz media info, links to other jazz resources, jazz photography, and more. Figure 21-26 shows the WNUR-FM Jazz Information Server home page.

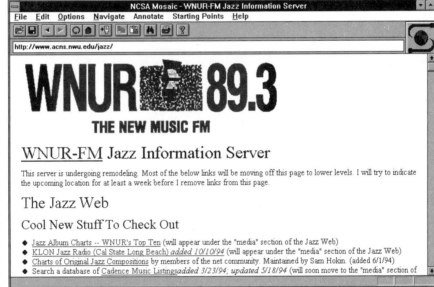

Figure 21-26: The WNUR-FM Jazz Information Server is a one-stop source for jazz resources on the Net.

Xerox PARC Map Viewer

http://pubweb.parc.xerox.com/map

The Xerox PARC Map Viewer site lets you use a point-and-click interface to view maps of the world. MapViewer is an interactive application that renders a map based on user input. Figure 21-27 shows the home page of this interactive site. Click a region, and MapViewer zooms in on it. You can also use a geographic name server to find a particular location by name. By entering the

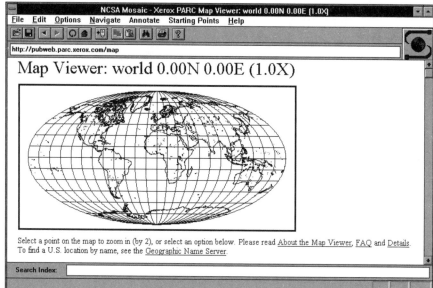

Figure 21-27:
The Xerox
PARC Map
Viewer site
lets you
interactively
navigate the
world via
maps.

name of a location, you can find its population and its location. The Geographic Name Server is located at the University of Buffalo. To find the map coordinates you're looking for, you need to click the hyperlink to the U.S. Geographic Name Server. Enter the city and state in the Search box, and the server displays the map coordinates for the location you want to view. The coordinates are hyperlinked. If you click them, you're returned to the MapViewer, and your location is plotted on the map.

The Zappa Page

http://carol.fwi.uva.nl/~heederik/zappa/

The St. Alphonzo's Pancake Homepage provides a complete discography of Frank Zappa and the Mothers of Invention. This site includes links to lyrics, sound bites, song and album lists, and album cover art from Freak Out! to the Yellow Shark. Clicking an album cover gives you the corresponding page from the discography. Interviews, articles, 1988 tour information, and information on other Zappa projects are all here.

Zarf's List of Interactive Games on the Web

http://www.cs.cmu.edu:8001/afs/cmu.edu/user/zarf/www/games.html

This is another hot game listing site. It divides the sites into two groups: Interactive Games and Interactive Toys. A handy icon system tells you what's needed to interact with a site. For example, if a site uses forms, a form icon is displayed next to the hyperlink for that site.

Glossary

analog line Voice-grade telecommunications line. The lowest level in the telecommunications food chain, analog lines require the use of modems for PC communications.

anchors Text or image links in a Web document that point to another resource.

annotations Personal or group messages that are attached to Web documents using Mosaic. When you or a member of a group view the Web document, these notes appear at the bottom of the document.

anonymous FTP A public FTP file archive, which can be accessed by any Net user. The term *anonymous* refers to the generic account username that any user can enter to log-in to an FTP server.

Archie A Net-based service that lets you locate files that are available for download-

The 5th Wave
Re´al Pro·gram·mers   By Rich Tennant

ELEVATOR CAPACITY
2100 LBS.

Real Programmers love to talk "computer-eze" while ordinary citizens are listening.

ing via FTP. Mosaic supports the Archie service.

articles Messages posted to network newsgroups. Most newsreaders keep messages together to provide a continuous thread of discussion. You can read articles using Mosaic.

ASCII Standard character set supported by most computer systems. ASCII stands for American Standard Code for Information Interchange.

AU Sound file format developed by Sun Microsystems. Mosaic supports the AU sound format by default.

AUI Auxiliary Unit Interface. A multiple-pin connector on an Ethernet card. Many external ISDN devices connect to an Ethernet card using this connector.

authentication A security feature that allows access to information on an individual basis.

bandwidth The amount of data that can flow through a channel. The higher the bandwidth, the more data that can travel at one time.

B-channels Bearer channels. The two channels within an ISDN line that can each handle up to 64 Kbps of data, for a combined capacity of 128 Kbps.

bearer services The communications capability to carry speech and any digital data that is handled by B-channels.

binary file A non-ASCII file, such as a program, video, or sound file.

bps Bits per second. The unit of measurement for data transmission speed over a telecommunications line.

BRI Basic Rate Interface. The term used to describe the three channels that make up an ISDN line: two B-channels (bearer channels) and one D-channel (data channel), which provides the call-control functions.

browser Any Web client program that lets you view HTML documents.

cache A storage area in your computer's memory in which data is stored for faster retrieval. By default, Mosaic caches the last two documents you viewed.

CERN (European Laboratory for Particle Physics) The Swiss organization that developed the World-Wide Web.

client Any computer remotely connected to a host computer, or any software program used to connect to a host version of the program. For example, Mosaic is the client program that connects to Web server software.

client-server computing The fundamental relationship of computers on the Net (or any network) in which one computer acts as the client by remotely connecting to another computer that acts as a server (also called a host).

CO Central Office. The central office location, or exchange, where communications switches provide connections to the telecommunications network.

compression The compacting of data to save storage space and reduce the time it takes to transfer files. A variety of compression formats and programs are available.

CSLIP A compressed version of SLIP that allows for faster transfer of information.

cyberspace A popular term coined by William Gibson in his book *Neuromancer*, it refers to the digital world of any network, but is commonly used to refer to the Net.

data traffic The amount of information traversing a network. On the Net, it refers to the number of TCP/IP packets moving through the network. Data moves slower as the traffic on a network or server increases.

dial-up IP account The entry level of Internet Protocol accounts. This low-cost type of account lets computer users dial up to a service provider's computer using a modem and a standard telephone line.

digital line A telecommunications line that transmits data in digital format, which is also the way computers handle data. A digital line allows high-speed data transmission.

DNS Domain Name System. The Internet addressing system that connects a domain name to a specified numeric IP address. A domain name is portable. In other words, it can stay the same even if a system's IP address changes.

domain Highest subdivision of the Net; usually by country or type of organization, such as .edu for education, or .com for commercial.

domain name A complete address, including the domain and the unique name of the organization — for example, bookware.com.

DSU/CSU Data Service Unit/Channel Service Unit. The equivalent of a digital modem, this device allows a computer to communicate via digital lines.

dynamic IP addressing An IP addressing scheme used by service providers for dial-up accounts. When users dial into the service provider to connect to the Net, they are assigned a random IP address for the current session.

e-journal An electronic publication, typically found in academic circles.

e-mail Electronic mail. A network service that enables users to send and receive messages. Communicating via e-mail is the number-one use of the Net.

e-zine A magazine published in electronic form.

encryption The scrambling of a message or file to make it unreadable except by the intended receiver, who unscrambles it.

Ethernet A networking standard developed by Xerox with Intel and DEC (Digital Equipment Corporation). Ethernet is capable of connecting as many as 1,024 workstations and transmitting data at a maximum speed of 10 Mbps.

FAQ Frequently Asked Questions. A text file that provides answers to questions that users may have about a particular topic, service, or product.

firewall A system that protects an organization's computer system from external access, such as through the Net.

flame An inflammatory remark or message, usually associated with e-mail or an article posted to a newsgroup.

freeware Software that you can use and distribute without charge.

FTP File Transfer Protocol. The medium that allows the transferring of files between computers on the Net using an FTP program or via Mosaic.

GIF Graphic Interchange Format. A graphics file format that originated with the CompuServe network. Mosaic supports the use of GIF files for inline images.

Gopher A popular protocol that lets clients retrieve Net resources. The Gopher protocol lets you access files and directories across the Net. A Gopher client can search for and retrieve information from the hundreds and hundreds of Gopher servers on the Net, thereby giving you a seamless view of the distributed information. You can access a Gopher server using Mosaic.

GUI Graphical User Interface. A computer interface based on graphical symbols rather than text. Microsoft Windows and Mosaic are examples of GUI environments.

hit A match to the criteria you've specified in a database search. You can search databases at numerous Web sites. If anything matches your query, it's a hit.

home page The first page of a Web site, and the starting point for navigating the Web using Mosaic.

host A computer that acts as a server. Users at remote computers (that is, client computers) are allowed to access information that's stored on the server, or host computer.

hotlists Lists of frequently accessed Web site document names and URLs.

HTML HyperText Markup Language. The scripting language used to create Web documents. HTML commands specify the layout of a document as it appears on a Web client.

HTML document A text-based document containing the HTML commands that tell Mosaic (and other Web browsers) how to create the Web document on the user's screen. An HTML document is also called a source document.

HTML editor A specialized text editor that simplifies the creation of Web documents using HTML commands. For example, with a Windows HTML editor, you add HTML commands to selected text by clicking buttons or choosing menu items.

HTML+ The newest version of the HTML scripting language. HTML+ includes a number of enhancements to HTML.

HTTP The HyperText Transport Protocol. The protocol that provides the foundation for communications between Mosaic and the Web.

hyperlinks Links within Web documents that can take you to almost any resource on the Net. By default, these links appear in Mosaic as blue underlined text, or as a graphic with a blue border.

hypermedia Links to any type of media, including the written word, graphics, video, and sound. Hypermedia is the foundation of the Web.

hypertext A text document that contains links to other documents, and thus can be read in a non-linear fashion. Ted Nelson coined the term *hypertext* in 1965.

IEC Inter-Exchange Carrier. The telephone companies that provide long-distance communications between local telephone companies, including AT&T, MCI, and Sprint.

inline images Graphics that are part of a Web document. These picture files are usually in the GIF or X-BitMap format.

interactive Systems that respond to

instructions that are entered by a user in different forms, such as with a keyboard or mouse.

Internet address The combination of the IP numeric address and the domain name, in which the IP numeric address is translated into a text-based address — for example, 198.171.58.166 (the computer's version) might become JBANKSTON@BCI-ASSOC.COM.

Internet tool Any application used on the Net that supports one or more protocols. For example, users work with FTP by using an FTP client program that operates under the File Transfer Protocol to transfer files across the Net. For every protocol, there is a tool that works with it. Mosaic supports multiple protocols.

IP Internet Protocol. The protocol that provides a basis for the Net. The Internet Protocol allows data to travel in packets that can be routed across different networks before being reassembled at their final destination.

ISDN Integrated Services Digital Network. A new generation of digital telecommunications lines. ISDN lines includes two bearer channels which can each handle up to 64 Kbps, for a combined capacity of 128 Kbps.

JPEG Joint Photographic Experts Group. An industry group that has defined a compression scheme that reduces the size of image files by up to 20 times. JPEG-compressed image files typically end with the filename extension .jpg.

Kbps Kilobits per second. A measurement of the speed at which data is transmitted over telecommunication lines.

LAN Local-Area Network. A group of interconnected computers usually connected by less than 1,000 feet of cable. LANs make it possible for computers to share files and peripherals. PC LANs are usually Ethernet based.

leased line A digital telecommunications line that is leased from a service provider or telephone company. Leased lines deliver more bandwidth at a fixed monthly rate instead of a measured rate. For businesses connecting multiple users to the Internet through a LAN or for users whose connect time is more than several hours a day, a leased line is usually the most economical option.

LEC Local Exchange Carrier. Your local telephone company.

local The computer and application at your end of a connection. For example, you run Mosaic locally to make a connection to a remote Web server.

mail bombing The bombarding of an e-mail address with messages sent by an angry person or a group of people. Mail bombing floods an e-mail account to the point at which it becomes unmanageable. In some cases, mail bombing may overload the mail server.

MIME Multipurpose Internet Mail Extensions. A protocol that allows Mosaic (and other programs) to recognize different types of files and deal with them accordingly.

modem The piece of equipment that connects a computer to an analog telecommunications line. A modem translates digital data to analog (MOdulate) and back again (DEModulate).

monospaced font A typeface that produces characters of equal width.

Mosaic The de facto standard for Web client programs. Developed by NCSA (National Center for Supercomputing Applications), versions of Mosaic are available at no charge for Microsoft Windows, Macintosh, and X-Windows platforms. Commercial Web clients are becoming available.

MPEG Motion Picture Experts Group. An industry group that created the MPEG video file compression format. MPEG files usually end with the filename extension .mpg.

MUD Multi-User Dungeon. Fantasy game in which players take on different roles in different environments or worlds. Users typically telnet to a site to play MUDs. Web interfaces are being developed for a growing number of MUDs.

multitasking operating system Allows multiple people to use a computer system to perform multiple tasks at the same time. UNIX is the most popular multitasking operating system. Windows NT is a PC-based multitasking operating system.

NCSA National Center for Supercomputing Applications. The organization that developed the Mosaic client program for the World-Wide Web.

network news A UNIX-based (USENET) distributed messaging system with thousands of ongoing discussions, called newsgroups, covering every topic imaginable. People who subscribe to network news communicate using a messaging system similar to e-mail.

newsgroup A discussion forum in the network news system.

NFS Network File System. A UNIX system protocol developed by Sun Microsystems that lets you use files and directories stored on another computer as though they're on your local computer. Many Windows TCP/IP software vendors offer NFS versions of their products.

NNTP Network News Transport Protocol. The protocol used to distribute network news.

NT1 Network Terminator 1. A device responsible for the termination functions of ISDN on the user premises.

packet A block of data sent over a network. The packet includes the identities of the sending and receiving stations, error-control information, and a message. TCP/IP is a packet-based protocol.

PDF Portable Document Format. The file format for documents created using Adobe Acrobat. PDF documents allow users to share formatted documents across different platforms. To create a PDF document, you use Adobe Exchange to print an existing document to a file. The Acrobat Reader, which is available for free, lets users view a PDF document.

POP Point of Presence. The closest telephone access number for a network or telephone company. Your telecommunication charges are affected by your proximity to a POP.

post To send a message, called an article, to a network news newsgroup.

PostScript Adobe's proprietary page description language, which is designed to relay instructions about fonts and objects to a printer. PostScript is the de facto standard for desktop publishing.

POTS Plain-Old Telephone Service. Term used to describe standard voice-grade telephone lines.

PPP Point-to-Point Protocol. A protocol that allows a computer to use the TCP/IP protocol and to be connected directly to the Net using a standard voice telephone line and a high-speed modem. PPP is the new standard that is rapidly replacing SLIP.

PRI Primary Rate Interface. The ISDN interface designed for high-volume requirements. It consists of 23 B-channels and a single D-channel.

protocol A specification that describes the rules and procedures by which computers can communicate. Most Net tools are named after the protocols they use.

publishing The placing of information on a server to make it available to Net users.

QuickTime A real-time video and multimedia data format developed by Apple Computer. QuickTime files can include text, sound, and video, among other formats.

RBOC Regional Bell Operating Company. The seven regional telephone service providers formed by deregulation of AT&T. They are Ameritech, Bell Atlantic, Bell South, NYNEX, Pacific Bell, Southwestern Bell, and US West.

RJ-45 A modular jack that can hold up to four pairs of wires. It looks similar to an RJ-11 jack (which is used for standard voice lines), but it's larger. ISDN connections use RJ-45 jacks.

router A hardware device connected to a host on a LAN that acts as a gateway between different types of networks. For example, a router connects an Ethernet-based network to the TCP/IP-based Net. Data traffic routes from individual computers to the router, and then through the telecommunications line to the service provider's computer.

RTF Rich Text Format. A text file format that includes such formatting as bold, italic, and underlined text.

server A computer, also called a host, that can distribute services or resources to users at remote computers — that is, clients. A server is the combination of hardware and software that provides access to information that is requested by client computers.

service provider An organization that provides connections to the Net.

server service A business that rents space on a server. The server service manages all the technical details of keeping the server running and connected to the Net. You rent space to place your Web document on the server, where it is available to Mosaic (or other Web browser) users.

SGML Standard Generalized Markup Language. A set of formatting codes for creating documents. These codes define the components of documents, such as headers, tables, and so on. HTML is a subset of SGML.

shareware Software that is available to try for a limited time with no obligation. If you like the software and want to continue to use it, you send the author a fee to register the product. Registering your copy of the software usually gives you access to technical support, documentation, and, in many cases, additional features.

shell account A UNIX-based account on a service provider's computer. This type of account doesn't let you use Mosaic.

signature A standard sign-off used by people for e-mail and newsgroup posts, often contained in a file that is automatically appended to an outgoing mail message or network news post.

SLIP Serial Line Internet Protocol. A protocol that allows a computer to use the Internet Protocol with a standard voice-grade telephone line and a high-speed modem. SLIP is an older protocol that is being superseded by PPP.

SMTP Simple Mail Transfer Protocol. The standard Internet protocol for distributing e-mail.

source document A text-based document containing the HTML commands that tell Mosaic (and other Web browsers) how to create the Web document on the user's screen. A source document is also called an HTML document.

Switched 56 Digital service at 56 Kbps provided by local telephone companies and long-distance carriers.

syntax The rules that specify how to work with the commands that make up a programming language. You can think of syntax as the rules of grammar and punctuation for a programming language.

system administrator The person who is responsible for the smooth running of a network.

tags Formatting codes used in HTML documents. These tags indicate how the parts of a document will appear in Mosaic. For example, the tag <TITLE>*Document Title Text*</TITLE> defines the text it surrounds as the document's title, which is displayed in the title bar of the Mosaic window.

TCP/IP Transmission Control Protocol and Internet Protocol. The suite of networking protocols that let disparate types of computers communicate over the Net.

TCP/IP is the standard protocol for the Net.

TCP/IP stack The software that allows a computer to communicate via TCP/IP.

Telnet A terminal emulation protocol that allows users to log-on to a host computer from remote computers using a Telnet program.

terminal adapter An ISDN phone or a PC card that emulates the phone. It connects a non-ISDN terminal to an ISDN network.

TIFF Tagged Image File Format. A graphics file format developed by Aldus and Microsoft.

transceiver A device that transmits and receives signals.

upload To send a file to a server or another computer.

URL Uniform Resource Locator. An addressing scheme used to link resources on the Web. Using URLs, a Mosaic user can point to most resources on the Net.

UNIX A popular multi-user, multitasking operating system developed by AT&T. UNIX served as a foundation for the development of the Net and continues to be the operating system of choice for most servers. TCP/IP is built into UNIX.

V.32bis Currently the fastest standard modem protocol used by 9,600 bps and 14.4 Kbps modems. Most V.32bis modems support V.42 error correction and V.42bis data compression. V.42 and V.42bis are error correction and data compression standards used in data communications.

V.34 The emerging 28.8 Kbps standard for modems. While V.34 was under development, some modem manufacturers implemented the unratified standard and called it V.Fast.

viewer A program used for presenting graphics, audio, or movies in Mosaic. These programs don't come with Mosaic, but they can be downloaded and set up to work with Mosaic.

virtual storefront The establishment of a full-service, on-line storefront, including the publishing of sales materials and the capability for processing credit card transactions.

WAIS Wide-Area Information Servers. A powerful system for searching and retrieving information from databases scattered across the Net.

Web The commonly used term for the World-Wide Web. WWW and W3 are also common terms that refer to the World-Wide Web.

Web browser Software that lets a user access and view HTML documents. Mosaic is a Web browser.

Web document An HTML document as it appears in Mosaic.

Webmaster A system administrator for a World-Wide Web server.

Web spider Automated software that crawls through the links of the Web and sends back a list of all the links it has traversed.

WinSock A program that conforms to a set of standards called the Windows Socket API. The Windows Socket is a standard for implementing Windows software with a TCP/IP stack. In other words, a WinSock program controls the link between Windows software and a TCP/IP program.

World-Wide Web A hypermedia-based system for accessing Net resources. Commonly referred to as the Web, it lets users download files, listen to sounds, view video files, and jump to other documents or Net sites by using hypertext links. The Web also includes gateways to sites using other Internet protocols, such as Gopher and FTP.

XBM X-BitMap. A graphics file format for X-Windows (UNIX) systems.

Index

IDG BOOKS WORLDWIDE REGISTRATION CARD

RETURN THIS
REGISTRATION CARD
FOR FREE CATALOG

Title of this book: Mosaic For Dummies, Windows Edition

My overall rating of this book: ❑ Very good [1] ❑ Good [2] ❑ Satisfactory [3] ❑ Fair [4] ❑ Poor [5]

How I first heard about this book:

❑ Found in bookstore; name: [6]   ❑ Book review: [7]

❑ Advertisement: [8]   ❑ Catalog: [9]

❑ Word of mouth; heard about book from friend, co-worker, etc.: [10]   ❑ Other: [11]

What I liked most about this book:

_____

_____

What I would change, add, delete, etc., in future editions of this book:

_____

_____

Other comments:

_____

_____

Number of computer books I purchase in a year: ❑ 1 [12] ❑ 2-5 [13] ❑ 6-10 [14] ❑ More than 10 [15]

I would characterize my computer skills as: ❑ Beginner [16] ❑ Intermediate [17] ❑ Advanced [18] ❑ Professional [19]

I use ❑ DOS [20] ❑ Windows [21] ❑ OS/2 [22] ❑ Unix [23] ❑ Macintosh [24] ❑ Other: [25]_____

(please specify)

I would be interested in new books on the following subjects:

(please check all that apply, and use the spaces provided to identify specific software)

❑ Word processing: [26]   ❑ Spreadsheets: [27]

❑ Data bases: [28]   ❑ Desktop publishing: [29]

❑ File Utilities: [30]   ❑ Money management: [31]

❑ Networking: [32]   ❑ Programming languages: [33]

❑ Other: [34]

I use a PC at (please check all that apply): ❑ home [35] ❑ work [36] ❑ school [37] ❑ other: [38] _____

The disks I prefer to use are ❑ 5.25 [39] ❑ 3.5 [40] ❑ other: [41]_____

I have a CD ROM: ❑ yes [42] ❑ no [43]

I plan to buy or upgrade computer hardware this year: ❑ yes [44] ❑ no [45]

I plan to buy or upgrade computer software this year: ❑ yes [46] ❑ no [47]

Name: _____ Business title: [48] _____ Type of Business: [49] _____

Address (❑ home [50] ❑ work [51]/Company name: _____)

Street/Suite# _____

City [52]/State [53]/Zipcode [54]: _____ Country [55] _____

❑ **I liked this book!** You may quote me by name in future
IDG Books Worldwide promotional materials.

My daytime phone number is _____

**IDG
BOOKS**

THE WORLD OF
COMPUTER
KNOWLEDGE

❏ **YES!**

Please keep me informed about IDG's World of Computer Knowledge.
Send me the latest IDG Books catalog.